*Fifth Ed*

# SOLUTIO
# SOCIAL PROBLEMS
## LESSONS FROM OTHER SOCIETIES

## D. Stanley Eitzen

*Emeritus, Colorado State University*

### Allyn & Bacon

Boston    Columbus    Indianapolis    New York    San Francisco    Upper Saddle River

Amsterdam    Cape Town    Dubai    London    Madrid    Milan    Munich    Paris    Montreal    Toronto

Delhi    Mexico City    Sao Paulo    Sydney    Hong Kong    Seoul    Singapore    Taipei    Tokyo

**Publisher:** Karen Hanson
**Editorial Assistant:** Courtney Shea
**Executive Marketing Manager:** Kelly May
**Production Editor:** Karen Mason
**Manufacturing Buyer:** Debbie Rossi
**Cover Administrator:** Kristina Mose-Libon
**Editorial Production and Composition Service:** Omegatype Typography, Inc.

**Library of Congress Cataloging-in-Publication Data**

Solutions to social problems : lessons from other societies / [edited by]
D. Stanley Eitzen.—5th ed.
   p.   cm.
  Includes bibliographical references.
  ISBN-13: 978-0-205-69834-9 (pbk.)
  ISBN-10: 0-205-69834-4 (pbk.)
 1. Social problems.  2. Social problems—United States.  3. Social policy.  4. United States—
Social policy   I. Eitzen, D. Stanley.
  HN17.5.S653   2010
  361.10973—dc22

                                                      2009024739

10  9  8  7  6            15

**Allyn & Bacon**
**is an imprint of**

**PEARSON**

**www.pearsonhighered.com**

ISBN 10: 0-205-69834-4
ISBN 13: 978-0-205-69834-9

# CONTENTS

# PREFACE

This collection of readings is intended to supplement traditional textbooks for courses dealing with U.S. social problems. It fills a void because social problems textbooks generally have two fundamental shortcomings: (1) they focus too much on U.S. society, and (2) they are long on the descriptions of social problems and short on the policies to alleviate them. The readings included in this text are from other societies and demonstrate successful alternatives for overcoming the social problems that plague the United States.

This unique approach is timely and important for at least four reasons. First, social problems in the United States are worsening. To illustrate: the number of the poor and the near poor is increasing; the income and wealth inequality gaps are widening; health care is rationed according to one's ability to pay; the inner cities continue to crumble from an inadequate tax base and a shortage of jobs; and the degradation of the environment continues. These social problems require solutions or the United States will continue to spiral downward.

Second, contemporary students must be prepared to live in a global environment. As workers and consumers they are vitally affected by the global economy and other elements of globalization. In our interdependent world the political and economic events from around the globe impinge on the United States, affecting expenditures, taxes, public policies, and military strategies. Expanding our knowledge and our appreciation of other societies is important as we adjust to being responsible citizens of the world, as well as citizens of the United States.

Third, since the presidency of Ronald Reagan, the U.S. government has been dismantling the welfare state, which began under President Franklin Roosevelt. This process has accelerated since the terrorist attacks on the World Trade Center and the Pentagon on September 11, 2001. Declaring a war on terrorism, the Bush administration with the support of Congress invaded Afghanistan to rid that country of al-Qaeda terrorists and the Taliban. This was followed by a preemptive war against Iraq. To fight these wars and the scourge of terrorism, the president asked for and received much higher budgets for the military and homeland security. Simultaneously, President Bush and Congress passed a series of tax cuts to, it was argued, stimulate the moribund economy. Higher military expenditures combined with lower tax revenues resulted in huge government deficits. Any attempt to reduce these deficits resulted in cutting expenditures for social programs and thus a further weakening of the social safety net. This raises key questions: Is the reduction or the elimination of the welfare state a good idea? What will be the likely consequences? Will it solve or intensify social problems? And, will the crises facing the United States during Obama's presidency reinvigorate government solutions along the lines of those found in other developed societies? Comparing the United States with more generous welfare states will help to answer these important questions.

Finally, a comparative examination of public policies regarding social problems will demonstrate what works and under what social conditions. This is a crucial precondition for the formation of creative and workable social policies that will reduce or eliminate social problems in the United States.

The book is divided into five parts. Part 1 focuses on two important foundational issues: first, a comparison of the United States with other advanced industrial societies on a number of dimensions; and second, a consideration of why the United States fails to adopt social policies that appear to solve social problems in other industrial societies. Part 2 examines inequality (poverty, income and wealth inequality, gender, sexual orientation, and age); Part 3 looks at institutional problems (families, schools, work, and health care delivery). Part 4 concentrates on problems of people, resources, and place (cities and environment); and Part 5 addresses the attempts by societies to control individual deviance (crime and drugs).

For each of the social problems considered, one or more articles have been selected. These articles either describe the situation in a single country or in multiple countries, or expressly contrast the situation in another country or countries with that of the United States. With two exceptions, South Korea and Argentina, I have limited the sample of countries to the major industrial nations (Canada, the countries of Scandinavia and Western Europe, Australia and New Zealand, and Japan). In each instance, we invite the reader to assess *critically* the situation in the United States and in the nation or nations under examination, considering questions such as, Will the successful public policies used elsewhere work in the United States? If not, why not? If possible here, how might they be implemented?

While engaged in this comparative exercise, we must guard against the tendency to be either overly defensive about the United States or, at the other extreme, too accepting of the social policies of other societies. Regarding the first instance, we must acknowledge the magnitude of our social problems as a precursor to finding appropriate solutions. Regarding the second possibility, we must recognize that we cannot simply import the social policies of other societies without some modification. As sociologist William Julius Wilson has said,

The approaches [used in Japan and the Western European nations] are embedded in their own cultures and have their own flaws and deficiencies as well as strengths. We should . . . learn from the approaches used in other countries and adapt the best aspects into our own homegrown solutions.[1]

## ACKNOWLEDGMENTS

I would like to thank the reviewers of this edition: Chris Adamski-Mietus, Western Illinois University; Douglas F. George, University of Central Arkansas; Eric Strayer, Hartnell College; and Beate Wilson, Western Illinois University.

## Note

1. William Julius Wilson, *When Work Disappears: The World of the New Urban Poor* (New York: Alfred A. Knopf, 1996), p. 220.

# Introduction

**Section 1** The Comparative Approach to Social Problems

# 1

■ ■ ■

# U.S. Social Problems in Comparative Perspective

**D. Stanley Eitzen**

*Social problems in the United States are worsening. Since 1971 the Institute for Innovation in Social Policy has compiled an "Index of Social Health" for U.S. society (Institute for Innovation in Social Policy, 2006). This index includes measurements on 16 major social problems, among them unemployment, percent of children in poverty, the gap between the rich and the poor, levels of child abuse, and health insurance coverage. This barometer of social problems, which is kind of a Dow Jones (stock market) average (the higher the score, the better), has declined from a composite score of 66 (out of 100) in 1970 to 55 in 2006, a decline of 17 percent. There have been improvements in the areas of infant mortality, teenage drug abuse, high school dropouts, poverty among the elderly, homicides, and alcohol-related traffic fatalities, but in general the trend is down. Among the declining scores are child abuse, child poverty, teenage suicide, average weekly earnings, health insurance coverage, food stamp coverage, access to affordable housing, and the gap between the rich and the poor (income inequality).*

*Not only are social problems in this country increasing for the most part, the United States does not compare favorably with other modern, advanced nations. This introductory essay addresses three fundamental questions. First, how does the United States compare to the other advanced industrial countries on a number of social problems? Second, what are the consequences of U.S. social policies regarding social problems? And, third, why doesn't the United States adopt public policies that other countries have found successful in reducing or eliminating certain social problems?*

## WE'RE NUMBER ONE: THE UNITED STATES COMPARED TO ITS PEERS ON SOCIAL PROBLEMS

Americans are extremely competitive. We want to be the best in all things: Olympic victories, world records, first to the moon, harnessing the atom, finding a cure for AIDS, or whatever. So far, we have done remarkably well in these and other competitions. But there is an area where we outrank the other modern nations that is not a source of pride—*we are number one, or nearly number one, in the magnitude of social problems.*

Compared with the other major industrial nations, the United States ranks number one in real wealth, number of billionaires, the amount of space in homes, defense spending and military capability, executive salaries, physicians' salaries, ethnic diversity, percentage of the population with access to safe drinking water, and the percentage of residents enrolled in higher education.

At the same time, however, the United States ranks first (i.e., worst) among its peers on a number of social problem indicators: murder rate, reported rapes, robbery rate, incarceration rate, the number of drunken driving fatalities, cocaine use, greenhouse gas emissions, contribution to acid rain, forest depletion, hazardous waste per capita, garbage per capita, the number of cars per capita (and the use of cars rather than public transportation), the number of children and elderly in poverty, homelessness, inequality of wealth distribution, bank failures, military aid to developing countries, divorce, single-parent families, reported cases of AIDS, infant mortality, the death of children younger than five, and teenage pregnancy.

Some additional facts underscore the depth of social problems in the United States relative to its peers: First, compared to its industrialized counterparts the United States had the highest incidence of poverty (12.5 percent in 2007, U.S. Census Bureau, 2008). Among the industrialized nations, the United States has the highest rate of child poverty (18.0 percent) for those under age 18. The United States ranks first in the percentage of its children under 6 in poverty (20.8 percent in 2007), a rate three to five times that of Western European nations. Moreover, in 2007, 8.1 million children (11.0 percent of all children) were not covered by health insurance. The United States also ranks next to last in reducing poverty through welfare subsidies out of 20 other developed nations (Drier, 2007:40, 43).

Second, the United States is the only industrialized nation *without* some form of universal health care. As a result, in 2007 about 45.7 million people, or 15.3 percent of U.S. residents, lacked health coverage for the year. A 2002 study estimates that 18,000 adults in the United States die each year because they are uninsured and cannot get proper health care (Sternberg, 2002). The United States, however, has the most advanced health care system in the world and it spends 35 to 40 percent more for health care than the other industrialized countries. But because health care in the United States depends on employment in a job with good benefits and ability to pay, the overall indicators of health are low, with the poor disproportionately disadvantaged. For example, the United

States has the highest infant mortality rate of the 19 countries in OECD (Organisation for Economic Co-operation and Development).

Third, the United States has the most unfair distribution of wealth and income in the industrialized world. There are several indications of this inequality gap in the United States.

- The United States ranks second, just behind Switzerland, in the concentration of wealth owned by the richest 10 percent of the population (Drier, 2007).
- The top 1 percent of Americans received 21.1 percent of all personal income in 2005, while the bottom 50 percent had 12.8 percent (Lardner, 2007). Looked at another way, data from the Congressional Budget Office found that the total 2005 income of the three million individuals at the top was roughly equal to that of the bottom 166 million Americans (reported in Johnston, 2007).
- The gap between the chief executive officers and the average blue-collar workers who make the products is enormous—around 411 times as much in 2006 (Pizzigati, 2006). This measure of income inequality is much higher in the United States than in the other industrialized nations. CEOs of America's 50 biggest companies are paid on average 75 percent more than their European counterparts (*The Economist*, 2008). In practice, the gap is even wider because the executives in the other countries pay higher taxes on their relatively lower incomes than do U.S. executives. Moreover, the workers in the other countries receive much more in nonmonetary compensation (e.g., universal medical care, subsidized child care) than do U.S. workers.
- In 2001 the median net worth for families of color was $17,100, compared to $120,400 for white families (United For a Fair Economy, 2004). In terms of income, in 2007 white households averaged $54,920 compared to $38,678 for Latino households and $33,916 for African American households (U.S. Census Bureau, 2008).

The historical evidence suggests that in the early part of the 20th century (the 1920s are the earliest period for which data are available), wealth inequality was much lower in the United States than in the United Kingdom; U.S. figures were comparable to Sweden. America appeared to be the land of opportunity, whereas Europe was a place where an entrenched upper class controlled the bulk of wealth. By the late 1980s, the situation appears to have completely reversed, with much higher concentration of wealth in the United States than in Europe. Europe now appears the land of equality (Wolff, 1995:21).

Fourth, as for cities: "None of the other industrialized democracies has allowed its city centers to deteriorate as has the United States" (Wilson, 1996:218). "No European city has experienced the level of concentrated poverty and racial and ethnic segregation that is typical of American metropolises. Nor does any European city include areas that are as physically isolated, deteriorated, and prone to violence as the inner-city ghettos of urban America" (Wilson, 1996:149). Many U.S. cities have child poverty rates higher than 35 percent and black child poverty rates of more than 50 percent.

Fifth, compared to its peers, the United States ranks first on a number of crime and criminal justice dimensions: the percentage of population who have been the victim of a crime; the murder rate (six times greater than the rate in Great Britain, five times that of Japan and Spain, and 22 times that of Austria) (Wellstone and Dauster, 2002); the murder rate of children; reported rapes (nearly three times higher than found in Sweden, the industrialized country with the second highest rate); and rate of imprisonment (Drier, 2007). U.S. citizens constitute less than 5 percent of the world's population, yet the number of U.S. prison inmates amounts to 25 percent of the world's prisoners. The United States incarcerates its citizens at a rate six times higher than Canada, England, and France, seven times higher than Switzerland and Holland, and ten times higher than Sweden and Finland (Street, 2001).

Sixth, a comparative study of child supports for families (e.g., housing, health, education, welfare allowances, and tax benefits) found in 15 nations that Luxembourg, Norway, France, and Belgium ranked among the most generous countries; Denmark, Germany, the United Kingdom, Australia, and the Netherlands among those providing middle range provisions; and Portugal, Italy, Ireland, Spain, Greece, and the United States among those nations with the least generous child benefit packages (Bradshaw et al., 1993). Since that study in 1993 the amount of government spending in the United States for social supports for families has declined further.

The litany of U.S. social problems could go on but the point has been made—*the United States has more serious social problems than those found in countries most similar to it.* These other societies, like the United States, are modern, affluent, industrialized, democratic, and capitalist. Why, then, are the social problems in the United States of such greater magnitude?

## COMPARING U.S. SOCIAL POLICIES REGARDING SOCIAL PROBLEMS IN THE UNITED STATES TO THOSE OF ITS PEERS

Most significant, the nations comparable to the United States devote a greater percentage of their gross domestic product (GDP) to social expenditures. The United States chooses not to have universal health insurance and spends a smaller proportion of its budget on social security and welfare programs (e.g., housing, food, family allowance to single parents) than other advanced industrialized nations.

The other industrialized countries also provide much more support for parents than the United States does, in such areas as family allowances, housing subsidies, publicly subsidized child care, and paid family leaves from work. In the United States, child care for working parents is tax deductible, which expands the benefits as income increases, thus providing the working poor with the least benefit. The other developed countries have programs that provide maternity (and sometimes paternity) leaves with pay, whereas U.S. law requires that only companies employing more than fifty workers must allow *unpaid* maternity leave. Workers in smaller enterprises may or may not receive family leaves depending on the whim of their employers.

The United States also differs from the other developed countries in the way public education is organized. Education in the United States is decentralized, with each of the 15,000 school districts responsible for much of the financing and curriculum decisions for the local schools. This is in sharp contrast to the other countries where national standards are set and schools financed much more equally nationwide. As a result of its heavy emphasis on financing education through local property taxes, the U.S. school system is rigged in favor of the already privileged, with lower class children tracked by race and income into the most deficient and demoralizing schools and classrooms (Sklar, 1997).

Prekindergarten programs are universal in the other developed countries, while dependent on parents' resources in the United States. Compensatory preschool programs for the disadvantaged are underfunded in the United States, with only about one-fourth of those eligible actually receiving programs such as Head Start. Contrast this with the almost 100 percent of four-year-old French children and 98 percent of Belgian and Dutch children enrolled in preprimary programs. As a result of these differences, American students graduating from high school are more varied in their skills and aptitudes (and this is correlated with parents' income and with the wealth of school districts) than are their counterparts in other industrialized countries.

Public education is taken more seriously elsewhere. In contrast to the United States, teacher salaries are higher, more resources are spent on public education, the school year is longer, and, for those eligible, higher education through graduate school is subsidized.

The differences in worker benefits are considerable when comparing the United States to its more generous peers. Take wages, for example, where total compensation (wages, health benefits, vacations) for the typical United States worker in manufacturing has either remained flat or declined since the mid-1970s, while it has increased by 40 percent for a European worker in a comparable job. In most of these societies, national law requires that workers receive such benefits as strong job security, four weeks of paid vacation, an ample minimum wage, and generous unemployment benefits. In the United States, in contrast, job security is weak, paid vacations are not universal but depend on seniority and job status, and unemployment benefits are meager and short in duration. Moreover, more than 12 million workers labor for wages that do not lift them out of poverty and are without health coverage or pension plans.

As we have seen, policies in the United States are much different in regard to its citizens than are the policies of the other developed nations. The other societies are much more generous to their citizens, providing social supports that encourage equal opportunity and provide for the basic needs of income maintenance, housing, job security, and health care. To reiterate, the other developed societies have much more comprehensive programs that minimize economic deprivation and insecurity. The few supports found in the United States are now under severe attack. Aid to Families with Dependent Children was eliminated in 1996 under a Democratic president. When George W. Bush was elected and the Republicans controlled both houses of Congress, programs such as food stamps, legal services to the poor, housing subsidies, vaccination for children, and school lunch programs were diminished further.

The generous benefits in the social democracies are costly, with income, inheritance, and sales taxes considerably higher than in the United States. The trade-off is that these other countries have comprehensive, universal health care systems; pensions and nursing home care are provided for the elderly; families are supported with paid parental leaves; jobs are well paid and relatively secure; and poverty, hunger, and homelessness are relatively rare. In short, the people in the high tax, industrial societies feel relatively safe from the insecurities over income, illness, and old age.

The United States, in sharp contrast, has the highest poverty rate by far among the industrialized societies, has a growing disparity between social classes, and is moving toward a two-tiered society. Regarding this last point, the United States is experiencing a dramatic rise in private schooling, home schooling, private recreational clubs, and in the number of walled and gated affluent neighborhood enclaves on the one hand and ever greater segregation of the poor and especially poor racial minorities in segregated and deteriorating neighborhoods and inferior schools, on the other. Personal safety is more and more problematic as violent crime rates increase among the young.

Finally, democracy is on the wane as more and more people opt out of the electoral process (e.g., in the 2008 election when Barack Obama was elected president and the turnout set a record, still 39 percent of those who could have voted *did not*. The United States consistently has the lowest voter turnout among the industrialized nations, presumably the consequence of so many potential voters being alienated when their issues are trumped by big money contributions to candidates and political parties.

In sum, the comparison of U.S. policies with those of the generous welfare states leads to the following conclusion: we ignore the problems of poverty, wealth inequality, and a rationed health care system at our own peril. If the United States continues on the present path of ignoring these and other social problems or reducing or eliminating programs to deal with them, Americans will be less secure and there will be more problems that require greater control at an ever greater social and economic cost.

## BARRIERS TO THE ADOPTION OF MORE GENEROUS WELFARE STATE POLICIES IN THE UNITED STATES

If the social policies of the other developed societies minimize social problems, why doesn't the United States adopt them or at least try to modify them to fit our situation? There are significant barriers that make such social changes very difficult.

First, there is the fundamental American belief in competitive individualism. Americans celebrate and support individual rights. Seymour Martin Lipset puts it this way:

> Citizens have been expected to demand and protect their rights on a personal basis. The exceptional focus on law here as compared to Europe, derived from the Constitution and the Bill of Rights, has stressed rights against the state and other powers. America began and continues as the most anti-statist, legalistic, and rights-oriented nation. (Lipset, 1996:20)

The high value Americans place on individualism has several implications, all of which work against efforts for the collective good. First, the individual is exalted, which makes working for group goals difficult. Americans typically do not want to pay taxes for the good of others. Opinion surveys taken in various developed countries, for example, reveal that Americans are much less prone than Europeans and Canadians to favor measures to help the underprivileged (Lipset, 1996:145). Second, government intrusions into personal lives or into local schools or communities are opposed. Third, there is a resistance against efforts to establish preferential rights for disadvantaged groups (e.g., affirmative action based on race or gender). Fourth, Americans combat government handouts to those they deem undeserving. And, finally, the strong emphasis on competitive meritocracy means that individuals are believed to be advantaged or disadvantaged because of their skills, effort, and motivation or the lack thereof. Thus, the affluent are venerated and the poor vilified.

A second barrier to the adoption of welfare state policies is political. To begin, the majorities in the federal and state legislatures since the Reagan administration have been political conservatives or centrists, which means that they tended to resist the expansion of or favored eliminating various dimensions of the welfare state. The political debate in these assemblies was from the right to the political center, with little, if any, voice from the political left. The political climate under George W. Bush obstructed spending for social programs by reducing the amount available in two ways. First, to stimulate the economy, tax breaks were given to the wealthy, presumably because they would invest it, resulting in companies hiring more workers and a growing economy. Using this "trickle down" strategy, huge tax cuts were passed with about 40 percent of this tax relief targeted to the wealthiest 1 percent of taxpayers, while the poorest 20 percent received about 1 percent of the total relief.

A second way to limit social spending is by increasing government spending for defense. The 2009 fiscal budget for military spending was $706 billion. Taking all military related expenditures into account, the United States alone spends 46 percent of the world total, distantly followed by the United Kingdom, France, Japan, and China with 4 to 5 percent each (Shah, 2008).

When the federal government cuts its tax income while increasing its budget for defense, the shortfall is made up by reducing or eliminating social programs. Jesse Jackson addresses defense this way:

> War abroad drowns out desperation at home. We can read about the
> conditions of every faction, ethnic group or tribe in Iraq. But we read
> nothing about the growing desperation of poor people in this coun-
> try. The president and the Congress have agreed to an unprece-
> dented increase in our military budget. . . . There is money to erect
> missile defenses against countries that have no missiles. It always
> pays to be prepared. But there is no money to ensure heat in the
> winter for the poorest families in America. (Jackson, 2003:15)

And, we would add, no money to provide adequate inoculations, school
lunches, Head Start, subsidized child care, legal services, unemployment compensation, health care, and the like as do the democracies in western Europe,
Scandinavia, and Canada.

Another political barrier is the two-party system, where both parties market their appeals to those categories most likely to vote—the affluent, the successful, and suburbanites, all categories interested in low taxes and the status
quo. Moreover, the major parties are financed by big business and wealthy individuals, both of which favor low taxes and reduced social programs (Green,
2002). Also, the two-party system that has evolved in the United States makes it
structurally difficult for third parties to emerge as viable alternatives.

The severe economic downturn of 2008–2009 has the potential to rebuild
the welfare state. The federal government, now controlled by a Democrat president and Democrat-controlled Congress, will address the financial disaster
with bailouts, greater oversight of the business sector, stimulus packages including job creation through the rebuilding of the infrastructure, and investments in various social programs. There is the potential to enhance the public
safety net, such as universal health care and public subsidies to the impoverished; however, this optimism is tempered by the huge federal and state debts,
the more than $1 trillion bailout of failed financial institutions and failed auto-
mobile manufacturers, and another massive stimulus package required to get
the economy "back on its feet." As a result, the center-left may not be able to en-
act costly programs to help the disadvantaged.

One of the necessary ingredients for a generous welfare state is the existence of a heavily unionized workforce. Strong unions use their collective clout to
support issues favorable to the working class, as evidenced in Canada and
the welfare states of Europe. The labor movement in the United States has
fought for Social Security, Medicare, Medicaid, FHA mortgages, the GI Bill,
civil rights legislation, voting rights legislation, student loans, and increasing
the minimum wage. In the past, U.S. unions were a powerful force for economic security and social justice. But that was forty years ago, when unions
were strong. In the mid-1950s, 35 percent of all U.S. workers belonged to
unions—80 to 90 percent in major industries such as auto, steel, and coal min-
ing. This percentage slipped to 28 percent in the mid-1970s and now is about
13 percent—in sharp contrast, 79 percent of the workers in Sweden belong to
unions (Drier, 2007). Weak unions do not present a countervailing force against

powerful business interests. The result is that efforts to expand the welfare state in the United States have no powerful ally.

## CONCLUSION

The political-social-economic system of a society does not just evolve from random events and aimless choices. The powerful in societies craft policies to accomplish certain ends, within the context of historical events, budgetary constraints, and the like. Addressing the issue of inequality, Fischer and his colleagues say:

> The answer to the question of why societies vary in their structure of rewards is more political. In significant measure, societies choose the height and breadth of their "ladders." By loosening markets or regulating them, by providing services to all citizens or rationing them according to income, by subsidizing some groups more than others, societies, through their politics, build their ladders. To be sure, historical and external constraints deny full freedom of action, but a substantial freedom of action remains. . . . In a democracy, this means that the inequality Americans have is, in significant measure, the historical result of policy choices Americans—or, at least, Americans' representatives—have made. In the United States, the result is a society that is distinctly *unequal*. Our ladder is, by the standards of affluent democracies and even by the standards of recent American history, unusually extended and narrow—and becoming more so. (Fischer et al., 1996:8)

In other words, America's level of inequality is *by design* (Fischer et al., 1996:125).

Social policy is about design, setting goals, and determining the means to achieve them. Do we want to regulate and protect more as the well-developed welfare states do, or should we do less? Should we create and invest in policies and programs that protect citizens from poverty, unemployment, and the high cost of health care or should the market economy sort people into winners, players, and losers based on their abilities and efforts? Decision makers in the United States have opted to reduce the welfare state. Are they on the right track or are there policies that the generous welfare states have adopted that might, with modification, reduce America's social problems? If societies are designed, should the United States change its design?

## References

Bradshaw, J., J. Ditch, H. Holmes, and P. Whiteford. 1993. "A Comparative Study of Child Support in Fifteen Countries." *Journal of European Social Policy* 3(4):255–271.

Drier, Peter. 2007. "The United States in Comparative Perspective." *Contexts* 6 (Summer): 38–46.

*Economist*. 2008. "What the Boss Pockets: Chief Executives' Pay at the Biggest Companies in Europe and America." (November 12). Online: www.economist.com/daily/chartgallery/PrinterFriendly.cfm?stor

Fischer, Claude S., Michael Hout, Martin Sanchez Jankowski, Samuel R. Lucas, Ann Swidler, and Kim Voss. 1996. *Inequality by Design: Cracking the Bell Curve Myth*. Princeton, NJ: Princeton University Press.

Green, Mark. 2002. *Selling Out: How Big Corporate Money Buys Elections, Rams through Legislation, and Betrays Our Democracy*. New York: Regan Books.

Institute for Innovation in Social Policy. 2006. *2006 Index of Social Health: Monitoring the Social Well-Being of the Nation*. Tarrytown, NY: Fordham University Graduate Center.

Jackson, Jesse. 2003. "Bush, GOP Give Cold Shoulder to Nation's Poor." *Progressive Populist* (January 1–15):15.

Johnston, David Cay. 2007. "Report Says That the Rich are Getting Richer Faster, Much Faster." *New York Times* (December 15). Online: www.nytimes.com/2007/12/15/business/15rich.html

Lardner, James. 2007. "The Richest Get Richer." *Inequality.Org* (October 22). Online: www.demos.org/inequality/article.cfm?blogid=C99DD3AC-3FF4-6C82-52162169B

Lipset, Seymour Martin. 1996. *American Exceptionalism: A Double-Edged Sword*. New York: W. W. Norton.

Pizzigati, Sam. 2006. "Beyond the Living Wage: Taking on CEO Excess." *Labor Notes* (November):11.

Shah, Anup, "World Military Spending," *Global Issues.Org* (March 1, 2008). Online: www.globalissues.org/article/75/world-military-spending

Sklar, Holly. 1997. "Imagine a Country." *Z Magazine* (July/August). Online: www.deanza.edu/faculty/yuen/poli5/sklar.htm

Sternberg, Steve. 2002. "Study Blames 18,000 Deaths in USA on Lack of Insurance." *USA Today* (May 22):1A.

Street, Paul. 2001. "Race, Prison, and Poverty," *Z Magazine* 14 (May):25–31.

United For a Fair Economy. 2004. "Wealth Inequality by the Numbers." *Dollars and Sense* 251 (January/February):20–21.

U.S. Census Bureau. 2008. "Income, Poverty, and Health Insurance Coverage in the United States: 2007." *Current Population Reports*, P60–235.

Wellstone, Paul, and Bill Dauster. 2002. "The Good Country." *Progressive Populist* (December 1):9–10.

Wilson, William Julius. 1996. *When Work Disappears: The World of the New Urban Poor*. New York: Alfred A. Knopf.

Wolff, Edward N. 1995. *Top Heavy: A Study of the Increasing Inequality of Wealth in America*. New York: The Twentieth Century Fund Press.

# 2

■ ■ ■

# The European Social Model

### T. R. Reid

*The following is from a chapter in T. R. Reid's* The
United States of Europe *devoted to describing
the European social model. The essence of this
model is that there is a shared commitment to a
welfare state with cradle to grave benefits for all.*

Access to the generous benefits of the social model is seen as a basic right of
every European—and the word *every* is crucial here, because the social model is
relentlessly egalitarian. At the same time, paying for the social model is seen as
a basic responsibility of every European. And this widely shared sense of the
government's social responsibility to everybody is another unifying force that
makes Europeans feel they all belong to a single place—a place, they believe,
that is definitely not American.

The responsibility for all to help pay is reflected in the tax structure that supports the continent's extensive welfare programs. European nations have the
same panoply of corporate and personal income taxes, inheritance taxes, property
taxes, and so forth as the United States, with the same type of exemptions that essentially exclude the poorest citizens from paying these wealth-based taxes. But
the European countries rely much more heavily than most of the world on sales
taxes—the Europeans call them value-added taxes—which are paid by just about
anybody who buys anything. This system was created deliberately to make sure
that lower-income people help pay for the social system. And do they pay! For an
American, even an American who lives in a "high-tax" state like California, New
York, or Washington, the VAT rates in European countries seem mind-boggling:

| | |
|---|---|
| Austria | 20 percent |
| Belgium | 21 |
| Czech Republic | 22 |

| | |
|---|---|
| Denmark | 25 percent |
| Germany | 16 |
| Estonia | 18 |
| Greece | 18 |
| Spain | 16 |
| Finland | 22 |
| France | 19.6 |
| Ireland | 21 |
| Italy | 20 |
| Hungary | 25 |
| Netherlands | 19 |
| Portugal | 19 |
| Slovakia | 19 |
| Sweden | 25 |
| United Kingdom | 17.5 |

Which is to say, when we paid that heavy 17.5 percent VAT tax on our purchases in Britain, we were actually living with one of the lightest sales-tax burdens in all of Europe. When I was traveling around Europe, I wasn't surprised to see that the Scandinavian countries had high rates of VAT tax; they are rich, and they are famous for their high taxes. It was surprising, though, to find that even the poorest countries in the EU—Greece, Portugal, Hungary, and Slovakia—imposed sales taxes at rates that would start a tax-payers' revolt in most of the United States.

But if the burden is spread fairly equally, the benefits of the public welfare programs in the European social model are also distributed with a fairly even hand. To Americans, it is simply a matter of common sense that rich families get better medical care and better education than the poor; the rich can afford the doctors at the fancy clinics and the tutors to get their kids into Harvard. But this piece of common sense does not apply in most of Europe. The corporate executive in the back seat of the limo, her chauffeur up front, and the guy who pumps the gas for them all go to the same doctor and the same hospitals and send their children to the same (largely free) universities. It's not that the truly rich are resented, or hated, in Europe. People who have made billions in business—people like Stelios Haji-Ioannou, the budget-airline wizard from Cyprus . . . or Britain's Richard Branson, or Austria's Dietrich Mateschitz . . . —are treated like heroes in their native countries. But no European would agree that a Stelios or a Mateschitz should get better health care or education just because they're rich.

This zeal for spreading the wealth fairly equally is reflected most dramatically in poverty rates. European nations certainly do have families living below the established poverty line (according to the definition preferred by the Organization for Economic Cooperation and Development, "poverty" means a family income at least 50 percent below the mean personal income in the nation as a whole). But they have a lot fewer poor families than the United States does. In America, about 20 percent of adults are living in poverty at any given time. In France, the comparable figure is 7.5 percent; it is 7.6 percent for Germany and 6.5 percent in Italy. Britain, with a somewhat leaner benefit system than its continental neighbors, has about 14.6 percent of its adults in poverty.

The helping hand of the social model is particularly evident when a worker becomes unemployed. Americans on the unemployment rolls tend to get a monthly government check, together with help in buying food and paying heat and light bills. At some level, when his savings fall low enough, an unemployed American worker may also apply for free government-supplied health care through Medicaid. In Europe, by contrast, a worker who is "made redundant"—that's the brutal British term for being laid off—will get a housing benefit, a heat and light benefit, a food benefit, a child care benefit, and a monthly unemployment payment that is almost always higher than the American standard. The European, of course, will have the same access as everybody else to the public health-care system. The American system, in which you lose your health insurance when you lose your job, strikes the Europeans as exactly backward. "I don't understand your approach to health care," a junior minister in Sweden's health department told me once. "It seems to me that your country takes away the insurance when people most need it."

Economists have a gauge to measure the relative generosity of unemployment assistance programs. It's called the replacement ratio—that is, how much of the worker's former income is replaced through benefits. In the United States, the figure varies from state to state, but overall a couple with two children and an income a little below average will have about 50 percent of earnings replaced by public assistance in case of unemployment. In France, the replacement ratio for the same family is 86 percent; in Britain, 83 percent; in Germany, 74 percent; in Sweden and the Netherlands, 90 percent.

This benevolent helping hand, funded by the taxpayers, tends to be described in the United States as a "welfare state," a phrase used derisively by American politicians to attack those who want to give away huge sums of public money. In Europe, too, the social safety blanket is known as the "welfare state," but in Europe people are proud of that term. I learned this on the campus of one of the world's greatest educational institutions, Oxford University. On a cold fall day, the students were holding a mass protest against one of Tony Blair's more daring government innovations: a tuition fee for college students. In Britain, as in most of Europe, nearly all universities are public institutions. Until 1999, university education was free in Britain, as it still is in most of Europe. To help balance his budget, Blair proposed a modest tuition fee, based on each student's family income, with a maximum payment of £1,000 per school year—about $1,500. Since then, Blair has raised the fee to a maximum of £3,000. Compared to, say, Princeton or Harvard (both running about $38,000 per year), this is a fantastic bargain. To Oxford students, it was an outrage, and that's why they were protesting. "Education Must Be Free," read the bedsheet banners draping from the leaded windows of the stately Gothic colleges.

Just for the sake of argument, I approached the student leading the demonstrations—Phillipa Warner Smith, the daughter of a lawyer from a tony London suburb—and suggested to her that education really isn't free. "Somebody is paying your professors," I said. "Somebody has to pay the light bill in the classroom." Ms. Warner Smith didn't flinch. "Education benefits society as a whole," she replied. "So the general society should pay the bursary." At that point, somebody turned on a microphone at the front of the crowd and a white-haired gentleman stepped up to give a speech. This turned out to be Tony Benn, a venerable leftist member of Blair's Labour Party, who took sharp issue with his prime minister on the subject of tuition fees. "Education benefits society as a whole," Benn declared, precisely echoing the student argument. "And government should pay for socially beneficial functions. This is an essential element of the welfare state that we have been building for the past century on this continent." The striking thing for me was the obvious pride in Benn's voice when he mentioned the welfare state, and the huge roar of approval from the crowd that greeted that term. "Protecting our welfare state," Ms. Warner Smith told me, "is probably the most important job that government has."

"Our welfare state"—that phrase nicely sums up the sense of ownership, the sheer pride, that Europeans feel toward their network of social support mechanisms. The social model is often cited as one of the basic elements that make a European country European. "Europe's welfare states," asserts the British analyst Will Hutton, "arise from . . . core European values and the European settlement. They define Europeanness. They are non-negotiable European realities." The Europeans argue that the generosity of their social model is the main thing that makes Europe different from other developed regions of the world. I heard the prime minister of Serbia, Zoran Djindjic, a Generation E member, make this point at a forum for Eastern European countries hoping eventually to be admitted to the EU. The session was a sort of beauty contest, to test whether the potential applicants were up to snuff, and Djindjic clearly passed the test. His great moment came when he was asked to give a Serbian view of what "Europe" is all about. "Modern societies are defined by three elements: political democracy, market economy, and social identity," the prime minister said in his smooth English. "It's in this third aspect—their attitude to social solidarity—that the Europeans seem to have an identity that is distinct from either Asia or America."

Citizens of the United States of Europe particularly like to brag that their social model makes them superior to the United States of America. "The simplest difference between the USA and Europe is that we have welfare states, and they do not," wrote the Irish political scientist James Wickham. Wickham applauds Americans' willingness to support charity and volunteer programs, but he argues that charity is not enough. "Social rights cannot depend on the voluntary goodwill of others. . . . The welfare state, enforced by law, is a defining feature of Europe."

Of course, the welfare state also forces Europeans to pay sky-high taxes. And the plush arrangements provided for people who are out of work may explain why Europeans who are laid off tend to accept their fate as a fairly permanent condition, rather than getting up and looking for a new job. But these problems tend to be ignored, except by a few marginal voices on the right, because Europe in general assumes the social model is preferable to what's going on in other parts of the world. "The reason why Europe compares so favorably with the US in respect of social and income mobility," Will Hutton says, "is that every European state sets out to offer equality of opportunity to all its people; the American neglect of the bottom 50 percent in the name of individualism is not reproduced in Europe."

The European social model involves a much bigger role for the public sector in daily life than Americans are comfortable with. The Public Broadcasting System (PBS) in the United States fills a fairly small niche in a TV and radio world dominated by giant private companies. In most European countries, by contrast, the public broadcaster tends to be largest and the most prestigious by far. Britain's BBC, funded by a tax of $170 per year paid by every home and office that has a television set, operates six TV and five radio stations. France's TFI, Germany's ARD, and Italy's RAI are more popular and more respected than any private network. Public transit systems are much more pervasive in Europe than in the United States, as are public art, public universities, and public medical systems. Public housing is so common in major European cities that it can't all be stuck away in a few big complexes. Instead, government-owned homes and apartment buildings are found in every neighborhood of every city and town. The inhabitants include not just the poor but a good proportion of the middle class as well.

# 3

# The Swedish Welfare State

## D. Stanley Eitzen

*The Swedish welfare state provides extensive public support for families and individuals, including universal health care insurance; family supports for parents and children; and programs to reduce the hardships of unemployment, elderly care, and poverty. Swedish taxes are high to pay for these programs, but an important benefit of this investment has been to level extremes in wealth and poverty.*

Sweden is a prosperous and productive nation of 9 million (the facts on Sweden throughout this essay come from the "Fact Sheets on Sweden" series, 2006–2008). For a long time Sweden's population was ethnically homogeneous, but this has changed with immigration after World War II, resulting in some 20 percent of Sweden's current population being either foreign-born or having at least one parent born outside the country. Contrary to common belief, it has a capitalist economy; that is, most businesses producing goods and services are owned by private enterprises. The government does own the railroads, mineral resources, a bank, and liquor and tobacco operations. Sweden has high taxes, which are used to provide for numerous generous cradle-to-grave public supports for its population, leveling extremes in wealth and poverty.

## COMPONENTS OF THE SWEDISH WELFARE STATE

The Swedish welfare state began with legislation passed in 1891 that provided some health insurance. Ten years later the legislature instituted compulsory employer responsibility in the event of occupational injury. In 1913 a general pension system began and in 1931 a system for sickness benefits was put into place. From 1932 the welfare state was further developed and expanded as the Swedish Social Democratic Party controlled the government with only brief

*Source:* This essay was written expressly for *Solutions to Social Problems: Lessons from Other Societies.*

interruptions for the next 60 years. "During the 20th century, at the price of the world's highest tax burden, Sweden built up what is often called the world's most generous general welfare system, with such elements as virtually free (that is, tax-financed) schools, child care, health care, pensions, elder care, social services, and various economic security systems" ("Sweden in Brief/The 'Home of the People,'" n.d.:1). In 1991, however, there was an economic crisis that resulted in relatively high unemployment and reduced government revenues. As a consequence the services and subsidies of the welfare state were reduced, including periods when no benefits were paid for certain welfare plans. In the late 1990s the economy recovered and the benefits of the welfare state were partially restored. The description that follows is of the current welfare system as it as evolved through good times and bad, expansions and constrictions.

The Swedish welfare state is based on the principle that the government is responsible for providing basic services for the entire population. In broad outline, the present welfare system includes the following provisions:

- *A national universal health insurance program.* In this plan patients choose their own physicians, and health services are subsidized for all residents of Sweden (the fees charged to patients in 2007 U.S. dollars were $12 per day for hospital stays, and about $21 for consultation with a doctor). Once a patient has paid $137, he or she is entitled to free medical care for the rest of the year. After a person has spent $252 for medicines, the remainder of pharmaceutical costs are free for the remainder of the year. The costs for health and medical care amount to approximately 9 percent of Sweden's gross domestic product (the United States spends 16 percent of its GDP on health care, yet 46 million are uninsured).

- *A family support program for parents and children.* Prenatal care, delivery, and postnatal care are free. All children under the age of 20 receive free medical and dental care. Family planning services and advice on contraception are provided throughout the country. Working parents may take a leave from work to care for their infant for a total of 480 days for both parents (divided as they choose), while being compensated at 80 percent of their wages. Either parent may also take time off for the care of a sick child (60 days a year per child) with compensation for loss of earnings. Parents receive a cash bonus of $133 per month per child up to the age of 16. Each child is guaranteed a place in child care programs (there is a sliding scale for this service, with no one paying more than $137 a month). All children ages 4 and 5 are provided three hours of free preschooling a day.

- *Education.* Education begins in day care centers and preschools, which an overwhelming majority attend. All education in the public school system is free, including school lunches. The schools are administered at the local level but financed at several levels so that there is equality in spending per pupil, regardless of the wealth of the local district. High school is free for those who qualify by passing in Swedish, mathematics, and English. For students who fail to qualify, individual programs can be tailored to meet their needs. University and college education is tax-financed, and therefore relatively free. In addition, there is a generous system of study loans and grants that make higher education accessible to students from all social classes.

• *Employment programs.* A laid-off worker has access to a state-run employment agency where employers must by law list their job openings. If no job is available, job retraining and unemployment insurance benefits are provided (at 80 percent of previous income). During difficult economic cycles, the government often expands public employment programs (e.g., building infrastructure such as roads, public buildings, pipelines) to reduce unemployment.

• *Care of the elderly.* Everyone who has lived in Sweden for at least three years is entitled to at least a minimum pension. Full pension is for those who have lived in Sweden for 40 years between the ages of 16 and 64. There are also pension programs for those incapable of working, and for widows and other survivors. The elderly receive a housing subsidy (means tested but not to exceed 90 percent of the rent). Institutionalized care is provided when needed but the preference is for the elderly to receive nursing care in their homes, which is subsidized whenever possible. The cost for all of the programs for the elderly is about 20 percent of the nation's GNP.

• *Subsidized housing.* The goal of Sweden's housing policy is to give everyone the chance for a good home at a reasonable price. The means to achieve these ends include planning for housing, non-profit municipal housing, establishing rent ceilings, subsidized financing, and housing allowances. The latter allows lower-income families to afford decent housing. The government's goal is for every family to have a housing arrangement that at a minimum has a bedroom for each child and a bedroom for the parents, plus a kitchen and living room.

## PAYING FOR THE WELFARE STATE: TAXATION

To provide these many and expensive services of the welfare state, Swedish taxes are relatively high. Direct taxes include taxes on income from employment and capital (e.g., dividends and capital gains from the sale of stocks, real estate, or other property), business income taxes, a national property tax on real estate, and an inheritance tax. Indirectly, there is a state sales tax (value-added tax) and consumption taxes used as a means to curb the consumption of energy (oil and gas, electrical power, motor vehicles), tobacco, gaming, and alcohol. As a result the total tax revenue for Sweden as a percentage of gross domestic product in 2000 was 54.2 percent, compared to 29.6 percent for the United States, 37.9 percent for Germany, 37.4 percent for the United Kingdom, and 35.8 percent for Canada (Organisation of Economic Co-operation and Development Report, cited in Francis, 2003).

## WHY DOES SWEDEN CHOOSE TO HAVE AN EXPENSIVE WELFARE STATE?

Sweden is a high-tax/high-benefit welfare state. There are at least four major reasons for the welfare state in Sweden. First, the Swedes have accepted the overarching goal of the Social Democrats that provides the basis for Sweden's expansive and expensive welfare state.

> The ambition is for financial security and social rights to be guaranteed to all citizens—not by being focused on certain hard-pressed groups in society, but by being given to all, without any application procedure or means-testing. . . . The basis of this policy is a tax system in which all taxpayers contribute, for the good of all, according to capacity, and in which funds are distributed with the objective of leveling out differences in people's living conditions, according to the principle of an egalitarian society ("Disability Policies in Sweden," 2000:1).

While there are complaints about the high taxes, opinion surveys reveal that the "majority of Swedes . . . are willing to pay higher taxes in order not to have such problems as chronic unemployment, homelessness, and health care rationed by income" (Feagin and Feagin, 1997:469). Further evidence of the general support of the welfare state in Sweden is the long-time support of the Social Democratic Party—even when this party is out of power, there is little retrenchment in the welfare policies.

Second, the Swedes receive many benefits. Directly, they receive health care, early childhood education, and various subsidies. In other societies, where these are not provided by society, the cost of these services is up to individuals and families, which means, in effect, that there is unequal access to these services. Indirectly, if poverty, hunger, homelessness, and other social problems are minimized, then so, too, is street crime.

Third, Sweden has strong labor unions, which represent the middle and lower social classes. Through pressure these unions have received considerable concessions from the capitalist class. In effect, "labor and capital worked out a cooperative agreement whereby labor got a welfare state and capitalists got labor peace" (Feagin and Feagin, 1997:468).

And, the fourth reason for the support of the welfare state is that all citizens of Sweden are represented in the decision-making. Sweden has a parliamentary democracy with one assembly of 349 seats. Seats in parliament are distributed proportionately between those parties that poll at least 4 percent of the national vote or at least 12 percent in any one constituency. Unlike the United States, which has a two-party system and a winner-take-all policy, minorities and groups with different agendas are represented in the Swedish legislature, guaranteeing a voice and the possibility of coalitions with other groups. This democratic tradition promotes citizen participation, with high voter turnout and subsequent attention by politicians to all citizens. Most important, it reduces the power of wealth in the decision-making.

## References

"Fact Sheets on Sweden" series, 2006–2008, The Swedish Institute. Stockholm, Sweden. Online: www.swedeninfo.com
  "Sweden in Brief/The 'Home of the People'" (n.d.).
  "Disability Policies in Sweden" (2000).
  "The Swedish Economy" (June 2006).
  "Swedish Health Care" (January 2007).
  "Swedish Support for Families with Children" (February 2007).
  "Social Insurance in Sweden" (March 2007).
  "Swedish Education" (April 2007).
  "Care of the Elderly in Sweden" (September 2007).
  "Taxes in Sweden" (February 2008).
  "Funding of the Swedish School System" (March 2008).
Feagin, Joe R., and Clairece Booher Feagin. 1997. *Social Problems: A Critical-Conflict Perspective*. 5th ed. Englewood Cliffs, NJ: Prentice Hall.
Francis, David R. 2003. "Tax Cuts as 'Stimulus'—A Global Reality Check." *Christian Science Monitor* (January 10):3.

# 4

# How Canada Stole the American Dream

**Duncan Hood**

*This essay from* Maclean's, *the Canadian equivalent of* Time Magazine *in the United States, compares Canada and the United States on a number of dimensions. Among the findings: Canadians have more wealth than Americans, they are healthier, they have fewer teenage pregnancies, and they spend more time with their families.*

To be an American is to be the best. Every American believes this. Their sports champions are not U.S. champions, they're world champions. Their corporations aren't the largest in the States, they're the largest on the planet. Their armies don't defend just America, they defend freedom.

Like the perpetual little brother, Canadians have always lived in the shadow of our American neighbours. We mock them for their uncultured ways, their brash talk and their insularity, but it's always been the thin laughter of the insecure. After all, says University of Lethbridge sociologist Reginald Bibby, a leading tracker of social trends, "Americans grow up with the sincere belief that their nation is a nation that is unique and special, literally called by something greater to be blessed and to be a blessing to people around the globe." Canadians can't compete with that.

But it turns out that while they've been out conquering the world, here in Canada we've been quietly working away at building better lives. While they've been pursuing happiness, we've been achieving it.

How do we know? You just have to look at the numbers. For our Canada Day special issue this year, *Maclean's* compared Canadians and Americans in every facet of our lives. We scoured census reports, polls, surveys, scientific studies, policy papers and consumer databases. We looked at who lives longer, who works more, who spends more time with friends, who travels more and who has more sex. We even found out who eats more vegetables.

*Source:* Duncan Hood, "How Canada Stole the American Dream," *Maclean's* (July 7, 2008), pp. 51–54. © 2008 by Maclean's Magazine. Reprinted with permission.

After digging through the data, here's what we found: the staid, under-paid Canadian is dead. Believe it or not, we now have more wealth than Americans, even though we work shorter hours. We drink more often, but we live longer and have fewer diseases. We have more sex, more sex partners and we're more adventurous in bed, but we have fewer teen pregnancies and fewer sexually transmitted diseases. We spend more time with family and friends, and more time exploring the world. Even in crime we come out ahead: we're just as prone to break the law, but when we do it, we don't get shot. Most of the time, we don't even go to jail.

The data [show] that it's the Canadians who are living it up, while Americans toil away, working longer hours to pay their mounting bills. The wealth numbers, in particular, are shocking. As of 2005, the median family in Canada was worth US$122,600, according to Statistics Canada, while the U.S. Federal Reserve pegged the median American family at US$93,100 in 2004. Those figures, the most recent available, already include an adjustment for our higher prices, and thanks to the rising loonie Canadians are likely even further ahead today. We're ahead mainly because Americans carry far more debt than we do, and it means that the median Canadian family is a full 30 per cent wealthier than the median American family. "The fact that we're now richer is a big reversal," says Jack Mintz, former president of the C.D. Howe Institute and the current Palmer Chair in public policy at the University of Calgary. "It's a huge change in the way we view the world."

---

**Canadians Are Wealthier Than Americans**

Americans used to be wealthier than us, but no more. Yes, they have bigger homes and nicer cars, but they bought it all on credit. When you look at our net worth, which is what we have when we add up the value of everything we own and subtract what we owe, you find that the median Canadian family is 30 per cent richer.

|  | Canada | United States |
|---|---|---|
| Median Family Net Worth (adjusted for purchasing power) | US$122,600 | US$93,100 |
| Median Household Income (adjusted for purchasing power) | US$44,325 | US$46,325 |
| Per Capita Personal Debt | US$23,460 | US$40,250 |
| Average Size of a One-Family House (in square feet) | 2,000 | 2,520 |
| Per cent of Annual Household Expenditure Spent on Housing | 19 | 34 |
| Per cent of Disposable Income Spent on Personal Consumption | 95 | 96 |

*Source:* Net worth: Statistics Canada's "Survey of Financial Security" (original 2005 figure: $148,400, adjusted by 2005 IMF PPP rate of 1.21) and U.S. Federal Reserve's "Recent Changes in U.S. Family Finances" (2004 data); incomes: StatsCan's "Household Income Groups in Constant 2005 Dollars" (original 2005 figure: $53,634 adjusted by 2005 IMF PPP rate of 1.21) and U.S. Census Bureau's "Median Household Income in Current 2005 Dollars;" per capita debt (2005, both adjusted from C$ to US$ by PPP): StatsCan's perspective on Labour and Income: Personal Debt," January 2007; house size; Canadian Home Builders' Association's "Pulse Winter 2008 Survey" and U.S. Census Bureau (2007); housing expenditure (2006); StatsCan and U.S. Bureau of Labor Statistics; disposable income (2008 Q1); TD Economics.

Mintz points out that it wasn't all that long ago that we were much poorer than the Americans. Just think back to the 1980s when our dollar was worth 69 American cents, inflation was raging, our real wages were dropping and our productivity was . . . well it was just embarrassing. "From 1987 to 1997 in particular, we had terrible economic growth," says Mintz. "By the time we reached 1999, we were way behind the U.S. in per capita incomes and everything else." Back then, he notes, the newspapers were packed with dire warnings of brain drain. Canadian incomes were so low compared to Americans, our best and brightest were fleeing the country.

Today, it's the reverse, and families such as Eric Nay, his wife, Polly, and their son are moving the other way. Nay, who's 41 and now works as associate dean at the Ontario College of Art & Design in Toronto, says he packed his bags and left his home in tony Monterey, Calif., for a new life in Canada two years ago. And get this: he did it for a bigger paycheque. "The academic salaries here are much higher," he says. "When I was working as an assistant professor in California, I was making $55,000, but in Canada, that magically becomes $70,000."

How did this happen? Canada often comes out ahead when you look at squishy things like quality of life. But since when were we richer? Mintz credits the rising loonie, the boom in commodities, and better public policy. He says that over the past decade productivity growth in the U.S. has slowed, while we've been hacking away at our government debt and lowering taxes. In short, as a nation, we've been doing everything right, while the U.S. has been doing everything wrong.

When you look at how individual Canadian and American families make and spend their money, it gets even more interesting. The numbers show that our median household incomes are about the same, or at least they were back in 2005 when the most recent figures came out. That year the median household income in Canada was about US$44,300, after you adjust it for the exchange rate and our lower purchasing power, while the American median was US$46,300. Since then, the loonie has gained on the U.S. dollar, so we've likely narrowed the gap. But while our incomes may be similar to American incomes, we're still much wealthier because we have less debt. What you make isn't a good measure of how rich you are—to figure out your true wealth you should add up everything you have and subtract what you owe. And Americans owe more. A lot more. Here in Canada the average amount of personal debt per person is US$23,460. In the U.S. it's a whopping US$40,250. And all those numbers are from 2005, just before their housing market slipped into a sinkhole. If you looked at the numbers now, you'd find that Americans are even further behind, because their largest asset—their home—is worth less. "There has been a lot of destruction of wealth in the U.S. over the past few years," says Mintz, "and that would affect the net worth figures significantly. I would suspect that they would be even worse off today."

Why do Americans owe so much? Because they spend, spend, spend. "In the U.S. spending is seen as patriotic," says Roger Sauvé, president of People Patterns Consulting and author of *Borderlines*, a book comparing Canada and the U.S. "After 9/11, the President said you have to support the economy, you have to get out to the malls." Mintz agrees, pointing out that the big tax break many Americans get on their mortgage interest also contributes to their debt. "The typical Canadian will borrow to buy a house and then over time he'll pay off the mortgage," Mintz says. "In the U.S. the behavior is very different. There, people borrow a lot to buy their house, but they never pay it off. They have a mortgage all through their life."

Certainly Canadians who venture down to live in the U.S. say there's a huge difference in how the two countries approach spending and debt. Gerry Van Boven grew up in southern Ontario but moved to the U.S. in 1985. Now he's 57 and living in Fort Lauderdale, Fla. He says his American friends seem genuinely puzzled by his reluctance to load on huge piles of debt so he can buy a big luxury car and a monster home. "Most of the people that I know who were born and raised here are a lot farther in hock than I am, and they think that's quite normal," he says. "They're like, 'Can't afford it? I'll just put it on plastic.' Whereas I was brought up to believe that if you can't afford to buy it in cash, you can't afford it."

The numbers confirm that Americans like to spend big. They have bigger homes than we do, averaging about 2,500 sq. feet, compared to only 2,000 sq. feet in Canada. They spend about 34 per cent of their annual household expenditure on their homes, compared to just 19 per cent here. They also love big cars. In the U.S., luxury cars and SUVs make up 21 per cent of the market, whereas in Canada, they make up only 11 per cent. The most popular model overall in the U.S. is the more upscale Toyota Camry, whereas we prefer the basic Honda Civic. "They like the big SUVs here especially," says Van Boven, "or at least they did. A good friend of mine went out and bought one of those big GMC Yukons a while back, but now gas is at $4 a gallon. I saw him the other day and asked when he was going to get rid of it. 'I can't,' he said. 'I don't own it yet.'"

Bibby, the sociologist, says the great American debt load is a direct result of their relentless quest for the best. "American culture is more consumer-oriented due to a more intense and more vigorous marketplace," he says. "My sense is that more dollars are spent per capita on advertising, for example. Little wonder then that per capita debt is considerably higher in the U.S. than in Canada. It is largely a function of the aggressive and successful marketing efforts of American companies."

Health care, too, is helping to keep Americans in a state of owe, and for all the same reasons. In the U.S., as long as you have a good insurance plan, you have access to the best health care in the world. MRI machines are available on an hour's notice, there's plenty of staff, and the specialists are the finest there are. But all of that comes at a cost, says Van Boven, and every American feels it. "The absolute biggest difference, financially, that I noticed was the cost of health insurance," he says. "When my wife got laid off, we found out that you could keep the insurance you got through work for a while as long as you paid for it. But it cost $5,000 a year, and that was back in 1986. We couldn't afford that. So since then I've had no health insurance." Eric Nay, who moved to Toronto from

California, says that even Americans with good insurance feel the pinch. "When I taught for the state of California, I had the best health coverage on the planet," he reports. "But when my son was born—and it was totally by the book, no complications—my insurance only covered the first $10,000 of the hospital costs. The remaining $8,000 came out of my pocket. And that's with full coverage."

Meanwhile in Canada, not only are we wealthier, but we don't even have to work as hard to make that wealth. In 2004, the average Canadian worker put in 35 hours of work per week, while our American counterparts put in 38. Only 30 per cent of Canadians work 45 hours a week or more, compared to 38 per cent of Americans. We also get—and take—much more vacation time. Employed adults in Canada get about 17 vacation days a year, and we take 16 of those days, leaving just one on the table. In the U.S., they get 14 days of vacation, but they only take 11, making them the world leader in yet another category: the working drudge.

Because we have more time off, Canadians tend to have a lot more fun. We spend more time with friends than Americans do, and we're much more

## Canadians Work Less and Spend More Time with Friends

Canadians work fewer hours than Americans and take more vacation time. As a result, we can spend more time with friends and family—and drink more too.

|  | Canada | United States |
| --- | --- | --- |
| Average Number of Hours Worked per Week | 34.6 | 37.9 |
| Per cent Who Work 45 Hours a Week or More | 30 | 38 |
| Number of Vacation Days Earned by the Average Employed Adult Each Year | 17 | 14 |
| Vacation Days Actually Taken | 16 | 11 |
| Per cent Who Spend 6 to 10 Hours per Week with Friends | 29 | 24 |
| Per cent of Parents Who Have Dinner at Home with the Family Every Night | 40 | 28 |
| Per cent Who Consume Alcoholic Drinks at Least "A Few Times a Week" | 27 | 19 |
| Per cent of Household Expenditure That's Spent on Alcohol | 1.3 | 1.0 |
| Per cent of Household Expenditure That's Spent on Vehicle Purchases | 4.5 | 7.1 |
| Luxury, Large and Sport Vehicles as a Percentage of Light Vehicle Sales | 11.0 | 21.3 |
| Top Car Model by Sales | Honda Civic | Toyota Camry |

*Source:* Hours worked (2004): Institute for Competitiveness and Prosperity; Gallup polls: 45+ hours worked (2004), time with friends (2004), dinner at home (2003), alcoholic consumption (2005); vacation (2008): Expedia.com's International Vacation Deprivation Survey; household alcohol and vehicle purchases (2006): Statistics Canada and U.S. Bureau of Labor Statistics; luxury vehicle sales (2007): DesRosiers Automotive Consultants; car models (2007): DesRosiers for Canada and *Automotive News* for U.S.

likely to have a sit-down dinner with the family at home each night. We also tend to drink alcohol more often, with 27 per cent of us having a drink at least a few times a week, compared to 19 per cent of Americans. Nay says that our richer social lives were one of the biggest differences he noticed when he moved to Toronto. "It was only in Canada that I found myself going to the pub with friends and colleagues," he says. "I spend more time in pubs here than I have in any other place that I've lived. It's partly the culture, and partly because the quality of beer is fantastic."

Christian Lander is another Canadian living among Americans. He grew up in Toronto, but the 29-year-old moved to Los Angeles 2½ years ago where he runs the popular Stuff White People Like website, and he's publishing a book under the same name on July 1. He also finds that Americans like to do things big, but that doesn't always mean better. "The expectations here are just different," he says. "There's more ambition. More ambition to acquire more in terms of money and career. Whereas Canadians seem to be more European in that we care more about enjoying life." He's lived all over the country and says that it's very difficult to sum up the differences between Americans and Canadians because Americans are so diverse. The gaps between rich and poor, or black and white within the confines of the U.S. are much deeper and wider than the gap between the two countries. And within that mix, he says there's a subset of Americans who are just like Canadians. "Left-wing urban Americans," he says. "Canada is just a country of left-wing urban Americans." Still, he says that the relentless zeal, the private schools, the long work hours, not to mention the fact that everyone in L.A. seems to carry a gun, well, it all gets him down sometimes. His wife, who's American, is pushing to move back to Toronto, he says. "And yeah, we probably will."

Reginald Bibby notes the irony of the situation. The U.S. is a country that aggressively pursues happiness, but Canada seems to have just stumbled onto it. While Americans are putting in overtime to pursue the American dream, we're at the pub having a few pints with friends. They may have bigger cars and bigger homes, but they're living under a mountain of debt. They look richer, but the numbers prove that they're not. The truth is that all of that competition, all of that keeping up with the Joneses, can take its toll. Getting ahead can be a lot easier when everyone is moving in the same direction. "The pursuit of happiness is ingrained in Americans as part of what it means to be an American," Bibby says. "But in Canada, happiness is almost something of a by-product of coexisting peacefully."

Be it sports, health care, business or wealth, Americans are still competing to be the best. And it's true that the best in the U.S. is the best you'll find on the planet. But when you look at the medians and the averages, their accomplishment pales. As the hard numbers in this report show, Americans have shorter lives, poorer health, less sex, more divorces, and more violent crime. Which may mean that perhaps America isn't the greatest nation on earth. After all, you can't judge a nation by the best it produces, you have to judge it by the success of the average Joe. And the average Joe in Canada is having a way better time.

# Problems of Inequality

# SECTION

# 2

■ ■ ■

# Poverty

## THE UNITED STATES CONTEXT

Using the official statistics on poverty (which understate the magnitude of this social problem), 12.5 percent of the United States population (37.3 million people) were poor in 2007. (The statistics throughout are from U.S. Bureau of the Census, 2008.) The likelihood of being poor is heightened for some categories: (1) *racial minorities* (24.5 percent of all African Americans and 21.5 percent of all Latinos); (2) *women* (22.2 percent of single women; two-thirds of impoverished adults are women); *children* (18.0 percent of all those under age 18 and 20.8 percent for those children under age 6); (4) *elderly women* (one in five women age 75 and over is poor, compared to only one in ten men); and (5) those *living in certain places* (in central cities compared to the suburbs, and those living in four rural regions—the Mississippi Delta, which is primarily African American; the Rio Grande/U.S.–Mexico border, which is largely Latino; the Native American reservations of the Southwest and Plains; and Appalachia, which is predominantly white).

The U.S. poverty rate is the highest in the industrialized world. Child poverty has worsened over time. Among those under 18, poverty has increased by more than 30 percent from 1970. Two experts on comparative poverty rates, Lee Rainwater and Timothy M. Smeeding, state that "Coincidentally, around the end of the twentieth century there were roughly the same number of children in the United States and the twelve European countries—around seventy-two million. But we find that as many as fourteen million American children are poor compared with some seven million poor children in our comparison European countries" (2003:17).

The safety net for the poor and their parents in the United States (e.g., Head Start, health care, housing subsidies) has declined steadily since the Reagan administration, and this decline has increased dramatically as the Bush administration and Congress have enacted tax cuts while increasing the budget allotments to homeland security and defense/war. The fiscal 2006 federal budget, for example, decreased the allocation to Medicaid (health services to the poor) by $10 billion while giving $131 billion in tax cuts (primarily going to the affluent). The poor in Europe, in contrast, have generous supports including universal health care, paid maternity leave, child care subsidies, and housing allowances.

## References

Rainwater, Lee, and Timothy M. Smeeding. 2003. *Poor Kids in a Rich Country*. New York: Russell Sage Foundation.
U.S. Bureau of the Census. 2008. "Income, Poverty, and Health Insurance Coverage in the United States: 2007," *Current Population Reports*, P60–235 (August).

# 5

■ ■ ■

# Poverty, Work, and Policy: The United States in Comparative Perspective

### Gary Burtless and Timothy M. Smeeding

*This is a portion of the testimony before Congress by poverty experts Gary Burtless and Timothy M. Smeeding. This segment shows that the United States has a higher poverty rate than other advanced countries and explains the reasons why.*

## LEVEL OF OVERALL AND CHILD POVERTY

Relative poverty rates in 21 nations are given in Figures 5.1 and 5.2 for all persons and for children. The overall poverty rate for all persons using the 50 percent poverty threshold varies from 5.4 percent in Finland to 20.2 percent in Mexico. The poverty rate is 17.0 percent in the United States, the second highest of all nations and the highest of all rich nations. The average rate of poverty is 10.8 percent across the 21 countries (Figure 5.1).

Higher overall poverty rates are found as one might expect, in Mexico, but also in Anglo-Saxon nations (United States, Australia, Canada, Ireland, and the United Kingdom), and southern European nations (Greece, Spain, Italy) with a relatively high level of overall inequality. Still, Australian, Canadian and British poverty are about 12–13 percent and are, therefore, below the United States levels.

The lowest poverty rates are more common in smaller, well-developed, and high-spending welfare states (Sweden, Finland) where they are about 5 or 6 percent. Middle level rates are found in major European countries, where social policies provide more generous support to single mothers and working

*Source:* Gary Burtless and Timothy M. Smeeding, "Poverty, Work, and Policy: The United States in Comparative Perspective," testimony to Congress, February 13, 2007, excerpt from pp. 5–11.

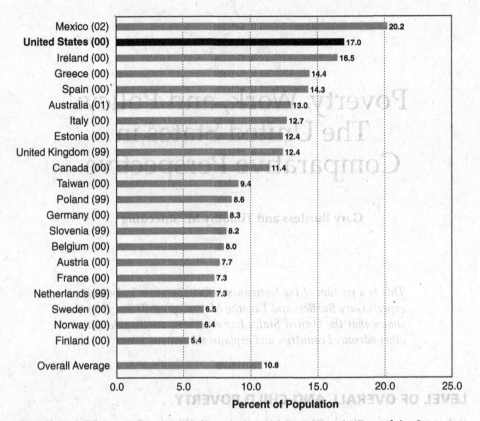

Mexico (02) — 20.2
United States (00) — 17.0
Ireland (00) — 16.5
Greece (00) — 14.4
Spain (00) — 14.3
Australia (01) — 13.0
Italy (00) — 12.7
Estonia (00) — 12.4
United Kingdom (99) — 12.4
Canada (00) — 11.4
Taiwan (00) — 9.4
Poland (99) — 8.6
Germany (00) — 8.3
Slovenia (99) — 8.2
Belgium (00) — 8.0
Austria (00) — 7.7
France (00) — 7.3
Netherlands (99) — 7.3
Sweden (00) — 6.5
Norway (00) — 6.4
Finland (00) — 5.4

Overall Average — 10.8

**Percent of Population**

**FIGURE 5.1** Relative Poverty Rates in Twenty One Rich Nations at the Turn of the Century for All Persons

(Percent of ALL Persons with Disposable Income Less than 50 percent of Adjusted National Disposable Median Income)

*Source:* Author's calculations from Luxembourg Income Study.

women (through paid family leave, for example), and where social assistance minimums are high. For instance, the Netherlands, Austria, Belgium, and Germany have poverty rates that are in the 8 to 9 percent range, while France is at 7 percent. Even the former Soviet block nations of Estonia, Poland and Slovenia, and Taiwan have much lower poverty rates than does the United States.

On average, child poverty is a slightly larger problem than is overall poverty in these nations, but the cross-national patterns are very similar (Figure 5.2). After Mexico, the United States child poverty rate is at 21.9 percent compared to the 11.8 percent average over these 21 nations. European child poverty rates are lower and Anglo-Saxon rates higher among these nations, but the United States is more than 4.0 percentage points higher than any other rich nation.

Moreover, note that the story is not one of poor immigrants, as two nations with substantially higher fractions of children born to foreigners, Canada and

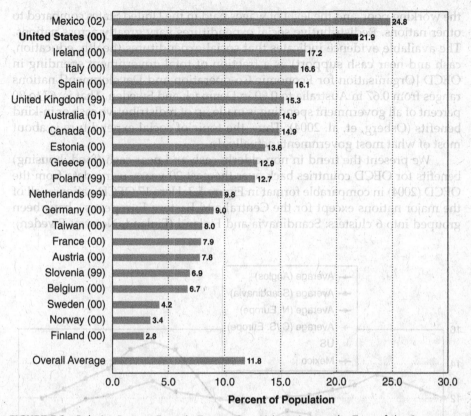

**FIGURE 5.2**   Relative Poverty Rates in Twenty One Rich Nations at the Turn of the Century for Children*

(Percent of CHILDREN with Disposable Income Less than 50 percent of Adjusted National Disposable Median Income)

*Persons 17 or younger.

*Source:* Author's calculations from Luxembourg Income Study.

Australia, have child poverty rates that are both 14.9 percent, a full 7 percentage points less than the United States rate.

We do not present trends in poverty rates here for any nations, but in many nations though not all, child poverty has risen since 2000. This is most certainly the case in the United States but not in the United Kingdom. . . .

## TOWARDS EXPLANATIONS: CROSS-NATIONAL SPENDING PATTERNS, AND RELATION OF SPENDING AND PAY TO POVERTY

We have seen clearly different patterns of poverty in the Unites States relative to other nations. What explains these differences? In short, the explanations are related to two things: the amount of support we give to the poor, especially the working poor, and the level of wages paid in the United States compared to other nations. Redistributive social expenditures vary greatly across nations. The available evidence indicates that social expenditures (health, education, cash and near cash support) as a fraction of total government spending in OECD [Organisation for Economic Co-operation and Development] nations ranges from 0.67 in Australia to 0.90 in Denmark and Sweden. That is, 67 to 90 percent of all government spending is made up of redistributive cash or in-kind benefits (Osberg, et. al. 2004). Thus, the topic of social expenditure is about most of what most governments actually do.

We present the trend in non-elderly cash and near cash (food, housing) benefits for OECD countries back over the past 20 years, using data from the OECD (2004) in comparable format in Figure 5.3. Here 17 OECD nations—all of the major nations except for the Central and Eastern Europeans—have been grouped into 6 clusters: Scandinavia and Finland (Finland, Norway, Sweden);

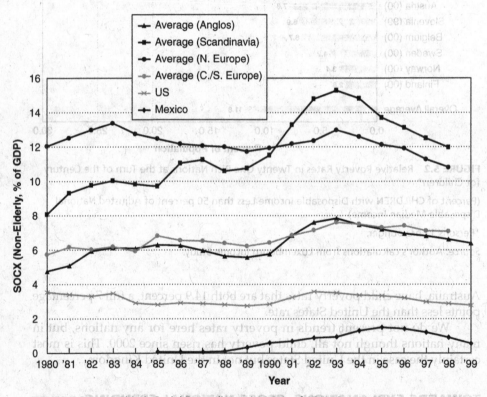

**FIGURE 5.3** Non-Elderly Social Expenditures in 6 Sets of 17 Nations*

*Total Non-Elderly Social Expenditures (as percentage of GDP), including all cash plus near cash spending (e.g., food stamps) and public housing but excluding health care and education spending. OECD (2004). Anglos include Australia, UK, Canada; Scandinavia includes Finland, Norway, Sweden; Northern Europe includes Belgium, Denmark, Netherlands; Central/Southern Europe includes Austria, France, Germany, Italy, Luxembourg, Spain.

Northern Europe (Belgium, Denmark, Netherlands); Central and Southern Europe (Austria, France, Germany, Italy, Greece, Luxembourg, Spain); Anglo Saxony (Australia, United Kingdom and Canada); the United States and Mexico.

The Scandinavian and Northern Europeans follow similar patterns—high levels of spending showing responsiveness to the recession of the early 1990s in Sweden and Finland, and a tapering after these events. The Central and Southern Europeans and the Anglo-Saxon nations show remarkably similar spending patterns, again with expenditures rising in the early 1990s, but overall at a level distinctly below that the other two groups. The United States is significantly below all these others and by the late 1990s is spending at a level closer, in terms of a fraction of GDP per capita, to Mexico than to the other richer OECD nations.

These figures illustrate the wide differences that one can find for both levels and trends in social spending, using figures that abstract from financing of health care, education and retirement for the elderly. They also correspond very closely to the measures of money and near-money income poverty used in the analytic literature in this area, including that presented above.

A substantial fraction of the variance in non-elderly cross-national poverty rates appears to be accounted for by the cross-national variation in the incidence of low pay (Figure 5.4). Because the United States has the highest proportion of

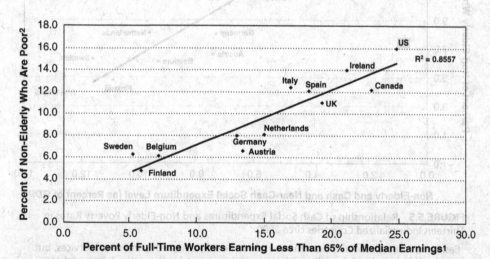

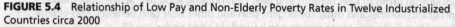

**FIGURE 5.4** Relationship of Low Pay and Non-Elderly Poverty Rates in Twelve Industrialized Countries circa 2000

[1]Data refer to the most recent year for which data could be found (2000 for US, UK, Italy and Canada; 1998 for Germany, Sweden and the Netherlands; 1996 for Austria; 1995 for Belgium, Spain and Ireland). Data for Italy refer to net earnings. Data for Greece are not available.

[2]Percentage of persons below 65 in poor households.

*Source:* OECD database on earnings (as reported in OECD Employment Outlook 2005) and authors' tabulations of the LIS data files.

workers in relatively poorly paid jobs,[1] it also has the highest poverty rate, even among parents who work half time or more (Burtless, Rainwater, and Smeeding 2001; Smeeding 2006). On the other hand, other countries that have a significantly lower incidence of low-paid employment . . . also have significantly lower poverty rates than does the United States.

But, the prevalence of low-pay workers is, in fact, not the only reliable predictor of poverty rates. While low pay is a good predictor of United States poverty rates, and while poorly-educated workers do not do well at keeping their families from poverty based on earnings alone, other factors, such as the antipoverty efforts of the government, are also important predictors of the poverty rate (Figure 5.5). Here we see that higher social spending reduces poverty.

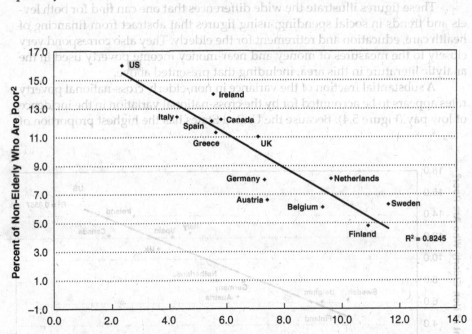

**FIGURE 5.5** Relationship of Cash Social Expenditures and Non-Elderly Poverty Rates in Thirteen Industrialized Countries circa 2000

[1]Cash and non-cash social expenditures exclude health, education, and social services, but include all forms of cash benefits and near cash housing subsidies, active labor market program subsidies and other contingent cash and other near cash benefits. Non-elderly benefits include only those accruing to household head under age 65.

[2]Percentage of persons below 65 in poor households.

*Source:* OECD (2004) and authors' tabulations of the LIS data files. Cash and non-cash social expenditures exclude health, education, and social services, but include all forms of cash benefits and near cash housing subsidies, active labor market program subsidies and other contingent cash and other near cash benefits. Non-elderly benefits includes only those accruing to household head under age 65.

As a result of its low level of spending on social transfers to the non-aged, the United States again has a very high poverty rate. Even though social spending in general has an inverse correlation with poverty rates, different patterns of social spending can produce different effects on national poverty rates. Antipoverty and social insurance programs are in most respects unique to each country. There is no one kind of program or set of programs that are conspicuously successful in all countries that use them. Social insurance, universal benefits (such as child allowances), and social assistance transfer programs targeted on low-income populations are mixed in different ways in different countries. So, too, are minimum wages, worker preparation and training programs, work-related benefits (such as childcare and family leave), and other social benefits.

The United States differs from most nations that achieve lower poverty rates because of its emphasis on work and self-reliance for working-age adults, regardless of the wages workers must accept or the family situation of those workers. For over a decade, United States unemployment has been well below the OECD average, and until recently American job growth has been much faster than the OECD average. The strong economy coupled with a few specific antipoverty devices (like the expanded EITC) has produced most of the United States overall and child poverty reduction in recent years, though it is decidedly below the effects found in other nations (Smeeding 2005; 2006). Simply put, the United States does not spend enough to make up for low levels of pay, and so we end up with a relatively higher poverty rate than do other nations.

## Note

1. There are no figures for low pay in the other nation[s] studied here, especially none for Mexico.

## References

Organization for Economic Cooperation and Development. 2004. "OECD Social Expenditure Database: 1980–1999." Paris: Organization for Economic Cooperation and Development at www.oecd.org.

Organization for Economic Cooperation and Development. 2005. *Employment Outlook*. Paris: Organization for Economic Cooperation and Development at www.oecd.org.

Osberg, Lars, Timothy M. Smeeding, and Jonathan Schwabish. 2004. "Income Distribution and Public Social Expenditure: Theories, Effects, and Evidence." In Kathryn Neckerman (ed.), *Social Inequality*. New York: Russell Sage Foundation.

Smeeding, Timothy M. 2005. "Government Programs and Social Outcomes: The United States in Comparative Perspective." In A. Auerbach, D. Card, and J. Quigley (eds.), *Poverty, Public Policy, and the Distribution of Income*. New York: Russell Sage Foundation, forthcoming.

Smeeding, Timothy M. 2006. "Poor People in Rich Nations: The United States in Comparative Perspective." *Journal of Economic Perspectives* 20(1) (Winter): 69–90.

# 6

■ ■ ■

# How Other Countries
# Fight the War on Poverty

### Sid Ryan

*Sid Ryan, a Canadian who grew up in Ireland, examines how
the Scandanavian countries and Ireland outperform Canada
and the United States in reducing poverty. He concludes that
"everything the pro-market, less government proponents say is
bad, is really good for working families and the poor."*

I grew up poor in a family of 10 children in the Republic of Ireland. At the time,
Ireland had one of the highest poverty rates among industrialized countries.
That was five decades ago, well before the Ireland of today where progressive
government social and economic policies have improved the standard of living
for many people there.

While policies like free post-secondary education, a living wage (not a
minimum wage) for low-income earners and co-operative job/economic strategies between labour, business and government have set Ireland on a better
course, the child poverty rate remains stubbornly high (it is on par with
Canada's at about 15 per cent).

That's because, according to recent studies measuring poverty, both Canadian and Irish government spending on family and social benefits falls far short
of where these investments can mitigate the growing gap between rich and
poor in global market economies, and show meaningful results in decreasing
poverty rates.

Where we should be looking for a socio-economic model that benefits
the majority of citizens and where poverty rates are lowest—between 2 and
5 per cent—is Denmark, Finland, Sweden and Norway.

Outperforming Canada and all the other Organization for Economic Co-
operation and Development (OECD) countries, in many quality of life indices,

*Source:* Sid Ryan, "How Other Countries Fight the War on Poverty," *Toronto Star* (January 19, 2007),
p. A13. Used by permission.

these Scandinavian countries have high taxation rates (between 42 per cent and 52 per cent of gross domestic product) compared to Canada's rate of 34 per cent of GDP, high social program spending, and high worker unionization rates of more than 80 per cent.

In addition, according to a UNICEF study, the government policies of these countries are the most effective at alleviating the effects of "market" forces on the poor, and conversely, in lowering child poverty rates.

Conscious that the income gap between rich and poor in a booming Irish economy was growing, Ireland tackled the problem of low incomes on several fronts.

These policies included raising the minimum wage to a living wage— about $12 an hour as of this January—taking low-income earners off the income tax rolls, increasing child care, housing and heat subsidies, and pumping more money into workers' training programs.

Ireland even increased welfare rates for those between jobs and targeted economically depressed communities for job-creation programs.

Without this aggressive government intervention, poverty rates in Ireland would be much higher than they are.

The naysayers in Canada, opposed to raising the minimum wage and government policies like social housing and universal child care, should take heed that the economic sky did not fall in Ireland. Rather, economic growth skyrocketed, and the standard of living of many people has increased.

In both Ireland and several of the Scandinavian countries, close links between business, trade unions and universities have boosted the skills of the workforce in the growing, knowledge-based economy.

In short, there is greater social cohesion, equality of opportunity and poverty rates are lower in countries where there is high tax, where governments redistribute a higher percentage of the national income to protect low-wage earners and the poor against market forces, where the majority of workers are unionized, and where child care is free or subsidized.

Go figure. Everything the pro-market, less government proponents say is bad, is really good for working families and the poor.

Of the OECD countries, only Mexico, with a 28 per cent child poverty rate, has a higher rate of child poverty than the United States at 22 per cent.

Marked by low taxes, low unionization rates, for-profit health care, low minimum wage rates, and great income disparity, the U.S. is not the socio-economic model Canadians should aspire to.

Yet, it is the model promoted by Prime Minister Stephen Harper who in the last election campaign said he believes "all taxes are bad," who has fronted organizations vehemently opposed to labour unions that help raise workers' wages and who favours tax cuts to investments in social spending.

In the coming federal election, voters can give Harper a strong message: Lower child poverty and improve the quality of life for poor and middle-income earners or else we will give the heave-ho to you and your "new" government.

# 3

## ■ ■ ■

# Income and Wealth Inequality

## THE UNITED STATES CONTEXT

Income and wealth inequality refers to the gap between the rich and the poor on these related dimensions. The United States has the largest inequality gap in the industrialized world. Moreover, the rate of growth in inequality is faster than in any other industrialized country.

Some of the facts concerning income and wealth inequality in the United States include:

- The total net worth of the 400 richest Americans was $1.25 trillion in 2006 (Forbes, 2006). At the other extreme, 37.3 million Americans were living below the poverty line in 2006.
- The top 1 percent of the population now owns 38 percent of the nation's wealth, while the bottom 40 percent own 1 percent. In short, the combined wealth of the richest 3 million Americans is nearly 40 times richer than 113 million at the bottom (Packer, 2003).
- The 13,000 wealthiest families in the United States earn more income than the bottom 20 million families (Sanders, 2004).
- In 1992 it took the combined wages of 287,400 retail clerks to equal the pay of the top 400 individuals. In 2004 it required the combined pay of 504,600 retail clerks to match the pay of the top 400 (Barlett and Steele, 2004).
- The Bush administration and Congress enacted massive tax cuts totaling $1.7 trillion in 2001 and 2003. The richest 1 percent of Americans reaped 54 percent of the total of these two tax breaks (Children's Defense Fund, 2004:xxviii).

This rising inequality gap in the United States has enormous consequences. If the trend continues, the number of people on the economic margin will rise. Homelessness and hunger will increase. Family disruption will escalate. Crime rates will swell. Public safety will become much more problematic. More generally, this phenomenon of economic inequality has implications for democracy, crime, and civil unrest. Economist Lester Thurow, wondering about this move toward a two-tiered society, asks: "How much inequality can a democracy take? The income gap in America is eroding the social contract. If the promise of a higher standard of living is limited to a few at the top, the rest of the citizenry, as history shows, is likely to grow disaffected, or worse" (Thurow, 1995:78).

## References

Barlett, Donald L., and James B. Steele. 2004. "Has Your Life Become a Game of Chance?" *Time* (February 2):42–44.

Children's Defense Fund. 2004. *The State of America's Children 2004*. Washington, DC: Author.

*Forbes.* 2006. "Forbes 400 Richest People in America." (October 9).

Packer, George. 2003. "The End of Equality." *Mother Jones* 28 (November/December):30–33.

Sanders, Bernie. 2004. "We Are the Majority." *The Progressive* 68 (February):26–29.

Thurow, Lester. 1995. "Why Their World Might Crumble." *New York Times Magazine* (November 19):78–79.

# 7

# Income and Wealth Inequality

## Americans for Democratic Action

*This report by the Americans for Democratic Action shows the extent of inequality in income and wealth in the United States and how it is worse than in other major industrial countries. Also provided is a list of policy shifts that would lessen this inequality gap.*

Inequality in the distribution of income and wealth and persistent poverty continue to jeopardize equal opportunity and democracy as the United States begins the 21st century. Extreme inequality of income and wealth gives vast economic and political power to big corporations and wealthy families and weakens the sense of community and common purpose essential to a democracy.

The rise in income inequality results from shifting policy choices and power favoring the wealthy. Each reinforces the other. Capital has taken power from labor, and local, state and national governments have pursued changes in policy that strengthen corporations and weaken workers.

Income inequality is worse in the United States than in other major industrial countries. Australia, Canada, and 10 European countries have much more equal distribution of income.

Recent U.S. Census Bureau statistics show the rich are getting still richer; middle income Americans are just barely raising their incomes; and the poor are falling still lower on the income ladder. The gap between rich and poor is now bigger than it has been since the 1930s. An incredible 98% of the 1979–92 gain in total household income went to the wealthiest 20% of households. The remaining 2% gain in total household income was shared by the remaining 80% of households.

In 2005 the richest fifth of families received 48.1% of total income and the poorest fifth received only 4.0%—a national income ratio of 12 to 1. The richest

*Source:* Americans for Democratic Action, "Income and Wealth Inequality," (2007). Online: www
.adaction.org. Reprinted by permission.

5% of families received 21.1% of income, which is approximately equal to the income of the lower 50% of families.

In 1995 the richest 10% of the population owned 70% of all the wealth—up from 50% in 1976—and the richest 1% owned 35.1% of all wealth, while the bottom 80% owned 31.5%.

In 2005 36.9 million Americans (12.6% of the population) lived in poverty: a rise of 1.1 million from 2003. A reported 12.8 million children under the age of 18 lived in poverty in 2005, a number that is still higher than the poverty rate for 18–64 year olds and people 65 and over. One out of every three Black and Hispanic children live in poverty—and the average income for families in poverty is half the poverty threshold; in fact, the number of families in poverty increased to 7.9 million in 2004 from 7.6 million in 2003.

Average hourly wages for private, non-farm production and non-supervisory workers (about 80% of all workers) were $16.13 in 2005. By contrast, in the last years of the 1970s, average hourly wages were about $15.00 expressed in 2004 dollars to adjust for inflation. In other words, the purchasing power of hourly wages rose only 7% in more than two decades (1978–2005)—scarcely $1/4$ of one percent a year while Corporate profits have been expanding rapidly and taking an ever rising share of national income.

The tax legislation promoted by President Bush has sharply worsened the already existing inequitable distribution of income and wealth through the elimination of the estate tax, disproportionate cuts in income tax rates, and other provisions favoring the most affluent families and powerful corporations.

## THEREFORE ADA RESOLVES THAT:

1. Deep cuts in programs designed to serve low-income families and individuals, the working poor, the disabled, and the elderly must be reversed. Needed funds can be gained through cuts in corporate welfare legislation, cuts in military spending, and a reversal of tax cuts for the wealthiest.
2. The federal government must assume a role in expanding job opportunities through such programs as public works and public service and increasing access to year-round full-time jobs. In the spirit of President Franklin D. Roosevelt's Economic Bill of Rights, the federal government must create year-round, full-time living-wage jobs when private industry does not provide enough jobs for all who want to work. All new programs must include strong anti-displacement and wage protection language.
3. Laws must be passed to require equal benefits for those at the top and bottom of employment rolls. Corporate executives should not be permitted to increase their pension and health care packages at the same time that they are cutting those for lower-income workers. The federal government also should require employers to provide a minimum level of health, pension and other benefits, as it does for the minimum wage. Additionally, corporations must be required to offer paid parental leave to all workers

so that parents do not have to choose between their jobs and the best interests of their children.

4. The federal government also must play a constructive role in elementary and secondary education, and ensure equality of educational opportunity across all income levels.

5. The extremely regressive tax cuts of 2001 give the top 1% of taxpayers almost 40% of the reduction. These cuts will cost the Treasury at least $1.8 trillion over the next decade. The tax bills of 2002 and 2003 add additional revenue losses. That huge drain has more than absorbed the surplus, and will force sharp erosion of funds needed for vital social and domestic programs, such as health, welfare, education, housing, and the environment. This reflects the Republican policies of curtailing a broad range of federal programs for meeting basic social and economic needs. The U.S. must return to a progressive system of taxation to mitigate inequality. Currently pending additional tax cuts, with the greatest benefit going to the wealthiest Americans, must be rejected in favor of a fairer system.

6. International trade pacts should be designed to bring other workers up to U.S. standards rather than pulling down the wages of U.S. workers. The U.S. must require its trading partners to adhere to environmental, labor and human rights standards at least equal to internationally recognized standards. U.S. companies that manufacture goods outside the U.S. and import them into the U.S. should be treated in the same manner as U.S. companies which manufacture goods in the U.S., paying their full share of taxes. Subsidies to corporations that export jobs must be ended. This will discourage companies from moving jobs overseas and across borders to increase profits and avoid taxes; any increase in revenue should be used to provide job training for displaced workers in the U.S. and to monitor conditions for workers in developing countries.

7. The Federal Reserve Board must focus on high employment/high growth instead of focusing only on potential higher inflation.

8. The federal government must act to encourage the growth of unions and to protect the rights of unorganized workers. Unions can thrive only when the rights to organize and collectively bargaining are guaranteed effectively and enforced by the government.

9. The government should fund the Trade Adjustment Assistant Reform Act of 2002 more fully to ensure that workers displaced by imports receive increased benefits, training and rapid assistance as they adjust to their new status.

# 8

# Inequality Here and There

## Claude S. Fischer, Michael Hout, Martin Sanchez Jankowski, Samuel R. Lucas, Ann Swidler, and Kim Voss

*The authors argue that inequality is not due to the distribution of talent in society nor to the natural workings of the market. Inequality in the United States is the result of societal choices based on the cultural support for rewarding difference and the resulting supply-side policies. In effect, inequality in the United States is by design. As the authors point out, other nations have designed systems that are less unequal than that of the United States.*

A glance behind us to American history shows that our pattern of inequality is far from fixed or naturally determined. A glance sideways to other wealthy nations makes the same point. The United States has the greatest degree of economic inequality of any developed country. It is a level of inequality that is not fated by Americans' talents nor necessitated by economic conditions but is the result of policy choices. The nations with which we will compare the United States are also modern, affluent, democratic, and capitalist—they are our competitors in the global market—and yet they have ways to reduce inequality and remain competitive.

The best and latest evidence on how nations compare in levels of inequality comes from the Luxembourg Income Study (so named because the project is headquartered in Luxembourg). Social scientists affiliated with the study have collected detailed, comparable data on earnings and income from over a dozen nations. Our first use of their research appears in Figure 8.1, which speaks to the question of inequality in *earnings*, specifically earnings of men, aged 25–54, who worked full-time, all year during the mid- to late 1980s. (Comparable data on

*Source:* Excerpt from Claude S. Fischer, Michael Hout, Martin Sanchez Jankowski, Samuel R. Lucas, Ann Swidler, and Kim Voss. 1996. *Inequality by Design: Cracking the Bell Curve Myth* (pp. 120–128). Princeton, NJ: Princeton University Press. Reprinted by permission of Princeton University Press.

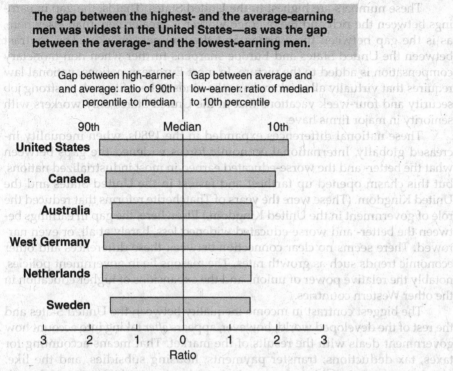

The gap between the highest- and the average-earning men was widest in the United States—as was the gap between the average- and the lowest-earning men.

| Gap between high-earner and average: ratio of 90th percentile to median | Gap between average and low-earner: ratio of median to 10th percentile |

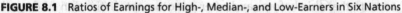

**FIGURE 8.1**   Ratios of Earnings for High-, Median-, and Low-Earners in Six Nations

*Source:* Adapted from Peter Gottschalk and Timothy Smeeding, 1995. "Cross-National Comparisons of Levels and Trends in Inequality." Working Paper no. 126, Luxembourg Income Study. Syracuse, NY: Maxwell School of Citizenship and Public Affairs, July.

earnings were available for only five nations. We are looking just at men here, because the situation of women in the labor force was in such flux and varied so much among nations.) The vertical line in the figure serves as an anchor for looking at inequality in each nation. It represents the earnings of the average (median) worker. The horizontal bars to the left of the median line display the ratio of the earnings that men near, but not at the top of, the earnings ladder received—those at the 90th percentile in earnings—to the earnings of men at the median. In 1986 the 90th percentile American male worker earned 1.8 times what the median worker earned. The bars stretching to the right represent the same comparison between the median earner and a low-paid worker, one at the 10th percentile of earnings. In the United States, the median worker brought home 2.8 times the amount the 10th percentile worker did. The left-hand bars, therefore, display inequality of earnings between the high-earners and the average; the right-hand bars display inequality between the average and the low-earners. Together, they display total inequality. In the United States, the 90th percentile worker earned five times that of the 10th percentile worker.

These numbers are highest in the United States. That is, the gap in earnings between the rich and the average worker is greater here than elsewhere, as is the gap between the average and the low-paid worker. The contrast between the United States and Europe sharpens further when non-monetary compensation is added to the picture. In most European nations, national law requires that virtually all workers have the kinds of benefits such as strong job security and four-week vacations that in the United States only workers with seniority in major firms have.

These national differences expanded in the 1980s, when inequality increased globally. International economic forces widened the gaps between what the better- and the worse-educated earned in most industrialized nations, but this chasm opened up farthest and fastest in the United States and the United Kingdom. (These were the years of Thatcherite reforms that reduced the role of government in the United Kingdom.) Elsewhere, the gap in earnings between the better- and worse-educated widened less, barely at all, or even narrowed. There seems no clear connection between these differences and other economic trends such as growth rates. The reasons lie in government policies, notably the relative power of unions and the expansions of higher education in the other Western countries.

The biggest contrast in income inequality between the United States and the rest of the developed world, however, appears *after* taking into account how government deals with the results of the market. That means accounting for taxes, tax deductions, transfer payments, housing subsidies, and the like. (Again, we note that this before- and after-government distinction underestimates the role of government. Where, for example, governments require employers to provide certain benefits, there is more market equality.)

To look at international differences in *household income*, we turn again to the Luxembourg Income Study. Peter Gottschalk and Timothy Smeeding compiled comparable data on households' disposable incomes—income after taxes and government support, adjusted for household size—in seventeen nations. In Figure 8.2, we use just the figures for nations with over ten million residents in 1980; our conclusions about the United States would be virtually the same if we showed the smaller nations, too. As in Figure 8.1, the bars to the left of the median display the ratio of a rich household's income (at the 90th percentile) to an average one's income, while the right-hand bars show the ratio of an average household's income to that of a poor one (10th percentile). The rich-to-average ratio is greatest in the United States, 2.1, as is the average-to-poor ratio, 2.9, and so the rich-to-poor ratio, 5.9 (not shown) is much higher than that of the next most unequal nations (4.0 for Italy, Canada, and Australia). In short, the United States has the greatest degree of income inequality in the West whether one focuses on the gap between the poor and the middle or the gap between the middle and the rich. Even these numbers underestimate America's distinctiveness, because they do not count the sorts of "in-kind" help that middle- and lower-income families receive in most other nations, such as free health care, child care, and subsidized housing and transportation. They also underestimate inequality

The income gap between the richest and the average household and the gap between the average household and the poorest are both wider in the United States than elsewhere.

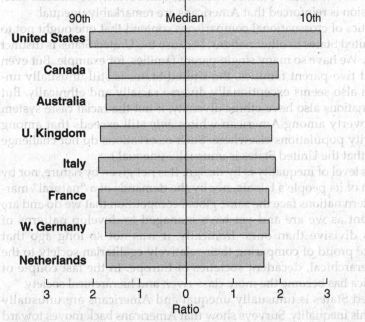

Gap between rich and average:  |  Gap between average and poor:
ratio of 90th percentile to median  |  ratio of median to 10th percentile

**FIGURE 8.2** Ratios of Incomes for High-, Median-, and Low-Income Households in Eight Nations

*Source:* Adapted from Peter Gottschalk and Timothy Smeeding, "Cross-National Comparisons of Levels and Trends in Inequality." Working Paper no. 126, Luxembourg Income Study. Syracuse, NY: Maxwell School of Citizenship and Public Affairs, July.

in America by not displaying the concentration of income at the very top of the income ladder.

Western nations generally take two routes to reducing inequality. . . . Some intervene in the market to ensure relatively equal distributions of *earnings* by, for example, brokering nationwide wage agreements, assisting unions, or providing free child care. Others use taxes and government benefits to reduce inequality of *income* after the market. A few do both seriously, such as the Scandinavian countries. The United States does the least of either. If one sets aside older people, who benefit a great deal from government action in the United States, the net effect of taxes and transfers here is to leave the degree of inequality virtually unchanged from the way it was determined by market earnings.

When everything is accounted for, the Western nation with the most income inequality is the United States. But the United States is also exceptionally unequal in terms of *wealth*. At the end of the 1980s, the richest 1 percent of families owned about 40 percent of household wealth here, more than in any other advanced nation; the richest 1 percent owned only 25 percent of the wealth in Canada and 18 percent of the wealth in Great Britain, for example. Add the less tangible features of "wealth," such as vacations and security of medical care, and the conclusion is reinforced that Americans are remarkably unequal.

(Some critics of crossnational comparisons contend that one ought not to contrast the United States to other nations, because the United States is distinct in certain ways. We have so many single-parent families, for example. But even looking only at two-parent families, the United States is still unusually unequal. America also seems exceptionally diverse racially and ethnically. But other Western nations also have ethnic diversity, if not the racial caste system we do. And poverty among American whites *only* still exceeds that among white or majority populations elsewhere. Such reservations do not challenge the conclusion that the United States is unusually unequal.)

America's level of inequality is by design. It is not given by nature, nor by the distribution of its people's talents, nor by the demands of a "natural" market. Other Western nations face the same global competition that we do and are about as affluent as we are and yet have managed to develop patterns of inequality less divisive than ours. Ironically, it was not so long ago that Americans were proud of comparing their relatively egalitarian society to the class-riven, hierarchical, decadent societies of Europe. In the last couple of decades, America has become the more class-riven and hierarchical society.

The United States is unusually unequal and Americans are unusually supportive of this inequality. Surveys show that Americans back moves toward expanding *opportunity* but oppose moves toward equalizing *outcomes.* They endorse wage differences among jobs that are pretty similar to the wage differences that they believe exist today (although the real differences are greater than Americans imagine), and they do not approve of government programs to narrow those differences. In a survey of people in six nations, only 28 percent of Americans agreed that government should reduce income differences. The next lowest percentage was 42 percent (Australians), while in the other countries majorities supported reducing income differences. Whether we have as much opportunity as Americans want is debatable but we seem to have a rough match between the desired and the perceived level of outcome inequality. That may be because Americans think that considerable inequality is needed for stimulating productivity and a high standard of living. Is it?

Some commentators straightforwardly defend our current level of inequality. A congressional report in 1995 conceded that the recent trends toward inequality were real but argued, "All societies have unequal wealth and income dispersion, and there is no positive basis for criticizing any degree of market determined [sic] inequality." Disparities in income and wealth, some analysts argue, encourage hard work and saving. The rich, in particular, can invest their capital in production and thus create jobs for all. This was the argument of "supply-side" economics in the 1980s, that rewarding the wealthy—for example, by reducing income taxes on returns from their investments—would stimulate growth to the benefit of all. The 1980s did not work out that way, as we have seen, but the theory is still influential. We *could* force more equal outcomes, these analysts say, but doing so would reduce living standards for all Americans.

Must we have so much inequality for overall growth? The latest economic research concludes *not;* it even suggests that inequality may *retard* economic growth. In a detailed statistical analysis, economists Torsten Persson and Guido Tabellini reported finding that, historically, societies that had more inequality of earnings tended to have lower, not higher, subsequent economic growth. Replications by other scholars substantiated the finding: More unequal nations grew less quickly than did more equal societies. . . .

Close examination of detailed policies also suggests that greater equality helps, or at least does not harm, productivity. Researchers affiliated with the National Bureau of Economic Research closely examined the effects on economic flexibility (that is, the ability to shift resources to more productive uses) of several redistributive policies used by Western nations—job security laws, homeowner subsidies, health plans, public child care, and so on. They found that such programs did *not* inhibit the functioning of those economies. Indeed, a study of over one hundred U.S. businesses found that the smaller the wage gap between managers and workers, the higher the business's product quality.

This recent research has not demonstrated precisely how greater equality helps economic growth, but we can consider a few possibilities. Increasing resources for those of lower income might, by raising health, educational attainment, and hope, increase people's abilities to be productive and entrepreneurial. Reducing the income of those at the top might reduce unproductive and speculative spending. Take, as a concrete example, the way American corporations are run compared with German and Japanese ones. The American companies are run by largely autonomous managers whose main responsibility is to return short-term profits and high stock prices to shareholders and—because they are often paid in stock options—to themselves as well. Japanese and German managers are more like top employees whose goals largely focus on keeping the company a thriving enterprise. The latter is more conducive to reinvesting profits and thus to long-term growth. Whatever the mechanisms may be, inequality appears to undermine growth. Americans certainly need not feel that they must accept the high levels of inequality we currently endure in order to have a robust economy.

A related concern for Americans is whether "leveling" stifles the drive to get ahead. Americans prefer to encourage Horatio Alger striving and to provide opportunities for everyone. Lincoln once said "that some would be rich shows that others may become rich." Many, if not most, Americans believe that inequality is needed to encourage people to work hard. But, if so, *how much* inequality is needed?

For decades, sociologists have been comparing the patterns of social mobility across societies, asking: In which countries are people most likely to overcome the disadvantages of birth and move up the ladder? In particular, does more or less equality encourage such an "open" society? The answer is that Western societies vary little in the degree to which children's economic successes are constrained by their parents' class positions. America, the most unequal Western society, has somewhat more fluid, intergenerational mobility than do other nations, but so does Sweden, the most equal Western society. There is no case for encouraging inequality in this evidence, either.

In sum, the assumption that considerable inequality is needed for, or even encourages, economic growth appears to be false. We do not need to make a morally wrenching choice between more affluence and more equality; we can have both. But even if such a choice were necessary, both sides of the debate, the "altruists" who favor intervention for equalizing and the supposed "realists" who resist it, agree that inequality can be shaped by policy decisions: wittingly or unwittingly, we choose our level of inequality.

# 4

∎∎∎

# Gender

## THE UNITED STATES CONTEXT

At the beginning of the Obama administration in 2009, women held many prominent posts in U.S. society. Hillary Clinton was Secretary of State. Nancy Pelosi was the House Minority Leader, the highest Congressional position ever held by a woman, and there were 17 women Senators and 74 women elected to the House of Representatives. These represent impressive gains from the past, but they fall way short of equality. Women make up only 17 percent of the 535 members of Congress. Moreover, gender inequality is a fact in wage differentials, possibilities for advancement in the workplace, equity in school sports, and the work load in families. There is a long list of occupations where the "glass ceiling" is the thickest, where women comprise 5 percent or less of the workers (e.g., pilots, navigators, truck drivers, mechanics, carpenters, telephone installers, loggers, material-moving equipment operators, construction workers, and firefighters). Women are overrepresented (90 percent or more) in such occupations as secretary, cashier, dental hygienist, child care provider, hairdresser, and receptionist. Generally, the more prestigious the occupation and the better the pay and benefits, the lower the proportion of women.

Gender inequality is also manifested in stereotypical media portrayals of women and men; the differences in the socialization of girls and boys at home, school, and church; the greater difficulty that women face from voters when running for electoral office against men; the much greater household demands on wives; and religious traditions that make women subordinate to men.

■ ■ ■

# 9

# Europe Crawls Ahead

## Megan Rowling

*The level of representation of women in politics is slowly rising in Europe. One reason for this is the use of proportional representation in many European countries, where political parties are allocated seats in political districts according to the number of votes they win. Multiple seats may ease gender imbalances because parties are more likely to select female candidates if more than one seat per constituency is allowed. This article addresses some of the barriers facing women in politics, and how many European countries are slowly breaking down these barriers.*

As Speaker of the Riksdagen, the Swedish parliament, Birgitta Dahl holds Sweden's second-highest political office. But when she was first elected back in 1969, as a 30-year-old single mother, she was regarded as "very odd."

"To be accepted and respected, you had to act like a bad copy of a man," Dahl recalls of her early years in politics. "But we tried to change that, and we never gave up our identity. Now women have competence in Parliament, and they have changed its performance and priorities."

Back then, women of her generation were eager for change. From the beginning, they based their demands on the right of the individual—whether male or female—to have equal access to education, work and social security. And as politicians, they fought hard to build a legal framework for good childcare and parental leave, for fathers as well as mothers. "We got this kind of legislation through," Dahl says, "even though it took 15 years of serious conflict, debate and struggle."

*Source:* Megan Rowling. 2002. *In These Times* (July 22), pp. 15–17. www.inthesetimes.com. Reprinted by permission.

And their efforts paid off. Sweden now has the highest proportion of women parliamentarians in the world, at 42.7 percent—up from just 12 percent in 1969. Two of its three deputy speakers are also women. Other Nordic countries too have high levels of female representation: In rankings compiled by the Inter-Parliamentary Union (IPU), Denmark takes second place behind Sweden, with women accounting for 38 percent of parliament members, followed by Finland and Norway with around 36.5 percent. (Finland also has one of the world's 11 women heads of state.) These nations' Social Democratic and far-left governing coalitions have made impressive progress toward equality in all areas of society in the past 40 years. But the nature of their electoral systems is also very important.

Julie Ballington, gender project officer at the Stockholm-based International Institute for Democracy and Electoral Assistance (IDEA), points out that the top 10 countries in the IPU ranking all use some form of proportional representation. This kind of voting system, in which parties are allocated seats in multi-member districts according to the percentage of votes they win, Ballington says, "offers a way to address gender imbalance in parliaments." With single-member districts, parties are often under pressure to choose a male candidate. But where they can contest and win more than one seat per constituency, they tend to be more willing to field female candidates. And by improving the gender balance on their slates, they widen their appeal among women voters.

Most European countries now use proportional representation or a combination of proportional representation and majoritarian voting, the system in use in the United States and the United Kingdom. In Europe, the widespread use of proportional representation has boosted the number of women politicians—particularly in the past three decades. And in the Nordic countries, where left-wing parties have enjoyed long periods in power and feminism has received strong support, the combination of these factors has led to significant progress toward gender parity in politics.

But even within Europe, some countries continue to lag behind. In Britain, which uses a single-member district plurality system, women members of parliament make up just 17.9 percent of the House of Commons. In the general elections of 2001, the ruling Labour Party stipulated that half those on its candidate shortlists be women. But research conducted by the Fawcett Society, a British organization that campaigns for gender equity, showed that some female hopefuls experienced overt discrimination and even sexual harassment when interviewed by local party members during the selection process.

"You are told things like 'your children are better off with you at home' . . . 'you are the best candidate but we are not ready for a woman.' They would select the donkey rather than the woman," said one candidate. Another complained: "They are absolutely adamant they will not consider a woman. . . . It was said to me . . . 'we do enjoy watching you speak—we always imagine what your knickers are like.' It is that basic." In light of such attitudes, it is not surprising that women candidates were selected for only four out of 38 vacant seats.

Thanks to new governmental legislation, however, the party is set to re-introduce the controversial method of all-women shortlists it used in the general election of 1997. The use of these shortlists saw the number of British women MPs double to 120 in that election, which swept Labour to power with a landslide victory. The technique was later ruled illegal because it was judged to discriminate against men. But in early 2002, the government returned to the idea, passing a bill that will allow political parties to take measures in favor of women when choosing parliamentary candidates—what's often referred to as "positive discrimination."

Judith Squires, a political researcher at Bristol University, believes that the new legislation got such an easy ride partly because it does not stipulate that parties must take action: "We had expected it to be a hard battle. But there has been a change of mood in the Conservative Party, and the fact that it is permissive, and there is a sunset clause [the legislation expires in 2015], all helped to push it through."

In France, where until the recent election women accounted for only 10.9 percent of National Assembly members, the government opted for a more extreme method: a law aimed at securing political parity between men and women. Now half of all contesting parties' candidates in National Assembly elections and most local ballots must be women. In National Assembly elections, which do not use proportional representation, parties that deviate from the 50 percent target by more than two percent are fined a proportion of their public financing.

The law's first test in the municipal elections of March 2001 saw the percentage of elected women councilors in towns of more than 3,500 almost double, to 47.5 percent. But in June's National Assembly elections, the proportion of women deputies increased by less than 1.5 points, to just 12.3 percent—way below expectations. The main factor behind this disappointing result was the success of right-wing parties that ignored the new law, says Mariette Sineau, research director at the Center for the Study of French Political Life. "The big parties decided it was better to incur the financial penalty than to sacrifice their 'favored sons.' And this was particularly so with parties on the right."

Another problem with the law, Sineau explains, is that it does not apply to regional assemblies, "which is a shame, because most National Assembly deputies are recruited there." And the recent victory of the right suggests that France's ruling—and predominantly male—elite are in no hurry to change the system that has allowed them to hold on to power up until now, law or no law. As Chantal Cauquil, a French deputy at the European Parliament and member of the Workers' Struggle Party, argues, other aspects of French society must change before real parity can be achieved. "There's no doubt that economic and social conditions—which weigh on women earning the lowest salaries, in the most precarious situations, and with the biggest problems caused by a notable lack of childcare infrastructure—have a negative impact on women's political participation," she says. Moreover, governing parties of both the right and left are influenced by social prejudices and are not inclined to regard women as full citizens. It requires real political will to go against such prejudices and allow women to take on the same responsibilities as men."

Such deep-rooted but hidden obstacles, faced by women everywhere, are precisely why proponents of the use of gender quotas on lists for both party and national elections believe positive discrimination is essential. "Everybody hates quotas, and everyone wishes they weren't necessary," says Drude Dahlerup, professor of politics at the University of Stockholm. "But we have to start from the point that there are structural barriers. Then quotas can be seen as compensation." Currently, political parties in some 40 countries appear to agree, with quota systems in operation from Argentina and India to Uganda.

The use of quotas in Europe varies significantly from country to country and from party to party, but where a quota system is applied, it tends to lead to a rise in women's representation. In 1988, for example, Germany's Social Democrats adopted a system of flexible quotas, under which at least one-third of all candidates for internal party elections must be female—and between 1987 and 1990, the number of Social Democratic women in the German parliament, the Bundestag, doubled. In Sweden, parties didn't introduce quotas until the '90s, but the principle of "Varannan Damemas" ("Every Other Seat A Woman's Seat") has been widespread since the '80s. Dahl, the Swedish speaker, argues that "it is not only legislation that changes the world, but convincing people that change is necessary."

Yet, as Dahlerup notes, women in some Scandinavian countries have worked to improve gender equality since the end of World War I, and "other countries are not going to wait that long—they are showing impatience." "Critical mass," or the level of representation above which women make a real difference to the political agenda, is widely judged to be around 30 percent. And in countries such as France and the United Kingdom, where that is still a long way off, measures such as parity laws and all-women shortlists are a way to speed up progress.

Even in countries that are close to achieving political parity, however, women are quick to warn against complacency. Dahlerup emphasizes the case of Denmark, where quotas have been abandoned. "Young women say they don't want and don't need quotas. The discourse is that equality has already been achieved. But I think Denmark could go backward again, and that is dangerous."

Squires of Bristol University also talks about a backlash in Britain's Liberal Democratic Party against what younger women regard as "old-fashioned feminist policies." At the party conference last year, she says, many women in their twenties and early thirties lobbied against any form of positive discrimination, wearing pink T-shirts emblazoned with the words "I'm not a token woman." But Squires suggests that this attitude is somewhat misguided: "All parties [in the United Kingdom] have set criteria that discriminate against women. It is not a supply-side problem, it is a demand-side problem."

In an attempt to address this "demand-side problem," activists are targeting not only national political institutions, but also those of the European Union. The number of women members of the European Parliament increased from 25.7 percent in 1994 to 29.9 percent in the 1999 elections—not very impressive considering that some countries introduced proportional representation voting, and some parties alternated women and men on their lists to boost women's chances. More worrying perhaps is the gender imbalance in the Convention on the Future of Europe, a body charged with the important task of drafting a new treaty for the European Union. Its presidium includes only two women among its 12 members, and the convention itself only 19 out of 118 members.

"The establishment of the convention is a response to the need for transparency and democracy. How can we explain the fact that women are not included?" asks Denise Fuchs, president of the European Women's Lobby. "It is simply not coherent." The EWL has launched a campaign to rectify the problem and is lobbying to achieve parity democracy across all other European institutions as well.

Yvonne Galligan, director of the Belfast-based Center for Advancement of Women in Politics, points out that "there has been a groundswell of support for women in political life across Western Europe, but this has not yet translated into numbers in the United Kingdom, Ireland and the European Union." In May's elections in the Irish Republic, for example, women parliamentarians in Ireland's Dail gained just one seat, and are now at 12.7 percent, according to the IPU.

Galligan is now working with political parties to set targets for Ireland's local elections in a couple of years' time—a tough job, because most parties oppose any form of positive discrimination. Parity in Ireland isn't likely to happen for a long while yet, but Galligan believes the social backdrop is improving. She cites a controversial referendum in March, in which the Irish electorate narrowly voted against a proposal to tighten the country's strict abortion laws even further. "That raised the status of women," she explains. "The underlying question was, how do we perceive the role of women? Now that is carrying over into elections. People are waking up and saying that it's not right that there are so few women in politics."

But where a sea-change in attitudes has not already occurred, it is almost certainly emerging. Naturally, there are fears that the apparent resurgence of the right in Europe could reverse the trend. But most of those interviewed for this article say women have already progressed far enough to prevent a significant decline in representation.

As Linda McAvan, deputy leader of Britain's Labour MEPs, argues: "If we look at how things were 20 years ago, they have changed enormously. Young women are different now. They see what has been done by women politicians before them, and they want to do it too."

# 10

# Gender Equality in Sweden

## Swedish Institute

*This report by the Swedish Institute provides the details for
how Sweden is structured to facilitate gender equality.*

Sweden is considered to be one of the countries with the greatest gender equality, and there is a fairly even breakdown by gender in most government bodies.
The percentage of gainfully employed women is 79 per cent and the birth rate
is among the highest in Europe. A well developed social welfare system makes
it easier to combine work and family.

## WORK WITH GENDER EQUALITY

The main objective of Sweden's gender equality policy is that men and women
have equal power to shape society and their own lives. To make this possible,
there are a number of government authorities whose task is to ensure that both
genders have the same rights, opportunities and obligations.

*The Minister for Integration and Gender Equality* coordinates the government's gender equality policy. Each minister is responsible for gender equality
in his or her area of responsibility.

*The Gender Equality Unit* under the Minister for Gender Equality is responsible for coordinating the government's work with gender equality and special
projects involving gender equality, as well as for developing methods for implementing the government's gender equality policy.

On each county administrative board, there is a person employed as a
specialist on gender equality.

*The Equal Opportunities Commission* can, under penalty of fine, enjoin employers to take active measures for gender equality.

*Source:* Swedish Institute, "Gender Equality in Sweden" (October 26, 2007). This text was first
published by the Swedish Institute on Sweden.se, Sweden's official website.

*The Office of the Equal Opportunities Ombudsman* oversees compliance with the Equal Opportunities Act.

## The Office of the Equal Opportunities Ombudsman

*The Office of the Equal Opportunities Ombudsman* is a government agency that was formed in 1980 and is responsible for ensuring that men and women have equal rights regardless of gender. The Ombudsman reviews rights in the workplace, at institutes of higher education, in the school system and in certain other areas, for instance, circumstances involving services, labour employment, labour market policy activities or social insurance. People can also notify the Ombudsman if they think they have been treated unfairly in connection with parental leave.

The Ombudsman also oversees compliance with the following five government laws: 1. *The Equal Opportunities Act*, which concerns conditions in the workplace; 2. *The Act concerning Equal Treatment of Students in Higher Education*, which concerns conditions at universities and university colleges; 3. *The Act Prohibiting Discrimination and Other Degrading Treatment of Children and School Students*, which concerns conditions in schools, including preschools, schools for students with intellectual disabilities and childcare facilities; 4. *The Prohibition of Discrimination Act*, with the Ombudsman supervising those parts concerning gender; 5. *The Parental Leave Act*, with oversight mainly concerning the prohibition of discrimination against one sex.

In accordance with the first three acts mentioned above, employers, institutes of higher education and schools are obligated to actively promote conditions for gender equality and prevent sex discrimination.

### Mainstreaming

Mainstreaming is a concept used both in Sweden and elsewhere in the world to describe how gender equality between men and women should be promoted in all government agencies, at all levels and in all operations. Gender equality is not to be carried out as an activity on its own, isolated from regular activities. The concept emerged in conjunction with the 1995 UN Conference on Women in Beijing.

### Statistics

Sweden can be considered a leader in the world concerning gender equality statistics, especially given its requirement that statistics be broken down by gender. Official statistics that concern individuals must be collected, analysed and presented by gender. Quantitative gender equality means equal apportionment (50/50) between men and women in all areas of society. Qualitative gender equality means that the knowledge and experience of both men and women are taken into consideration and can enhance development in all areas of society.

# GENDER EQUALITY IN SOCIETY
## Power

The percentage of female heads of Swedish private limited companies (with more than one employee excluding the managing director) was 25 per cent in 2005, a decrease of seven percentage points compared to 2004. The corresponding figure for publicly quoted companies was 31 per cent, a decrease of three percentage points. The share of women in senior management groups in quoted companies was 12.3 per cent.

In government bodies, the numbers are higher (in 2007). Women make up 47 per cent of Parliament members in the Riksdag and 10 of the 22 government ministers. Among elected politicians in local authorities and county councils, women constitute 41 per cent.

## Schools

Girls in Sweden have consistently higher grades than boys on average. In the last two decades, girls have also caught up with boys in math and science.

A greater proportion of women than men completes upper secondary school. Women constitute roughly 60 per cent of students in undergraduate university studies. Almost two-thirds of all degrees are awarded to women. Significantly more women than men participate in adult education. In postgraduate studies, there has been a leveling out so that women now constitute almost half of all new students. Women account for about 44 per cent of doctoral degrees.

## The Workplace

The Equal Opportunities Act has two main sections concerning the workplace. First, there is the requirement that all employers must work actively and pursue specific goals to promote equality between men and women. Second, there is a prohibition against discrimination as well as an obligation to investigate and take measures against harassment. Nor may an employer treat unfairly any employee or job applicant who is, has been or will be on parental leave.

Pay differentials between men and women can largely be explained by differences in their profession, sector, position, work experience and age. But there are pay differentials that cannot be explained in this way but may instead be attributable to gender, what are called unwarranted pay differentials. On average, women's monthly salaries are 92 per cent of men's monthly salaries when differences in the choice of profession and sector are taken into account. Pay differentials are greatest in the private sector.

## The Family

According to one estimate of the economic consequences of parenthood over a ten-year period, 1994–2003, it was determined that parenthood costs more for mothers than fathers. The typical case is a couple living together with two children. The man is a white-collar worker in the private sector and the woman is employed by the local authority. During the ten-year period in question, the couple has two children, and the woman is at home for eleven months and the man one month for each child. The woman also works part-time (75 per cent) for seven years during the ten-year period.

Calculations show that the loss of after-tax income during the ten-year period is SEK 304,000 for the mother and SEK 10,000 for the father. The accumulated [loss] of after-tax income is 23 per cent for the woman and less than one per cent for the man compared to the case if the couple had not had any children. The pension proceeds for the ten years are roughly SEK 50,000 lower for the woman and SEK 1,000 lower for the man. Both the lower pension proceeds and loss of income are largely attributable to the woman working part-time.

## Parental Insurance and Parental Leave

A parental allowance is paid out for a total of 480 days when a child is born or adopted. This is taxed like other income and is pensionable income. For 390 of the 480 days, payment is paid at the "sickness cash benefit level", that is, 80 per cent of benefits-based income (in Swedish SGI), which as a rule is the current annual salary. The highest parental allowance is SEK 874 a day.

The remaining 90 days are "lowest level" days and give an allowance of SEK 180 a day for children born as of 1 July 2006.

Each parent has 60 days' leave which can be allotted as determined by their benefits-based income and which are reserved specifically for them. These days are often called maternal or paternal months and so cannot be transferred to the other parent.

The father of a newborn may, in connection with the birth of his child, get ten extra days' leave on a temporary parental benefit in addition to the parental allowance. With the birth of twins, a father is entitled to 20 days' leave.

A parent adopting a child is entitled to take leave from work for one and a half years, calculated from the time the child comes under his or her care.

## Healthcare

The Swedish National Board of Health and Welfare indicates that there are certain gender differences regarding healthcare for men and women in comparable age groups, for instance, in cardiac intensive care and in cataract treatment. Women do not get the access to bypass surgery to the extent that is warranted, and have less access to cataract surgery.

In addition, there are clear differences between age groups: older patients get less frequent treatment than younger patients. This restrictiveness in treating older patients affects considerably more women than men. New and expensive technologies and pharmaceuticals are made available primarily to middle-aged men.

## Violence Against Women

In 2006, some 25,500 cases of male violence against women were recorded. But the number of unrecorded cases is large, and according to estimates from the Swedish National Council for Crime Prevention violence reported to the police constitutes only about 20–25 per cent of actual violence. According to the Swedish study "Slagen Dam" ('Battered Woman', published in 2001), 46 per cent of the women (over 15) asked had been subjected to some form of violence in their life. About 16 women are murdered each year by a man with whom they have or have had a close relationship.

Women's shelters in Sweden have two national organizations: The National Organisation for Women's Shelters and Young Women's Shelters in Sweden (ROKS) and the Swedish Association of Women's Shelters (SKR). SKR was formed as a spin-off to address children's issues in particular. There are a total of some 160 women's shelters in Sweden, and operations are based largely on volunteer work.

# LAWS

## The Abortion Act

Sweden has had free abortions since 1975. This means that a woman can decide for herself whether to have an abortion through the 18th week of pregnancy, without having to indicate why she wants an abortion. After week 18, an abortion can be performed if there are "special reasons" up to week 22, when the National Board of Health and Welfare, after conducting an investigation, decides whether the abortion will be performed. There are some 35,000 abortions performed in Sweden each year.

## The Act Prohibiting the Purchase of Sexual Services

The Act Prohibiting the Purchase of Sexual Services, which entered into force in 1999, makes the purchase of sexual services illegal. This sets the focus more on the purchaser, rather than women and children, as was the case previously, in the work to curtail prostitution. The Swedish policy has had great importance for changes internationally.

## The Act on Violence against Women

The Act on Violence against Women entered into force in 1998. Violations of the act are defined as violation of a woman's (or child's) integrity and gross violation of a woman's integrity, that is, repeated abuse and degradation of a woman. The act takes a cumulative approach to the abuse of women. What is new about the Act on Violence against Women is that the violence and abuse a woman has been subjected to are added up. Each blow and instance of sexual and psychological degradation of the woman that the man is in a close relationship with is taken into account. Before, each blow or instance of degradation had to be so serious as to be considered on its own as a violation of the law. Now, the total amount of degradation serves as a basis for prosecution. The sentence for the new crime, gross violation of a woman's integrity, is up to six years in prison.

## HISTORY

1250s  King Birger Jarl passes a law on violence against women (prohibition of rape and abduction).

1921   Women get the right to vote and run for office.

1922   Kerstin Hesselgren becomes Sweden's first female member of Parliament.

1965   Sweden is the first country in the world to have a law against rape in marriage.

1974   Parental insurance is introduced.

1975   New abortion law. Women decide for themselves about abortion through the 18th week of pregnancy.

1979   Female succession to the throne.

1980   The Office of the Equality Opportunities Ombudsman is introduced.

1995   The first paternal month, as it is known, is introduced in the parental insurance system, which means that 30 days' parental leave must be taken by the father (there is also a corresponding month for the mother).

1998   The Act on Violence against Women.

1999   The Act Prohibiting the Purchase of Sexual Services.

## Links

The Equal Opportunities Commission
    www.jamstalldhetsnamnden.se (only in Swedish)

Gender equality statistics at Statistics Sweden
    www.scb.se

The Ministry of Integration and Gender Equality
    www.sweden.gov.se

The Office of the Equal Opportunities Ombudsman
    www.jamombud.se (information available in other languages)

ROKS (The National Organisation for Women's Shelters and Young Women's Shelters in Sweden)
    www.roks.se (only in Swedish)

SKR (The Swedish Association of Women's Shelters)
    www.kvinnojour.com

The Swedish Secretariat for Gender Research
    www.genus.se

The Women's Business Research Institute
    www.wombri.se

# SECTION

# 5

■ ■ ■

# Sexual Orientation

## THE UNITED STATES CONTEXT

Variance from the societal norm of heterosexuality is not a social problem, but *the societal response to it is.* (Much of this section introduction is taken from Eitzen and Baca Zinn, 2009, Chapter 10, and Baca Zinn and Eitzen, 2008.) Consequently, people who differ from the socially approved sexual orientation (gays, lesbians, bisexuals, and the transgendered) are objects of derision and contempt by members of society and discriminated against by individuals and by the normal way the institutions of society operate. Society imposes the norm of sexual identity (compulsory heterosexuality) through negative sanctions on those who are sexually different and by granting privileges to those in heterosexual relationships.

The Judeo-Christian tradition considers homosexual behavior a heinous sin. Thus, many (but by no means all) contemporary churches deny pastorates to gays and lesbians, refuse to conduct marriage ceremonies for them, and do not allow them as members unless they vow sexual abstinence.

The laws deny equal rights to gays and lesbians. In mid-2009, same-sex marriage was not recognized in all but six states, Massachusetts, Connecticut, Maine, Vermont, Iowa, and New Hampshire. California, Hawaii, New Jersey, Oregon, and Washington also allow civil unions or domestic partnerships with spousal benefits. In response, many states have passed laws banning same-sex marriages. Congress has passed the Defense of Marriage Act, which denies federal recognition of same-sex marriage and allows states to ignore such unions licensed elsewhere.

Parenthood has become the latest battleground for lesbian and gay rights. The legality of homosexual parenthood varies from state to state, and the interpretation from judge to judge. Thus, there is considerable legal ambiguity regarding the rights of same-sex couples to adopt and to obtain custody of children following a heterosexual marriage.

Gay Americans won a historic victory in 2003, when the U.S. Supreme Court, reversing the Court's ruling in 1986, struck down a Texas law banning sodomy (oral or anal sex) as an unconstitutional violation of privacy. This invalidated anti-sodomy laws in 13 states.

The armed forces have always discriminated against gays and lesbians, with lesbians about three times more likely to be removed from the military for homosexuality than gays. The Clinton administration instituted the "don't ask, don't tell" rule in an attempt to reduce discrimination against homosexuals in the military. This meant that the military was not to ask its personnel about their sexuality, and to prosecute only if gay and lesbian service members were blatant about their sexual orientation. In short, as long as homosexual service members "stayed in the closet," they were allowed to remain in the military. In 2009 President Obama rescinded the "don't ask, don't tell" policy, allowing gays and lesbians to serve in the military openly.

## References

Baca Zinn, Maxine, and D. Stanley Eitzen. 2008. *Diversity in Families,* 7th ed. Boston: Allyn and Bacon.
Eitzen, D. Stanley, and Maxine Baca Zinn. 2009. *Social Problems,* 10th ed. Boston: Allyn and Bacon.

# 11

# Social Shift Opens Door to Gay Marriage Plan

**Clifford Krauss**

*Canada has become a more tolerant society, decriminalizing possession of small amounts of marijuana, permitting "safe-injection" clinics for heroin addicts, and allowing gay marriage. The author asserts that the main reason for this transformation is that Canada in the last generation has become a multicultural society.*

TORONTO—Canada's decision to allow marriage between same-sex couples is only one of many signs that this once tradition-bound society is undergoing social changes at an astonishing rate.

Increasingly, Canada has been on a social policy course pursued by many Western European and Scandinavian countries, gradually moving more out of step with the United States over the last few decades.

Even as the government announced Tuesday that it would rewrite the definition of marriage, it was transforming its drug policies by decriminalizing possession of small amounts of marijuana and permitting "safe-injection" clinics in Vancouver for heroin addicts in an effort to fight disease.

The large population of native peoples remains impoverished, but there are growing signs that they are taking greater control of their destinies, and their leaders now govern two territories occupying more than a third of Canada's land mass.

Canada has never had a revolution or a civil war, and little social turbulence aside from sporadic rebellions in the 19th century and a splash of terrorism in Quebec in the 1960s and 1970s.

Regarding ease of social change, Canada is virtually in a category by itself.

The transformation of the country's demographics, for example, has been breathtaking since the 1970s, when the government of Pierre Trudeau opened wide the country's doors to Africans, Asians and West Indians as part of an attempt to fill Canada's huge, underpopulated hinterland. Eighteen percent of the population is now foreign-born compared with about 11 percent in the United States, and there is little or no public debate over whether a sea change in culture, demographics and even national identity is good or bad for the country.

In only the last generation, Toronto, Montreal and Vancouver, where a third of the population lives, have become multicultural polygots where the towers of Sikh temples and mosques have become mainstays of the skyline and where cuisine and fashion have become concoctions of spices and patterns that are in the global vanguard.

Toronto, once a homogeneous city of staid British tradition, is now a place where more than 40 percent of the people are foreign-born, where there are nearly 2,000 ethnic restaurants and where local radio and television stations broadcast in more than 30 languages.

"Everything from marriage laws to marijuana laws, we are going through a period of accelerated social change," said Neil Bissoundath, an immigrant from Trinidad who is a leading novelist here. "There is a general approach to life here that is both evolutionary and revolutionary."

He said that the balance goes all the way back to the ideals of the Tory founders of Canada, who remained loyal to the British crown and who instilled a laissez-faire conservatism "that says people have a right to live their lives as they like."

That philosophy was a practical necessity in a colony that was bilingual after the British conquered French Quebec, creating relative social peace by allowing greater religious freedoms than even Catholics in England had at the time.

The live-and-let-live approach was codified by the 1992 Charter of Rights and Freedoms, Canada's Bill of Rights. Being as young as it is, the charter occupies a vivid corner of the Canadian psyche. So when three senior provincial courts ruled recently that federal marriage law discriminated against same-sex couples under the charter, the Liberal Cabinet decided to go along and not appeal the decisions.

While the new law will have to be passed by the House of Commons, little organized resistance has risen.

Few here have complained that a national policy pertaining to something as intimate as marriage would be set by courts in Quebec, British Columbia and Ontario rather than by a federal body. In part that reflects the great relative political strength that regional governments have developed in what is known as the Canadian Confederation, where Canada's federal government is weaker than most central governments in the West.

But it also reflects poll results that show a majority of Canadians support expanding marriage to gay couples. Last year, the Quebec provincial assembly unanimously enacted a law giving sweeping parental rights to same-sex couples, with even the most conservative members voting in favor despite lobbying by the Roman Catholic Church.

"Canada has always been in the vanguard in relation to many societies in the world," Prime Minister Jean Chretien said Tuesday, speaking in French to reporters after he announced the Cabinet's decision. "We have met our responsibilities."

Nowhere has the social change been more dramatic than in Quebec, which as recently as the 1960s was a deeply conservative place where the church dominated education and social life. Since the baby-boomer generation launched the "Quiet Revolution" in favor of separatism, big government social programs and secularism, abortion and divorce rates there rose to among the highest in Canada while church attendance plummeted.

Now the pendulum is moving in the other direction, ever so slightly.

"There is a centrist mentality in Canada that translates into the political system not tolerating the Pat Buchanans nor the leftist equivalent," noted Michel C. Auger, a political columnist for *Le Journal de Montreal*. "There is a unified fabric here that is a lot stronger on social issues than it seems to be in the United States."

# 12

# Gay Rights and European Citizenship

**Joydeep Sengupta**

*The European Union leads the way in gay rights advances.
Unlike the United States, where the government and state legislatures have been unwilling to grant gays and lesbians the
"rights" of minority groups, the nations of Europe and Scandinavia have granted these group rights to prevent discrimination
by the majority.*

The European Union (EU) has been cautiously approaching the notion of the
"European citizen"[1] as a person endowed with certain rights, privileges, and
responsibilities traditionally held as the exclusive jurisdiction of nation states.
Including gay rights within this evolving notion of EU citizenship requires a
negotiation of rights in transnational space while utilizing the slowly widening
apertures at the national level.

Citizenship is the legal expression of membership in the national family,
carrying with it the obligation for its defense and welfare. Exclusions from the
rights and duties of citizenship—such as banning homosexuals from the military or denying them the right to marry and create a family—are a symbolic os-
tracism from the national family. Attempts to redress the systematic exclusion of
gays from full citizenship in Europe must reconcile a reprehensible history of in-
justice rooted in prohibitions on homosexuality in the Judeo-Christian religious
traditions, and (with a few exceptions) in the criminalization, pathologization,
or mere omission of homosexuality in legal code until the 20th century.

The progressive expansion of gay rights corresponds to the growing understanding of gays and lesbians as a "social group" having claims to rights
similar to those of other minorities—ethnic, religious, and linguistic ones,

*Source:* Joydeep Sengupta, "Gay Rights and European Citizenship," *The Gay and Lesbian Review*
9 (November/December 2002), pp. 28–30.

among others—traditionally the target of discrimination. Many demands for greater rights and protections for gays and lesbians are similar to those sought by women or other minority groups, such as nondiscrimination in laws governing employment, housing, or access to public office and government services. On the other hand, most other minorities in Europe have not had to worry about laws governing marriage, property, inheritance, taxation, divorce, joint adoptions, custody rights, insurance and employer benefits, and immigration, as these rights have traditionally been derived automatically from heterosexual marriage.

The law plays a critical role in constructing group identity, affecting how the group is perceived by society at large. While minority legislation broadly addresses the group, the particular application of it to the individual forms the basis for contesting rights and benefits. Especially in the Anglo-American common law tradition, and to a large extent within continental civil law systems, the individual is afforded primary legal personhood; the individual, not the group, is the subject of the law. As Nathan Glazer has observed, the Fifth Amendment to the U.S. Constitution, which provided the legal foundation for the minority rights protections of the subsequent Fourteenth Amendment, emphasizes the "person" and the "citizen" in its guarantees for due process, privileges and immunities, and equal protection of the law.

In the U.S., right-wing opposition to civil rights advancements is sometimes veiled as a principled rejection of "special" rights for minority groups and women, since they explicitly recognize certain groups and provide protections that supposedly are not applicable to, say, white heterosexual males. In *Inclusion of the Other: Studies in Political Theory* (1998), Jurgen Habermas observes that the "legislation of identity," especially minority identities, in Western liberal democracies stands on precarious ground. Group rights are critiqued as weakening an individual rights culture, which has strengthened civil rights claims. Additionally, claims for state protection of a group's identity as distinct from the majority's religious and cultural value system are viewed as threats to national unity. Claims for rights by one group occasionally [necessitate] the controversial and divisive subjugation of the claims of another, such as religious conservatives and gay rights advocates. Habermas observes that "protection of collective identities comes into competition with the right to equal individual liberties (subjective *Freiheiten*)—Kant's one original human right—so that in a case of conflict a decision must be made about which takes precedence."

In an article in *Journal of Politics* (May 1996), Haider-Markel and Meier propose an explanation for the evolution of gay and lesbian collective rights in the American context. They claim that "two competing coalitions [are] often formed around conflicting ideological camps and/or partisanship, and are brought to a public vote."[2] The process resembles that of redistributive politics, except that groups seek to redistribute values rather than money through government action. The "government stamp of approval" is viewed as validation of their interests and affirmation of its rights as citizens. In *Multiculturalism and*

*"The Politics of Recognition"* (1992), Amy Gutmann asserts that minority groups within pluralistic democracies seek "public recognition as equal citizens," thereby requiring two forms of legal respect from the majority: respect for unique identities, and respect for activities, practices, and world views. Thus, for group-identified sexual minority cultures, legislative protection serves not only to guarantee fundamental rights against prejudice or discrimination from the majority culture, but also to assert the right to enter into alternative social units and pursue autonomous cultural expression regardless of majority opinion against it.

In modern liberal democracies, group rights are broadly derived from the authority vested in elected leaders, who must then promote social justice while upholding the primacy of individual equality. This is complemented by a progressive, positivist legal culture in which the rights of minorities are upheld to prevent discrimination by the majority. Indeed, group rights have a long historical lineage in the West: Roman and Justinian law, for instance, provided special protections for politically weaker groups, such as women and slaves. In the utilitarian tradition of Jeremy Bentham and John Stuart Mill, protection of individual rights (entitlements) and liberties within the democratic state is favored over paternalistic prohibitions on behavior deemed harmful to the group. Mill's famous "harm principle" strongly resonates with the modern legal concept of "proportionality": Mill asserts that the potential tyranny of an all-powerful state must be restrained by forbidding state intervention in private choices that do not directly harm the general welfare of others.

The harm principle is what deprives the government of the right to interfere in the practice of private same-sex behavior between consenting adults, an act that does not inflict a proportional harm upon other citizens. In the gay marriage cases in Hawaii and Vermont, moral opposition or a paternalistic commitment to preserving "traditional values" is insufficient [reason] for restricting rights. But the sweeping passage of anti-gay-marriage legislation in many states and at the federal level reveals that a moralistic ethic still wins the day with the argument that gay marriage would so harm the majority of citizens as to abolish the minority's claim to equal rights. Even John Stuart Mill, who advocated the full enfranchisement of one excluded group, women, simultaneously supported English efforts against colonized peoples, and he approved the imposition of "civilization" on traditional societies as a necessary evil.

In *History of Sexuality*, Foucault argues that in the 18th and 19th centuries, European society increasingly embraced a monolithic norm of heterosexual monogamy. This bourgeois norm translated into laws that restricted sexual behavior and forced the diverse sexual identities of Europe into the closet. As Foucault amply demonstrates, these identities were painstakingly enumerated in the law, which regulated extramarital sex, premarital sex, incest, sodomy in all its forms, miscegenation, prostitution, and so on. Thus did a category of "moral degenerates" join a number of other social categories—women, the landless, Jews, Gypsies, and so on—as legally excluded from the full benefits and privileges of citizenship. The persecution of what Foucault called "peripheral sexualities" thus shares a common heritage with the persecution of these other minorities.

Despite the continued occurrence of systemic homophobia and legally enforced inequality for gay and lesbian people in parts of Western Europe, the continent leads the world in gay rights advances. Legal equality began to emerge slowly with the growing acceptance of homosexuals in postwar Europe. All EU countries have decriminalized same-sex behavior, and most have repealed higher age-of-consent laws for homosexual acts. In the last two decades, dramatic advances have occurred in the areas of employment non-discrimination, access to reproductive technologies, partner recognition for taxation, immigration, and co-adoption, and protection from hate speech and hate-motivated violence. As in the U.S., support for equal rights varies regionally, being strongest in the north and the west, weakest in the south and east. Political support for gay rights in most EU countries rests on coalitions built by left-leaning parties, which have brought gay rights under their traditional banner of minority rights.

Scandinavian countries and the Netherlands continue to provide the most comprehensive legal protections to gays and lesbians. By 1989, Denmark had enforced employment non-discrimination, removed barriers to full military service, and led the world in the revolutionary Danish Registered Partnership Act or DRP. The DRP became the world's first national-level legislation recognizing the rights of homosexual couples almost on a par with heterosexuals (except in access to reproductive technologies from public health officials, church weddings, and joint adoptions). Currently all five Nordic countries offer some form of domestic partnership and adoption provision. In 2000, the Netherlands became the only government in the world to extended full marriage benefits, including adoption rights, to same-sex couples. Between 1999 and 2001, both France and Germany instituted partnership acts that permit the official registration of same-sex couples and many benefits of marriage. Within the EU, Belgium, Denmark, Finland, France, Germany, Holland, Sweden, and the UK all offer immigration rights for binational couples.

Still, the principle of equality for gay people does not have the status of an indisputable universal human right in the manner of, say, freedom from involuntary servitude. Two key international courts, the European Court of Justice (ECJ) and the European Court of Human Rights (ECHR), have enforced EU treaties and international human rights treaties with varying success when they've come into conflict with national laws. Created to interpret and uphold EU treaties, the ECJ has taken a conservative approach in adjudicating discrimination claims stemming from treaty provisions on gender equality. In ruling against granting equal employer benefits for homosexual couples otherwise available to heterosexuals, the ECJ has repeatedly recommended more explicit EU legislation on gay partnerships. While not an EU Court, the ECHR upholds the European Convention of Human Rights and Fundamental Freedoms (ECHRFF), to which the EU is formally committed through the Maastricht Treaty. For example, archaic sodomy laws in Northern Ireland were famously struck down in the *Dudgeon v. United Kingdom* case at the ECHR, and ruled a violation of the right to privacy. Catholic opposition to gay rights had preserved largely unenforced sodomy laws in the Republic of Ireland. In *Norris v. Ireland*, the ECHR ruled that Ireland should repeal its sodomy laws, and invalidated the Irish High Court's claim that the "Christian and democratic nature" of Ireland was sufficient justification for upholding the laws. The Irish Parliament complied in 1993, striking down all legal discrimination by instituting gender-neutral language.

But standard gay rights legislation for the whole EU remains sparse, causing wide regional disparities in the law. Unlike heterosexual marriage, for instance, same-sex marriage and domestic partnerships do not enjoy uniform reciprocal recognition among all EU states. As the European Court of Justice has repeatedly urged, more explicit EU legislation by way of directives on gay rights issues is necessary, since significant exclusions from the benefits of EU citizenship cannot be adequately addressed by national legislatures. The Treaty of Amsterdam of 1997 introduced for the first time a provision (Article 13) that authorizes the Community to "take appropriate action to combat discrimination [based on sexual orientation]." This article made possible a Council directive in 2000, the first explicit piece of EU legislation prohibiting discrimination on the basis of sexual orientation in private and public employment. While major gains have been made on nondiscrimination in employment, privacy rights, and sodomy laws, areas that are only now being addressed include same-sex marriage, reproductive choice, and immigration rights for gay partners.

With the fragmented, contested, and occasionally triumphant process of integrating a diverse continent, European leaders have long envisioned common values and principles upon which a shared democratic identity of contemporary Europe may be constructed. Embracing the human rights cause has been one such manifestation, and EU governments have consistently supported promotion of human rights worldwide, protection of existing mechanisms for human rights protection, strengthening of human rights organizations, and creation of new institutions for enforcement of international human rights law. In 2000, the European Council adopted the ambitious *Charter of Fundamental Rights of the European Union*, which provides a sweeping non-discrimination provision: "[A]ny discrimination based on any ground such as sex, race, colour, ethnic or social origin, genetic features, language, religion or belief, political or other opinion, membership in a national minority, property, birth, disability, age or sexual orientation shall be prohibited."

Despite a lack of binding force, the Charter provides additional authority to EU institutions when interpreting community principles and adjudicating discrimination claims. Efforts to create a transnational European identity deeply rooted in respect for human rights requires stronger leadership of member states and continued commitment towards democratic values and minority protections. EU leadership has led to the repeal of anti-gay laws in several non-EU countries, as a condition of future membership. By strengthening support for human rights enforcement and providing moral leadership in promoting equal rights for sexual minorities, the EU can simultaneously consolidate its position as a modernizing, pluralizing, diversifying, progressive force, committed to just and humane social values. The answers that emerge on the citizenship debate must reach to the very soul of the European Union project, and what it seeks to become.

## Notes

1. See Title I, Article B, the Treaty on European Union, one of the key goals of which is "the introduction of citizenship of the Union," and "to develop close cooperation on justice and home affairs."
2. Key U.S. examples include Colorado Amendment 2 (1992); Oregon Ballot Measure 9 (1993); California Knight Initiative (2000), all of which sought to restrict gay rights and opposed broadening of existing definitions of family/marriage.

# SECTION

# 6

# ...

# Age

## THE UNITED STATES CONTEXT

Similar to what is occurring worldwide, the population of the United States is aging. In 1900 about one in 25 residents was 65 or older. By 1950 it was about one in 12. In 2000 one in eight was 65 and over, and by 2030 it will likely be about one in five. In effect, by 2030 there will be more grandparents than grandchildren.

There are two major problems brought about by an aging society. (The following is from Eitzen and Baca Zinn, 2009, Chapter 5.) The first is that the Social Security system will become increasingly inadequate to meet the needs of the elderly. This program, when compared to similar programs in other industrialized societies, provides only minimal support. Instead of a universal system that allows the elderly to live comfortably, the Social Security program: (1) does not cover all workers; (2) pays benefits according to the length of time workers have paid into the system and the amount of wages on which they paid a Social Security tax; (3) provides such meager benefits for some that 30 percent of those relying exclusively on Social Security are *below* the poverty line; and (4) is biased against women. These problems will escalate in the future as more people become eligible for Social Security, people live longer, and relatively fewer workers—in comparison with the proportion who are old—pay into the Social Security system.

The second problem for the elderly in the United States is paying for health care. Of all age groups, the elderly are most affected by ill health, especially from age 75 onward. The United States does provide universal health care for those 65 and over through Medicare, but this government program is insufficiently financed. From the perspective of the elderly, only about half of their health care bills are paid through the program, leaving them with substantial costs. The affluent elderly are not hurt because they can afford supplemental health insurance. The poor are not hurt because they are covered by Medicaid, a separate program that pays for the health care of indigent people. The problem is that with the high federal debt (over $10 trillion in 2009) and huge budget deficits, the federal government and many of the states are slashing the funds available for Medicaid. The near-poor, however, do not qualify for Medicaid and they cannot afford additional health insurance.

More than four out of ten of today's elderly will use a nursing home in their lifetimes. This is a special concern for the elderly in the United States because nursing home care may cost as much as $3,000 to $5,000 a month. Nursing home patients must pay these costs until their assets reach a point low enough that Medicaid takes over. The problem, of course, is that few resources remain for the surviving spouse. In other industrialized nations, the government pays for nursing home costs when needed.

## Reference

Eitzen, D. Stanley, and Maxine Baca Zinn. (2009). *Social Problems*, 10th ed. Boston: Allyn and Bacon.

# 13

■ ■ ■

# As Good As It Gets:
# What Country Takes the
# Best Care of Its Older Citizens?

**Mike Edwards**

*The American Association of Retired Persons (AARP) conducted a survey of sixteen nations on seventeen dimensions related to the quality of life of older people. The Netherlands ranked first and the United States was next to last. Even the highest ranked nations (i.e., the Netherlands, Australia, and Sweden), however, have room to improve.*

Every week, Anna Sophia Fischer greets a clutch of tourists in the medieval central square of Utrecht and, with a spring in her step, guides them on a stroll among 14th-century Dutch monasteries and houses. She knows every arch, garden, and alley and, at 75, goes about her daily business by bicycle, as do the swarms of people around her. "You have to go by bike if you live in town," she says. (Could this be one reason that the Dutch live longer than we do—an average 78.6 years, compared with 77.3 in the U.S.?) A retired physician, Fischer is living her dream. "I wanted to do something different," she says. "I'm not rich, but I can do the things I want to do."

Wim van Essen, 69, is a former teacher, tall, vigorous, an ardent hiker, a fanatical chess player—and a one-man pep squad for the Dutch way of retirement. "You see how we live," he says, inviting a guest into his brick home in the leafy city of Amersfoort. There's a fireplace in the living room, a wildflower garden out back. Extra bedrooms upstairs await visiting grandchildren. On a coffee table are photos of Van Essen trekking in the Austrian alps with his wife,

Lamberta Jacoba Maria, nicknamed Bep. (Every year, the two of them take a major trip, partly subsidized by the government.) The couple receive government and work pensions and various perks. All told, it's a wonderful life, based on what Van Essen calls "a beautiful pension," which, when everything is added up, comes to about $45,000 a year.

In a world that is rapidly aging, the Netherlands, perhaps more than any other country, has created a society in which people have the luxury of growing old well, according to a survey conducted by AARP THE MAGAZINE. We weighed 17 criteria (see chart, page [84]) in selected industrialized nations that approximate as closely as possible the lifestyle of most AARP members. We focused on key quality-of-life issues such as health care, work, education, taxes, and social programs.

But if you're already thinking of packing your bags, stop right there. The purpose of this report is not to encourage American retirees to immigrate to the Netherlands or to some of the other top scorers in our study. Most nations aren't keen to share their pensions and health care benefits with noncitizens just off a plane. Rather, our goal is to shed light on what retirees enjoy elsewhere in the world as a reference point for our own country's policies.

In the Netherlands, all citizens receive the full old-age pension at 65 if they've lived in the country for a minimum of 50 years between ages 15 and 64. Unlike our Social Security, however, the pension doesn't require a work history. The full amount per month is nearly $1,000 for singles and nearly $1,400 for couples, married or not. The old-age pension is in addition to an occupational, or employer-provided pension based on payments over the years by worker and employer. And every pensioner gets a "holiday allowance" of about $700, thoughtfully paid in May, just in time for spring.

Pension generosity is a major reason that, by international measurements, only 6.4 percent of the elderly fall in the bottom quarter of income distribution, as compared with the U.S. percentage of 20.7. Although the U.S. has a far larger per capita income than the Netherlands—$26,448 a year versus $17,080—it scores poorly in two other comparisons: First, all Dutch citizens have government insurance for medical conditions and nursing-home care; 45 million Americans have no health insurance at all. Second, prescription drugs are available to all Dutch citizens, with few if any copayments: Americans get drugs in many different ways and those without insurance pay top dollar. Even when Medicare drug coverage begins in 2006, most enrollees will still face substantial out-of-pocket costs.

How do the Dutch do it? How do their euros stretch further than our dollars? The key factor is lower costs. Although medicine isn't completely socialized—physicians and pharmacists, for example, aren't state employees—the government regulates almost all health expenses. That helps explain why, in the view of Professor Gerard F. Anderson of the Johns Hopkins Bloomberg School of Public Health, "in the U.S. we pay a lot more than anybody else for pretty much the same stuff." In analyzing health systems in the Netherlands and other industrialized nations, Anderson found that drugs, hospitals, and physicians' services were from 30 to 50 percent more expensive in the U.S., "and their health status is as good or better than ours."

Another factor is attitude. A strong feeling of "social solidarity," as Anderson sees it, makes Europeans inclined to be generous to older people, more willing to support them. "Their attitude is, we're in this together and sooner or later we're going to become older and we'll need some help," he says. "The U.S. attitude is, we're all rugged individualists and we're going to take care of ourselves, not others."

The Netherlands demonstrates its attitude toward older citizens (2 million are over 65) by showering them with numerous friendly perks, in addition to the big-ticket items such as pensions and health care. One example: seven days of free travel a year on the efficient rail system. "I go as far as possible," says Joris Korst, a 65-year-old civil servant in Nieuwegein. That's never very far in the Netherlands, which is only a third the size of Pennsylvania, but the destinations can be exhilarating—like the windswept beaches that Korst strolls in the West Frisian Islands. Museums, movies, concerts, campgrounds, and holiday bungalows are discounted, too. All this and a country that's worldly, prosperous, tolerant, steeped in art, and graced by canals, windmills, and tulip fields. What's not to like?

## HEALTH CARE

The Dutch are accustomed to paying minuscule copayments for expensive treatment.

Dutch health insurance took care of teacher Van Essen when he needed a heart pacemaker. "He never saw a bill," his wife, Bep, recalls. Neither did civil servant Korst, who remembers that there were no charges when his wife, Trees, had cancer surgery followed by 32 chemotherapy treatments. "The whole country paid," he says, referring to the state-regulated insurance. In the U.S., those 32 treatments alone could have cost $30,000 or more, depending on the type and number of drugs used. Medicare might cover 80 percent, but the patient still could owe thousands.

Compare Trees's experience with that of Harold Powers, 79, and his wife, Ozelle, 82, retired educators in Tennessee. Powers paid about $200 of the bill for his bypass heart surgery because Medicare picked up 80 percent of the tab and his private Medigap insurance (which costs extra) paid most of the rest. But, in addition, he and Ozelle spend about $3,000 a year for medicines, and Medicare won't cover any of that until 2006. Van Essen, on the other hand, pays nothing for the medicine he takes to prevent migraines. In 2003, however, the Dutch health ministry proposed that everyone make a copayment of $1.75 for each prescription—but backed down when the people protested.

There is also a government limit on the amount a hospital may bill an insurance company for a pacemaker—Van Essen's was $5,750, plus the expense of the procedure. In the U.S., a pacemaker can cost as much as a car—$15,000 to $20,000, just for the device. The whole procedure can zoom up to $50,000. In the

**And the Winner Is . . . The Netherlands, which scored highest on key quality-of-life issues important to older people and society in general.**

| On a scale of 1 to 5, five is tops | Mandatory Retirement | Age-Discrimination Laws | Unemployment Rate | College Education | Per Capita Income | Total Tax Burden | Home Care | Retirement Age for Full Benefits | Public Pension Replacement Rate | Employers Pension Coverage | Economic Inequality | Economic Inequality for the Elderly | Public Spending on Social Programs | Total Health Costs | Universal Health Care | Universal Rx | Life Expectancy at Birth | TOTAL |
|---|---|---|---|---|---|---|---|---|---|---|---|---|---|---|---|---|---|---|
| Italy | 1 | 3 | 2 | 1 | 2 | 1 | 2 | 2 | 2 | 2 | 3 | 1 | 1 | 3 | 5 | 5 | 2 | 48 |
| Germany | 1 | 1 | 3 | 3 | 3 | 1 | 3 | 2 | 3 | 3 | 3 | 3 | 3 | 5 | 5 | 1 | 3 | 49 |
| United Kingdom | 1 | 5 | 5 | 5 | 1 | 2 | 4 | 1 | 2 | 3 | 3 | 3 | 1 | 5 | 5 | 4 | 2 | 49 |
| United States | 5 | 5 | 4 | 5 | 5 | 5 | 2 | 1 | 2 | 3 | 1 | 2 | 1 | 1 | 4 | 3 | 1 | 50 |
| Spain | 1 | 5 | 5 | 1 | 2 | 4 | 3 | 3 | 5 | 1 | 3 | 3 | 1 | 5 | 5 | 5 | 3 | 52 |
| Ireland | 1 | 5 | 5 | 2 | 4 | 3 | 2 | 4 | 3 | 1 | 5 | 3 | 1 | 3 | 5 | 5 | 1 | 53 |
| Canada | 5 | 5 | 4 | 5 | 3 | 3 | 4 | 4 | 1 | 3 | 3 | 2 | 1 | 1 | 5 | 1 | 5 | 55 |
| France | 1 | 1 | 3 | 3 | 3 | 1 | 5 | 2 | 4 | 3 | 3 | 3 | 5 | 5 | 5 | 3 | 5 | 55 |
| Japan | 1 | 1 | 5 | 5 | 3 | 5 | 2 | 1 | 3 | 3 | 3 | 3 | 3 | 5 | 5 | 3 | 5 | 56 |
| Denmark | 1 | 1 | 4 | 4 | 3 | 1 | 5 | 1 | 3 | 5 | 4 | 5 | 5 | 5 | 5 | 1 | 3 | 57 |
| Norway | 1 | 1 | 5 | 5 | 5 | 2 | 4 | 1 | 3 | 3 | 5 | 5 | 3 | 5 | 5 | 3 | 3 | 58 |
| Switzerland | 1 | 1 | 5 | 5 | 3 | 5 | 2 | 1 | 3 | 5 | 4 | 3 | 3 | 4 | 5 | 5 | 4 | 58 |
| Finland | 1 | 5 | 4 | 5 | 3 | 3 | 5 | 3 | 4 | 3 | 5 | 5 | 5 | 5 | 5 | 4 | 2 | 59 |
| Sweden | 1 | 5 | 5 | 5 | 3 | 1 | 5 | 1 | 3 | 5 | 5 | 5 | 5 | 5 | 5 | 3 | 3 | 61 |
| Australia | 1 | 5 | 5 | 4 | 4 | 5 | 4 | 4 | 3 | 5 | 5 | 5 | 1 | 5 | 5 | 4 | 3 | 62 |
| Netherlands | 1 | 5 | 5 | 4 | 4 | 3 | 3 | 3 | 5 | 5 | 5 | 5 | 5 | 5 | 5 | 2 | 4 | 64 |

**UNDERSTANDING THE CHART**

**Mandatory Retirement** Australia and the United States are the only countries on the list above that prohibit companies from making their employees retire at a certain age. The EU expects to have laws by 2006, but experts are skeptical that all countries will make the deadline.

**Age-Discrimination Laws** The U.S.

**Unemployment Rate** In 2003, the Netherlands averaged lowest (3.89%); Spain, the highest (11.3%). The U.S. had 6%.

**College Education** The U.S. and Norway both get an A on this one: 28% of adults ages 25–64 have a college degree.

**Per Capita Income** Compared with the countries above, the U.S. has the highest average standard of living; Norway is next.

**Total Tax Burden** Sweden collects the most taxes (51.4% of GDP).

**Home Care** In Australia and Denmark, more than 20% of those 65 and older receive home help—from medical care to tidying up. (In the Netherlands, it's 12.8%; in the U.S., less than 10%.)

**Retirement Age for Full Benefits** Most grant benefits at 65. France is lowest—at 60—with citizens strongly protesting change; Denmark is 67.

**Public Pension Replacement Rate** Spain's retirement benefit as a percentage of an average worker's earnings is highest, at 88%. Spain also has a high tax burden and the lowest income.

**Employers Pension Coverage** About 50% of U.S. workers have pension coverage at work. In some countries—Finland and Australia—employer pensions are required by law.

**Economic Inequality** Using an international definition, this is the percent of those whose income is in the lower quarter.

**Economic Inequality for the Elderly** In the U.S., the elderly fare slightly better than the general population.

**Public Spending on Social Programs** Income-support programs, such as social security and welfare, vary widely. Scandinavian countries traditionally offer the most.

**Total Health Costs** Americans spend the most (14.6% of GDP); Finland and Ireland, the least (7.3%).

**Universal Health Care** The U.S. is odd man out: 45 million—41% have no health insurance, though most seniors have Medicare.

**Universal Rx** Canada has limitations and some gaps at the provincial level; 88% have coverage. The U.S. scores lowest, but changes in Medicare represent progress for the elderly.

**Life Expectancy at Birth** In the U.S., babies born in 2004 can expect to live to 77.3; in the Netherlands, to 78.6. Japan is highest at 81.9.

Netherlands, government pressure on hospitals, doctors, and manufacturers helps to keep costs down.

These kinds of controls are not always painless. Just this past year, the Dutch government hit a nerve when it decided to boost the $6-per-hour cost of home care by 250 percent. Half a million citizens, most of them beyond the age of 65, have been receiving subsidized home visits by health professionals or workers who clean and tidy up (like most developed countries, the Netherlands wants to help people maintain their independence and avoid going into nursing homes as long as possible). However, at the increased rate of about $15 an hour, despite government subsidies, home care is rapidly climbing out of sight for many low-income retirees. This increase takes effect, moreover, at an awkward time when the country has a nursing-home waiting list of some 50,000.

Still, all things considered, the Dutch like their health care. In a Harvard School of Public Health survey (taken before the increase in home-care costs), 70 percent said they were satisfied with the system. The same study rated the satisfaction level in the U.S. at 40 percent. And this even when the U.S. spends far more on health care than any other nation in the world—an average of $5,440 per person, with a large share of that going toward retirees.

Canada, by the way, doesn't score much better. Just 46 percent say they are satisfied. Although Canadians receive low-cost prescription drugs, thanks to government controls, health services are underfunded and waiting periods for treatment are long.

Waiting. That seems to be the tradeoff. Someone who needs open-heart surgery in the Netherlands might have to wait 14 weeks before a time slot and hospital space become available. Hip surgery? You're maybe looking at eight weeks. Like much of Europe and also Canada, the Netherlands is short of hospital beds and medical staff. Dutch officials say no one has to wait for emergency attention, and some patients are being sent to Germany and Belgium for faster treatment. Still, the delays underscore a major difference between Dutch and U.S. care. Says one not-so-happy Dutch resident: "I don't care what they say. If you need open-heart surgery here, you can die before you get it."

"In America we love responsiveness," says Anderson, the Johns Hopkins expert. "We're the best on responsiveness." But ready access to care, he adds, is one reason why Americans pay more than people in other countries. Anderson is among the many health specialists and economists who have been pointing out the built-in inefficiencies of U.S. care. Some critics argue that the huge number of health-insurance providers—HMOs, PPOs, Medicare, Medicaid, and all the rest—consumes far more in overhead than would one or two providers and that their many forms and complicated rules drive up hospital administrative costs. Others point to the huge sums spent advertising and marketing drugs and hospitals.

## TAXES

The Dutch in particular pay quite a lot to take care of one another. The personal income tax rate in the Netherlands isn't Europe's highest, but it's well up there, with a top rate of 52 percent on any income over $60,000. (The top U.S. rate has

## FINLAND

### Model Home

Drop a few coins into a slot machine in a local casino in Finland and you contribute to the care and comfort of retirees. Legal gambling in Finland is the exclusive province of the Slot Machine Association, a government-controlled nonprofit that pumps more than $50 million a year into the welfare of the country's 65-plus population (800,000 out of a total of 5.2 million).

Slot machine profits, for example, helped build the four-story Saga Senior Center, a complex of 138 units in Helsinki, with cheerful apartments that are emphatically uninstitutional and that allow older people to have their own space and their own life. "It's the classiest senior home in Finland," says Leif Sonkin, a housing expert. "It's really like a spa." Indeed. Sunshine pours through the glass roof of the atrium, nourishing a lush semitropical garden. The swimming pool is indoor-outdoor and heated in winter. In the basement are saunas, essentials of Finnish life, and a well-equipped gym. (Pay no attention to its thick steel doors: the government requires bomb shelters in all buildings, a holdover from Cold War days.)

"The Saga center isn't a place for rich people," says administrator Mariana Boneva. A small apartment rents for about $600 a month. Most retirees can afford that, but "if they need it to live here, people can get a government housing subsidy," she adds.

Saga is owned by the non-profit Ruissalo Foundation. Although municipalities are charged by law with caring for older people, nonprofits have taken a major role; they operate more than half of Finland's "service housing" for the elderly. This shared responsibility is an extension of the egalitarian streak that started permeating policy in the 1950s, when Finland, along with Sweden, Norway, and Denmark, embraced an unabashedly liberal form of tax-supported welfare.

Finland's taxes are formidable. "I cannot say we love taxes," says Erkki Vaatanen, who lives with her husband, Orvokki, in the Wilhelmiina House, a new senior center. "But we know that schools, hospitals, and highways would go down if we didn't pay." Still, Vaatanen recently faced a drawback. After waiting a year for surgery for an arthritic wrist, she applied again, only to be told: "Little lady, you must wait two years more." So she went to a private physician for treatment and paid herself.—*M.E.*

been going down during the presidency of George W. Bush and now stands at 35 percent. A family of four with an income of about $60,000 would be in the 25 percent tax bracket.)

Almost half of Dutch taxes go to the universal pension fund, known as the AOW, which provides the basic pension that everyone receives at age 65. The AOW takes a salary bite of 17.9 percent. Most Dutch workers have an employer-provided pension based on payments by worker and employer—that's another salary bite of 6 or 7 percent.

Then comes a bigger bite: a 12.05 percent contribution to help pay for basic state health insurance, known as the AWBZ, which, like the basic pension, is universal. Besides paying for care for grave illnesses and a place in a nursing

### SWEDEN

## Shrinking Benefits

In a suburb of Stockholm, care for Aina Karlsson, 85, arrives twice a day, seven days a week. In the morning a *vårdbiträde* (care assistant) helps her bathe and dress; in the evening she helps her get ready for bed. Once a month she cleans the apartment that Aina shares with her husband, Einar. And twice a week she takes Aina to a gymnasium for exercise.

Life expectancy in Sweden is 80.4, one of the highest in Europe. Good care could be one reason. Aina has been receiving *hemhjälp* (home help) assistance since she suffered a stroke four years ago. Cost to the Karlssons: $159 a month. "Not very much," says Einar, a retired union official. To the municipal government, which provides Aina's care, the real cost is about five times greater. And if the Karlssons couldn't afford even $159, the government would provide a subsidy. "That's why Swedish taxes are so high," Einar says cheerfully, noting that income taxes shrink his own pension of $4,400 a month by a third.

Sweden is democratic, capitalistic, high-tech, and industrialized, well known for Ikea and Volvo. It is also well known as a prime example of a welfare state. Social spending, which includes payments such as pensions and welfare, equals 28.5 percent of GDP. In the U.S. it's 16.4 percent.

The income tax rate tops out at a breathtaking 58.2 percent, and there's a 25 percent VAT tax on most purchases. "Of course, many people say taxes are too high," remarks Nils-Erik Hogstedt, a home-care manager. "But the complaint isn't against the elderly. The great majority favor the care." Adds Pernilla Berggren, the manager of a retirement home: "People in Sweden are used to the community doing everything. You grow up expecting society to help take care of Mom."

Tens of thousands use *hemhjälp,* which enables people to remain in their own homes. "Sometimes we visit just once a month to clean," says Chatrin Engbo, head of a Stockholm district care office. "But if needed, we may go several times a day and at night."

This sounds nice—but expensive. To contain costs, the government recently sanctioned sharps cuts in home care by the municipalities, a move that upset many. "Home care used to include visits just to sit and have coffee two or three times a week, or just to take someone for a walk," says Berggren. "We do the essentials, but we can't afford those social moments anymore."

Reductions are also in the pipeline for the pension system, but for now a worker on the job for 30 years is customarily rewarded with a pension that replaces about 60 percent of his pay. (In the U.S. the Social Security replacement rate ranges from about 30 to 60 percent.)

The government's worry about future solvency began in the 1990s. The percentage of 65-plussers, almost one in five of the 8.9 million Swedes, is one of Europe's highest. As with U.S. Social Security, pension payments made by active workers support retirees. With low birth rates and the increase of pensioners, experts estimate that by 2035 the system will be seriously out of balance, with about two workers supporting each older person. (By then, America will be in the same boat.)

Looking ahead, the parliament recently approved drastic, complicated revisions. Out the window went the defined-benefit pension—a set amount based on salary and years of service—replaced by a system based on contributions by worker and employer. The benefit will be indexed to wage growth, with a built-in expectancy that the rate will grow 1.6 percent annually. If wages don't grow that much, the benefit drops. The plan phases in fully in 2019, with the retirement of those born in 1954.

There's yet another new wrinkle: mandated private investments. Besides paying into the pension's main part (employee and employer contribute a total of 16 percent of the worker's wages), all workers are required to put an additional 2.5 percent into their choice of investments—an idea that has become popular among world pension experts. A voluntary form of this setup is favored by President George W. Bush.

Swedes were optimistic in 2000, when this change took effect, even though many were confused by the hundreds of funds, Swedish and foreign, competing for their kronor. The timing proved terrible. The return averaged 3.5 percent in 2001, and then *katastrof!* Or so said a civil servant who saw a thousand dollars vanish from her stock account as markets toppled worldwide. More than 2 million Swedes lost 30 to 40 percent of their mandated investments. (By July 2004, the average fund had recovered nearly 19 percent.)

One likely outcome of the radically revised system: to earn higher pension benefits more Swedes will work beyond the typical retirement age of 60. Says Barbro Westerholm, president of the Swedish Association of Senior Citizens: "I've recommended to my children that they plan to work until they are 70."—*M.E.*

home (after a wait), it also covers part (but less now) of the cost of home care. Most workers also have government-regulated insurance with private or non-profit companies for lesser medical expenses and medicines. Employers usually pay most of this cost: the worker's share is only about 1.7 percent of income.

On top of that formidable raft of outlays, there's also a stiff value-added tax (VAT tax) of 19 percent on most things you buy. And 12 percent on food. And a whopping tax of as much as 40 percent on new cars (plus roughly $6 for a gallon of gas). Yet costs like these haven't stopped Wilhelmina and Cornelius van der Hoop, both retired teachers, from driving all around Europe towing a trailer. The couple's combined pension is about $41,000 after all deductions. "We have no reason to complain," Wilhelmina says. "All those taxes help other people."

In fact, polls show that most Dutch citizens don't object to the large salary deduction that sustains the AOW. "The general attitude in the Netherlands—if you ask the man in the street—is that people who have worked their entire lives should be protected from poverty," says pension expert Maarten Lindeboom, an economist at the Free University of Amsterdam.

Dutch citizens with higher-than-average incomes usually invest in a private pension plan or annuities. That's what tour guide Anna Sophia Fischer did years ago. These investments put her annual income in the $60,000 range, where the taxman ordinarily takes a large bite. But thanks to reductions

## O CANADA!

The pain in her back was terrible, recalls Diane Tupper, who lives in a Vancouver suburb. When she finally got a consultation with a neurosurgeon—after waiting eight months—he said he could fix her spine. Then he delivered the bad news: "Our surgery waiting time is a year and a half to two years."

If Tupper, a 63-year-old lawyer, could hold out, her surgery would be free under Canada's universal-care system. But if she hopped over the border to St. Joseph Hospital in Bellingham, Washington, she could be in the operating room in days. The cost would be about $47,000. "I'm not a well-off person," Tupper says, "but I felt I didn't have any choice." Tupper took out two lines of credit, borrowed $14,500 from a friend, and went to Bellingham.

To many Americans, Canada may look like health care's promised land. Care for all 32.5 million citizens is paid for from taxes. Drugs are typically 30 to 50 percent cheaper than in the U.S.—which is why more than a million statesiders now get prescriptions filled in Canada.

But recently, Canada's system has fallen behind, hobbled by budget cuts, regulations, and shortages of physicians, nurses, and sophisticated equipment such as MRI machines. A recent survey put the backlog of unperformed procedures at 876,584. The waiting time for a hip replacement in Tupper's province, British Columbia, is nearly a year, even longer for a knee replacement.

Filling that gap are U.S. border cities such as Buffalo, New York, and Great Falls, Montana. Minot, North Dakota, attracts people needing CT scans and MRIs, for which they'd wait months in Saskatchewan. Randy Schwan of Trinity Health in Minot says Canadians are amazed to find that "a doctor says we've got to get a test, and the same day someone wheels them down the hall for that test." At the globally famous Mayo Clinic in Rochester, Minnesota, Canadians are the largest foreign-patient constituency.

Some provinces cover care outside of Canada under special circumstances. To trim the waiting list of cancer patients needing radiation treatment, Ontario picked up the bill for 1,650 people who went to the U.S. in 2000 and 2001.

So, get to a Canadian hospital's emergency room after a heart attack and you'll be treated promptly—with no worry about cost. But the system, once the nation's pride, has become, as one official says, "functionally obsolete."—*M.E.*

granted to people over 65, her tax is only about 30 percent of her income. As a former physician, Fischer is well acquainted with the fabled liberality of the health system. "If you want a sex-change operation, the government will pay for it," she says. "I do think that goes a bit too far." A recent innovation: marijuana available by prescription for pain.

A noticeable difference in Europe's treatment of older people is the absence of laws that forbid discrimination and age-based mandatory retirement. In the U.S., mandatory retirement has been illegal for most jobs since 1986. Says one Dutch pension expert: "Here it is automatic that at 65 the job is over." The European Union has mandated that its 25 member states introduce laws against age discrimination by 2006, but the word is that loopholes will permit mandatory retirement to continue. Laurie McCann, senior attorney with AARP Foundation Litigation, concludes that the EU is a long way from either "talking the talk" or "walking the walk" when it comes to eliminating age discrimination.

Today some 14 percent of Americans 65 and over—about 4.8 million people—are still on the job; that's one of the highest rates in the industrialized world. Most Europeans retire at 60 or so, taking advantage of pension generosity.

The need for a ban on mandatory retirement hasn't seemed all that urgent. Frits Velker, a foreman at a Dutch plumbing and sheet-metal company, was 59 when the company was sold. "I looked around and saw so many other people who had retired early," he says. So Velker did too. His company pension is about $27,000, and when he turns 65 he and wife Gerrie will receive about $14,000 a year from the AOW, the state pension fund. In general, a Dutch worker in the Netherlands can expect a total pension equaling about 70 percent of his salary if he worked for 40 years. Thanks to cost-of-living adjustments, former teacher Van Essen's pension is slightly higher—72 percent of his salary—even though his teaching career stopped after 38 years.

Such generous retirement benefits are under siege all across Europe (and Japan). Cutbacks and proposed cutbacks in care and pensions provoked angry strikes last year in France, Italy, Germany, and Austria. Even in Sweden, shining star of the Scandinavian welfare-state constellation, benefits have shrunk. With increasing concern, governments are facing challenging demographics: swelling ranks of longer-living older citizens and thinning ranks of workers able—and willing—to pay for benefits.

If we can get pensions right, demographic change may not be the disaster often painted. Provided we can afford it, living in an older society may be rather pleasant. There ought to be less pressure on resources, less congestion, less crime and a generally calmer society.

But only if we get pensions right. At the moment there are 3.2 people of working age for every person aged over 65. By 2015 that ratio will have fallen to 2.7 and by 2050 when the twentysomethings now entering the workforce will be drawing pensions, to 1.7. (If that sounds alarming, projections suggest that in Italy and Spain the ratio will be around 0.8 in 2050. There'll actually be more pensioners than workers.)

That is the problem with the present pay-as-you-go state pensions schemes, where each generation of working people pays the pensions of the preceding generation. When these were extended after the Second World War, there were about seven workers for every pensioner, so the burden on people of working age was quite modest. But the combination of earlier retirement and longer lifespans has changed the arithmetic. The average age of retirement and average lifespan for men crossed over in the USA in the late 1950s but it will only be in the next five or 10 years when the baby-boomers born in the post-war era retire...

# 14

# We Should Rejoice in an Ageing Society, So Long as We Plan Properly for It

**Hamish McRae**

*Europe, like the United States, has a rapidly aging population. This article discusses some strategies for ensuring that adequate pensions will be available for people after they retire and suggests some methods for deferring retirements by adjusting mandatory retirement ages.*

If we can get pensions right, demographic change may not be the disaster often painted. Provided we can afford it, living in an older society may be rather pleasant. There ought to be less pressure on resources, less congestion, less crime and a generally calmer society.

But only if we get pensions right. At the moment there are 3.2 people of working age for every person aged over 65. By 2015 that ratio will have fallen to 2.7 and by 2050, when the twentysomethings now entering the workforce will be drawing pensions, to 1.7. (If that sounds alarming, projections suggest that in Italy and Spain the ratio will be around 0.8 in 2050. There'll actually be more pensioners than workers.)

That is the problem with the present pay-as-you-go state pensions schemes, where each generation of working people pays the pensions of the preceding generation. When these were extended after the Second World War, there were about seven workers for every pensioner, so the burden on people of working age was quite modest. But the combination of earlier retirement and longer lifespans has changed the arithmetic. The average age of retirement and average lifespan for men crossed over in the US in the late 1950s. But it will only be in the next five or 10 years, when the baby-boomers born in the post-war era retire,

*Source:* Hamish McRae, "We Should Rejoice in an Ageing Society, So Long as We Plan Properly for It," *The Independent—London* (December 18, 2002), pg. 16. Reprinted by permission.

that the arithmetic of these pay-as-you-go schemes becomes really unmanage-able. So there is a short window when reforms have to be put in place. That is what the Government's pensions reform is about.

The UK is relatively lucky by European, though not US, standards. We are ageing more slowly than most Continental countries: the size of our workforce will be stable for some years, while that of most Continental countries will shrink. We have a high participation rate—a larger proportion of the people of working age do actually work. And we have one of the most substantial private pension networks in the world. Private pensions, unlike state ones, are funded in the sense that there is a pot of money that can be drawn down to pay the pen-sion. True that pot has in most cases been cut in size with the fall in share prices. But at least there are some funds.

So we have a more manageable problem than most countries—but not manageable enough. Whatever happens, young people now entering the work-force will have a bad deal from the state. They will have to pay far more in tax-ation than they will receive in pensions and other services. There is no way of changing that. But the greater the success of the Government in persuading people to save more and retire later, the less the burden on the people in jobs who have to pay for them.

So the tests to be applied to the Government's plans are simple. Will they encourage people to save more? And will they encourage people to stay in work longer?

Save more? Not sure. Whether people choose to save or not has long been something of a puzzle. Tax incentives to save probably have had some effect on the scale of saving, but there is also some evidence that people simply save dif-ferently. In other words people decide how much they want to spend and then look for the most tax—effective way of saving the rest. From a macroeconomic point of view, it really does not matter if people save in a company pension, a private pension, a PEP, Tessa or whatever. It is perfectly sensible, too, for people to dip into their retirement funds and invest the money instead in a flat or two for their university-aged children.

There is, however, one important reason for preferring people to invest in a structured way. If people have to set aside money each month and that money is deducted immediately from their wages, then the chances are that the pot re-ally will be available for retirement and not cashed in early. We also know that the relative attraction of saving in a pension fund, rather than the various alter-natives, has been decreased by the present Chancellor. His tax raid on pension funds in his first budget did not attract much attention at the time. But now it has begun to eat into the size of those pension pots—though most people will not feel anything until they come to draw their pensions.

So whatever view one takes of the changes to private-pension legislation proposed yesterday (and my instinct is that they are less important than they seem), the fact remains that this Government has, over its two terms, on bal-ance discouraged people from saving more for retirement. But we will only know in 20 years when we see what happens to the long-term trend in savings.

So a possible fail on test one. What about test two, the working longer one?

Here I think there may be a pass. The adjustment of the state pension to reward later retirement will have two effects. There will be the direct one on people's desire to carry on working and defer retirement. But there will also be an indirect one on the job market. The signal to employers is that there will be many more older workers seeking to extend their working lives. That will encourage companies to think more, not just about the way they organise their pay scales but also about the way jobs are defined.

For example, most jobs are defined by hours worked. But that is only a secondary element in the work/pay relationship. What employers are really interested in is the amount of work done, not the time taken to do it. While time may be an appropriate element in the contract for most workers it is hardly relevant to the elderly. Maybe they take more time to do the job, but so what? They need to be paid for what they do, at their own pace, rather than how long it takes them.

The more that the Government can undermine the notion that there should be a single retirement age, the better. The idea that there should be a state retirement age was set by Bismarck, the German Chancellor, in the 1890s. He chose 70, by the way, at a time when the life expectancy of the German male was in the 40s.

But while these proposals to soften the single retirement are helpful, they won't be really convincing until the Government changes its own practices as an employer. Senior civil servants and diplomats retire on indexed pensions at the age of 60—often to go on to have a second career in the private sector. Many police and local authority workers retire early—police officers often on spurious health grounds. It is no good for the Government to preach to people that they have to work on to 70 or 75 and meanwhile allow their own employees to bunk off at 55.

Look, this is a start. At least we are talking about the problem. The more there is a vigorous debate, not just about pensions but about the whole nature of retirement, the better. The more we think as individuals what we are going to do in our "third age," the more likely we are to make decent preparation for it. On any measure of human values, it is far, far better for people to live to a healthy old age than to die unnecessarily young. So we should rejoice in our ageing society. But we have to plan for it.

# 15

# We're Not Finnished with You Yet

## Gail Edmondson

*Finland, like many advanced countries, has a problem—a shrinking labor pool and an aging workforce. This article documents how Finland is addressing this issue by helping companies boost the productivity of older workers and by increasing the average retirement age.*

He's trim, fit, and runs six miles after work every evening. Finnish machine operator Juha Voutilainen, 57, doesn't even think of retirement, though he's racked up more than three decades at Abloy, a $214 million maker of locks and door systems in Joensuu, Finland. An avid runner who competed in the Aug. 18 Helsinki marathon and trains along the verdant pathways circling Finland's eastern lakes, Voutilainen may be headed for a marathon-like career. And Abloy is in the vanguard of a revolutionary global shift in the management of older workers. Abloy and many other Finnish companies are suddenly treating older employees like a precious resource. Instead of nudging them into early retirement, they're coaxing gray-hairs to work longer with better health benefits, extra weeks of paid vacation, and more. But these companies aren't just feeling charitable. Finland's workforce is aging faster than any other country's—40% of Finns will reach retirement age during the next 15 years. Nearly a quarter of Abloy's 820 workers, for instance, are already over age 55. And companies now recognize that seasoned hands are an important source of knowledge and productivity. "If all our older workers were to leave suddenly, we would lose a lot of knowhow," says Antti Piitulainen, vice-president of operations at Abloy.

The combination of an aging workforce and a shrinking labor pool will affect countries around the world. In Japan, more than 26% of workers are already

*Source:* Gail Edmondson, "We're Not Finnished with You Yet," *Business Week* (September 17, 2007), p. 62. Reprinted by special permission, copyright © 2007 by The McGraw-Hill Companies, Inc.

over 55. And Spain is set to become the world's grayest country by 2050, with half its population older than 55, according to the World Bank. In the U.S., some 19% of workers will be 55-plus by 2012, up from 15.6% in 2005.

Finland is the farthest along in dealing with the aging-worker issue, thanks to a national program called "age ability" launched in 1998. Programs like Abloy's "Age Masters" are spreading, and they're helping companies boost the productivity of older workers and nudge up the average retirement age. At Ores—a $185 million maker of faucets and valves that offers older workers up to 25 extra days off—the average retirement age is now 63, up from 58 in the late 1990s.

## REVERSE COURSE

Some Finnish companies have done an about-face on retirement policies. Swedish-Finnish bank Nordea, which spent a decade restructuring and pushing older workers to retire early, reversed course starting in 2003. It has launched training, mentoring, and health-care initiatives and is all but begging them to stay. Before the program, "people gave up earlier and waited for their career to be over," says Minna Rautakoura, head of human resources at Nordea Finland. "Now they remain in their prime until retirement."

The Finns are lavishing perks on these experienced hands. At Abloy, Age Masters enjoy free massages, company-sponsored golf lessons, language training, and free outings to the theater. The only requirement for the program: A 55th birthday and a cardiac checkup. "They pamper us," says lock assembler Liisa Sutinen, 63, a 35-year veteran. Of course, all this coddling is expensive. Extra vacation time for Abloy's 200 Age Masters costs the company roughly $430,000 a year. But that's money well spent, management figures, since big companies in Finland must shoulder pension payments for workers who retire before age 63.

Programs such as Age Masters are sparking a broader rethink in Finland of how to manage the health of younger workers, too. Abloy, for instance, now offers free access to fitness clubs and swimming pools with an employee ID card. "If you aren't in good condition when you're 55, you can't improve a lot," says Abloy's Piitulainen. And that's key, because in Finland, at age 55, most workers have long careers ahead of them.

# Institutional Problems

3

# Institutional Problems

# 7

# Families

## THE UNITED STATES CONTEXT

The situation of families in the United States is similar in some respects to that found in other industrialized nations: a high divorce rate, both spouses in the workforce, and a relatively high number of single parents. Families in the United States differ considerably when compared to families in similar countries, however, in the relative lack of support they receive from the government and from their employers.

The United States has the highest incidence of unwed teenage births of any of the industrialized countries. Two obvious reasons for this are that it is much more difficult to obtain contraceptives and sex education is woefully inadequate in the United States. About 60 percent of all pregnancies in the United States are unplanned, occurring because contraceptives are misused, unreliable, or not used at all. Their cost is expensive. The free distribution of condoms in schools and health clinics is challenged by many in the United States because they believe that it leads to sexual promiscuity. Current law requires that schools will receive federal money if they use an abstinence-only message. In those countries with cheaper contraceptives and fully-informed sex education, teens who are as sexually active as those in the United States have much lower teen pregnancy rates (England and Wales have half the U.S. rate and the Netherlands has one-tenth the U.S. rate).

The maternity and nursing benefits given to working mothers in the United States are the least generous in the industrialized world. Working mothers in Europe receive, on average, 80 percent of their wages while staying at home with their infants. The United States merely "permits" 12 weeks of *unpaid* maternity leave (a few employers provide paid maternity leave). Many industrialized countries provide paternity leave as well.

Child care is imperative for families where both parents are in the workforce and for working single parents. Child care in the United States is often expensive and difficult to find. By contrast, in France virtually all of 3-, 4-, and 5-year-olds attend preschools at minimal or no charge. Daycare facilities for younger children are heavily subsidized by the government.

# 16

# Atlantic Passages:
# How Europe Supports Working
# Parents and Their Children

**Janet C. Gornick**

> *Janet Gornick documents how Europe and the Nordic countries*
> *support working families and their children by providing paid*
> *family leave, public early-childhood education and care,*
> *and flexible work hours. She concludes that these countries are*
> *able to perform productively and competitively while at*
> *the same time granting generous rights and benefits that*
> *recognize the realities of contemporary family life.*

Many rich countries do a far better job than the United States does of supporting workers who are balancing the competing demands of employment and parenthood. Several European countries, especially in northern and western Europe, provide extensive work/family reconciliation policies—including paid family leave, public early-childhood education and care, and working-time measures that raise the quality and availability of reduced-hour work. The European Union puts a common floor under several of these national standards.

Parents in much of Europe have access to multiple forms of paid family leave, for both mothers and fathers. Equally important, these programs provide wage replacement, usually financed by social insurance, in order to spread the costs between women and men, across generations, and among enterprises. Social-insurance financing also minimizes employers' resistance to hiring young workers, especially women, who they anticipate will be leave-takers.

*Source:* Reprinted with permission from Janet C. Gornick, "Atlantic Passages: How Europe Supports Working Parents and Their Children," *The American Prospect* 18(3) (February 19, 2007), pp. A19–A20. www.prospect.org. The American Prospect, 1710 Rhode Island Avenue, NW, 12 Floor, Washington, DC 20036. All rights reserved.

The Nordic countries—including Denmark, Finland, Norway, and Sweden—provide especially generous family leave rights and benefits. Most new parents have the right to take approximately one year of leave, and they receive about two-thirds or more of their pay. Family leave policies in the Nordic countries also offer parents substantial flexibility. Denmark and Sweden allow parents to take their allotted leaves in increments until their children are eight years old. Norway and Sweden allow parents to combine pro-rated leaves with part-time employment, and Finland and Norway permit parents to use portions of their leave benefits to purchase private child care instead. Recent reforms add incentives for fathers to take leaves, to encourage more gender-egalitarian usage.

Across Europe, publicly supported child care serves a large proportion of infants and toddlers while their parents are working for pay. In Denmark, for example, three-quarters of one- and two-year-olds are now served in publicly financed child-care settings; half of the children in this age range are in public care in Sweden and more than a third in Norway. In many European countries— including Belgium, France, and Italy—nearly all children from age three to the start of primary school are enrolled in full-day preschools. Throughout Europe, public policy measures assure that early childhood education and care are affordable. Parents typically pay income-scaled fees for infant and toddler care, while educationally oriented preschools (for children age three and older) are usually free for all families.

Parents are further aided by a package of working-time measures, some of which are required by the European Union. European countries set their standard weekly work hours individually and, across western and northern Europe today, full-time work is generally defined as between 35 and 39 weekly hours. All EU-member countries are required to grant workers a minimum of four weeks of paid time off each year. Furthermore, EU law requires that all member countries ensure part-time workers pro-rated pay and benefits comparable to what full-time workers receive, in order to make shorter-hour work more economically feasible. In addition, since 2000, several countries—including Germany, the Netherlands, and the United Kingdom—have granted workers new rights to request work-schedule changes; employers may refuse, but their refusals are subject to public review.

These work/family measures are provided alongside universal health insurance, which adds crucial economic support for families, and gives workers flexibility when seeking employment that best meets their families' needs. All told, the comprehensive work/family policy packages operating in several European countries offer parents considerable latitude in allocating their time between paid work and care, and indemnify them against substantial fluctuations in disposable income.

Generous work/family policies are good for parents, children, and worker productivity, and especially benefit lower-income workers who tend to have less bargaining power and cannot afford to pay for help privately. Public systems equalize access and affordability, across family types and throughout the income spectrum, leading to outcomes that are more equitable than what market-based systems produce.

Moreover, expansive work/family policies are compatible with good economic outcomes. Consider GDP-per-hour-worked, a powerful indicator of productivity. The six top-ranked countries in the world are European countries with comprehensive work/family policies, including France, the Netherlands, Belgium, and Norway. Furthermore, the World Economic Forum's Competitiveness Index includes, among the top five countries globally, Denmark, Sweden, and Finland—three countries with extensive work/family policies.

In recent decades, many European countries have restructured their social policies to trim costs and improve economic outcomes. However, programs that support workers with family responsibilities—including paid leave, child care, and rights to high-quality reduced-hour work—were singled out for protection and growth rather than cutbacks, both by the EU and in many individual countries. Clearly, high-income industrialized countries can perform productively and competitively while granting workers rights and benefits that recognize the realities of family life.

# 17

# The Father Generation

**Rainer Stumpf**

*On January 1, 2007, Germany passed legislation regarding the new parenting benefit rules. Under this legislation, the government pays working mothers and fathers a parenting benefit for twelve months, amounting to 67 percent of the average net monthly income compared to the previous year. If both parents participate in child care the benefit is paid for two additional months. Compared to the previous rules, the new legislation gives more opportunities for fathers to participate actively in raising their children.*

Jörg Sattler has a new boss. She wants him now—immediately. She wants her bottle. And then a change of clothes. His boss shouts and wets herself: Zoe is barely half a metre long—and her 37-year-old father can imagine nothing better than spending every available minute with his newborn baby daughter. Instead of attending meetings, he spends his time giving consolation—also at four in the morning. For one year, Sattler has exchanged his job as manager of the lost property office and deputy manager of the passenger service department at Fraport, the company that runs Frankfurt Airport, for a place in front of the baby's changing unit. These precious months have been made possible by a new parenting benefit *(Elterngeld)*. The first time he saw the ultrasound images of his daughter in the womb was "the most beautiful experience," says Sattler. "The birth was simply unbelievable! It was clear to me from the very start that I wanted to play a big part in looking after her. This opportunity came at just the right time." Zoe is now lying contentedly in his arm, sucking on her bottle and enjoying having papa at home. The Fraport employee is one of the first fathers to take advantage of the new parenting benefit rules that came into force on 1 January 2007 and are thus pioneers for a new understanding of the family

*Source:* Rainer Stumpf, "The Father Generation," *Deutschland* (April/May 2007), pp. 23–25. Reprinted by permission.

in Germany. "Almost 70% of all fathers see themselves primarily as educators of their children, only 33% regard themselves mainly as breadwinners," explains gender researcher Robert Richter. Jörg Sattler is also convinced: "It is perfectly normal today for men to do housework. Equally, it will soon be perfectly normal for them to play an equal part in bringing up their children. Parenting benefit is the first step towards that."

## NEW OPPORTUNITY FOR FATHERS

The key date for the new parenting benefit was 1 January 2007: the government will pay working mothers and fathers a parenting benefit for twelve months in place of earnings for all the children born on or after that date. The monthly allowance amounts to 67% of the average net monthly income over the previous twelve months—up to a maximum of 1,800 euros. If both parents actively participate in childcare, the parenting benefit is paid for two additional months, in other words, a total of 14 months. Mothers and fathers can flexibly divide this time between them. That means more hours together with their children. Above all, however, the scheme offers new opportunities for fathers. Previously, payments of child-raising benefit (*Erziehungsgeld*) of roughly 300 euros a month had been made, but this was usually not enough to replace the normally higher earnings of fathers. Now even men with management jobs, like Jörg Sattler, can devote time to their children without having to take a great financial risk. The system is a success: whereas last year only 3.5% of all applications for parental leave were submitted by men, the total already doubled during the first quarter of 2007. Ulrich Schmidt has also handed in his application. "Unfortunately, after the birth of my first daughter I couldn't take any parental leave. When our second child is born in November, I'll be taking a two-month break from work." The 35-year-old journalist didn't hesitate this time around: he now wants to and can help his wife from immediately after the birth. Stefan Schmidt wants to do the same: "When my daughter Anna Dora was born, my head of department immediately asked when I would be taking parental leave. There was no question about that for her." His colleagues, family, friends—everyone supported his decision. Several friends, also fathers-to-be, want to follow his example and take advantage of the new rules. A baby furlough of eight weeks is planned for spring 2008. He is not the only person looking forward to these two months. After twelve months of parental leave, his wife, a biologist, wants to set up her own business next year. The support from her husband comes at just the right moment. "You don't want to give up everything for the child. We need a middle path—between career and family," says the 38-year-old mother. For men and women.

That is also the goal of Federal Family Minister Ursula von der Leyen. "It's the beginning of a new era, a family-friendly era," explains the politician, who is herself a mother of seven. Within a short period of time she has made family policy a central focus of domestic policy in Germany. With the introduction of parenting benefit, the government has made it easier for highly qualified mothers and fathers to decide to have a child. Now a nationwide expansion of creche and nursery places also aims to enable them to return to work easily. 500,000 additional childcare places, largely for children under three, are planned by 2013. That means there will be a childcare place for roughly one third of all infants. Additionally, the ministry is supporting multi-generational houses and planning a system of nursing leave. This aims to enable sons and daughters to look after parents who need care without them having to give up their jobs. These are decisions from which society as a whole will benefit, insists von der Leyen: "Family policy is a definite growth engine." That is also confirmed in a study by the Cologne Institute for Economic Research. Economically, European countries will be left behind by the United States if they do not take measures to increase their low birth rates. Good family policy secures rising birth rates and thus maintains prosperity.

## FAMILY-FRIENDLY EMPLOYMENT

It is also becoming increasingly important for business. Demographic change in Germany means the proportion of old people in the population is steadily growing and this is already creating personnel shortages in some industries. There is growing competition between companies for the best minds. It is clear to Patrik Speier, a team leader at the R+V insurance company who has just become a father, that only those firms that enable their employees to achieve a balance between work and family will be able to retain their personnel in the future. The 46-year-old has himself experienced how important that is—thanks to the support of his superiors and colleagues he was able to take five weeks' leave after the birth of his daughter Kira and defer his parental leave to 2008 when his wife will go back to work: "A satisfied worker is a better worker," says Speier. Although it would involve a greater planning effort for the leader of a group of 10 employees, he would like to see more flexible working arrangements. "Companies should offer more part-time jobs. That would help many parents and also strengthen employees' commitment to their firms." According to a survey by the German Society for Personnel Management (DGP), there is a good chance that will happen. Some 85% of German personnel managers expect that family-oriented corporate policies will become increasingly important. Fraport demonstrates what parent-friendliness can mean. Just recently, the airport operator was named as one of the 500 most family-friendly firms in Germany by berufundfamilie, a national families initiative. The company is currently launching a fathers' network and encourages fathers to take advantage of the new parenting benefit rules. Lost property office manager Jörg Sattler will certainly have a lot to tell there—about his one-year period of parental leave, his new boss that he would like to hold in his arms around the clock and about his professional future: he is enjoying the time he spends with his daughter Zoe so much that he only wants to work part-time when his parental leave comes to an end.

# 18

## ■ ■ ■

# Teen Pregnancy:
# Trends and Lessons Learned

### Heather Boonstra

*During the 1990s, teenage pregnancy rates and birthrates declined to record low levels. Even with this progress, however, the U.S. teen birthrate is one of the highest in the developed world. This article addresses these trends.*

Many of the provisions of the 1996 law overhauling the nation's welfare system will expire at the end of the current fiscal year on September 30. The reauthorization process likely will set the stage for a major debate over one of the law's main stated goals, reducing out-of-wedlock births, and how best to achieve it. Social conservatives favor programs and policies encouraging marriage and promoting abstinence from sexual intercourse outside of marriage for people of all ages. Others suggest that it would be more appropriate and more effective for policymakers to concentrate on finding ways to sustain recent declines in *teenage* pregnancy and childbearing, since half of first nonmarital births are to teens and almost eight in 10 teen pregnancies are unintended.

The declines in recent years in teen pregnancy rates and birthrates are impressive: Both now stand at record low levels. However, the United States still lags far behind other developed countries, whose rates have fallen to much lower levels. New research suggests that going forward, more realistic views of young people's sexuality and their needs as they make the transition to adulthood, along with more-comprehensive approaches to meeting those needs, may be in order.

*Source:* Heather Boonstra, "Teen Pregnancy: Trends and Lessons Learned," *The Guttmacher Report on Public Policy* 5(1) (February 2002), pp. 7–10. Reprinted by permission.

## KEY TRENDS OVER TIME

### Childbearing

The rate of teen childbearing in the United States has fallen steeply since the late 1950s, from an all time high of 96 births per 1,000 women aged 15–19 in 1957 to an all time low of 49 in 2000 (see Figure 18.1). Birthrates fell steadily throughout the 1960s and 1970s; they were fairly steady in the early 1980s and then rose sharply between 1988 and 1991 before declining throughout the 1990s. In recent years, this downward trend has occurred among teens of all ages and races.

### Unmarried Childbearing

Even though teen childbearing overall has declined steeply over the last half-century, the proportion of all teen births that are nonmarital has increased equally dramatically, from 13% in 1950 to 79% in 2000 (see Figure 18.1). Two factors are at play. The first is that marriage in the teen years, which was not uncommon in the 1950s, has by now become quite rare. (By the mid-1990s, the typical age of first marriage in the United States had risen to just over 25 for women and 27 for men.) The second is that this trend has extended to pregnant teens as well: In contrast to the days of the "shotgun marriage," very few teens who become pregnant nowadays marry before their baby is born.

### Abortion

Birthrates rise and fall as a result of changes in the rate at which women become pregnant or resolve their pregnancies in abortion, or a combination of

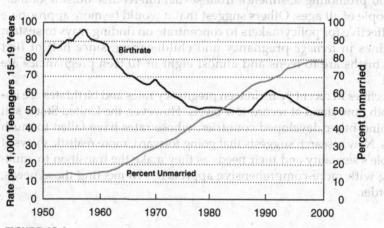

**FIGURE 18.1**

*Note:* Data for 2000 are preliminary.

*Source:* National Center for Health Statistics, "Births to Teenagers in the United States, 1940–2000." *Natial Vital Statistics Report,* 2001. Vol. 49, No. 10.

both. Among teens in the United States, at least in recent years, declining birthrates are not the result of more pregnant teens opting to have an abortion. The U.S. teen abortion rate, after rising through the 1970s and holding fairly constant during the 1980s, then began a steady decline. By 1997, the rate was 28 abortions per 1,000 women 15–19—33% lower than the rate a decade earlier.

## Pregnancy

Recent declines in teen birthrates, then, are attributable to reductions in pregnancy rates. In the 1970s and early 1980s, the U.S. teen pregnancy rates rose. They remained steady through the 1980s, even as sexual activity among teens increased, due to improved contraceptive use among those teenagers who are sexually active. The rates declined 19% from 117 pregnancies per 1,000 women aged 15–19 in 1990 to 93 per 1,000 in 1997—the lowest rate in 20 years. The recent decline is particularly encouraging, because—as with the teen birthrate decline—all population groups followed a similar pattern, regardless of young women's age, marital status, race or ethnicity.

## WHY THE RATES ARE DOWN

If recent declines in teen childbearing are the result of fewer teens getting pregnant in the first place, the obvious next question is: why? Are fewer teens avoiding pregnancy by abstaining from sex, or are those who are having sex using contraception more successfully?

Not surprisingly, the answer is: both. But deconstructing that answer is critical, because it goes to the heart of a number of relevant and timely public policy questions, among them the debate over public funding for abstinence-only education and for more-comprehensive approaches. . . .

In 1999, researchers at The Alan Guttmacher Institute (AGI) analyzed the reasons behind the recent declines in the U.S. teen pregnancy rate, using data from two comparable, large-scale government surveys, the 1988 and 1995 cycles of the National Surveys of Family Growth, and recent information on rates of teenage pregnancies, births and abortions. AGI's methodology follows the consensus of a group that was convened by the National Institute of Child Health and Human Development to examine measurement issues regarding teen sexual activity and contraceptive use, which included researchers from AGI, the National Center for Health Statistics, The Urban Institute, Child Trends and the National Campaign to Prevent Teenage Pregnancy.

The AGI analysis concluded that approximately one quarter of the decline in teenage pregnancy in the United States between 1988 and 1995 was due to increased abstinence. (The proportion of all teenagers who had ever had sex decreased slightly, but nonsignificantly, during this period, from 53% to 51%.) Approximately three-quarters of the drop resulted from changes in the behavior of sexually experienced teens. (The pregnancy rate among this group had fallen 7%, from 211 per 1,000 to 197.)

The researchers considered a number of behavioral changes that could explain why a smaller proportion of sexually experienced teenage women became pregnant in 1995 than in 1988, including the possibility that they were having less sex. However, they found that, overall, there was little change between the two years in how often sexually experienced teenagers had intercourse.

Instead, the researchers found that overall contraceptive use increased—but only slightly, from 78% in 1988 to 80% in 1995. More importantly, teenagers in 1995 were choosing more-effective methods. A significant proportion had switched to long-acting hormonal methods that were introduced to the U.S. market in the early 1990s, namely, the injectable contraceptive (Depo-Provera) and the contraceptive implant (Norplant). By 1995, more than one in eight teen contraceptive users (13%) was using a long-acting method, and primarily because of this shift, sexually active teens became increasingly successful at avoiding pregnancy.

## U.S. STILL LAGS

Despite all this good news, the fact remains that teenagers in the United States continue to experience substantially higher pregnancy rates and birthrates than do teens in other Western industrialized countries (see Figure 18.2). The adolescent pregnancy rate in the United States, for example, is nearly twice that in Canada and Great Britain and approximately four times that in France and Sweden. Moreover, teen birthrates have declined less steeply in the United States than in other developed countries over the last three decades.

In order to learn more, AGI initiated a large-scale investigation in collaboration with research teams in Canada, France, Great Britain and Sweden.

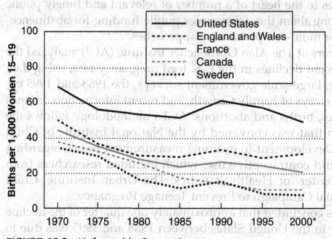

**FIGURE 18.2** Unfavorable Comparison
Teenage birthrates declined less steeply in the United States than in other developed countries between 1970 and 2000.

*Data are for 1997 in Canada, 1998 in France and 1999 in England, Wales and Sweden.

*Source:* Darroch J.E. et al., *Teenage Sexual and Reproductive Behavior in Developed Countries: Can More Progress Be Made?* Occasional Report. New York: AGI, 2001, No. 3, page 14.

Between 1998 and 2001, each team prepared a case-study report for their country, including quantitative data on sexual and reproductive behavior, information documenting social attitudes and service delivery, and examples of relevant policy and program interventions. AGI synthesized key findings in a report, *Teenage Sexual and Reproductive Behavior in Developed Countries: Can More Progress Be Made?*, published in November 2001.

The research explored the roles of several key factors expected to contribute to variation among countries, including two commonly given explanations for why rates are so much higher in the United States: that U.S. teenagers are more sexually active and that the United States has a higher proportion of its residents living in conditions of poverty and social disadvantage.

In fact, the study found that levels of sexual activity and the age at which teenagers initiate sex do not vary appreciably across the countries and are simply too small to account for the wide variations in teen pregnancy rates. Rather, teen pregnancy and childbearing levels are higher in the United States, they found, largely because of differences in contraceptive use. Sexually active teens in the United States are less likely to use any contraceptive method and especially less likely to use highly effective hormonal methods, primarily the pill, than their peers in other countries (see Figure 18.3). U.S. teens who become pregnant are also less likely to opt to have an abortion, whether due to lack of

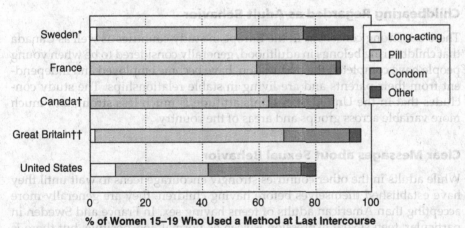

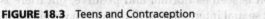

**% of Women 15–19 Who Used a Method at Last Intercourse**

**FIGURE 18.3** Teens and Contraception
U.S. teens are less likely to use a contraceptive method, and to use a hormonal method, than teens in other developed countries.

*Data are for 18–19-year-olds.
†The condom category includes all methods other than the pill, but the condom is the predominant "other method."
††Data are for 16–19-year-olds.

*Note:* Users reporting more than one method were classified by the most effective method. Data are for early to mid-1990s.

*Source:* Darroch, J. E. et al., *Teenage Sexual and Reproductive Behavior in Developed Countries: Can More Progress Be Made?* Occasional Report, New York: AGI, 2001, No. 3, page 33.

abortion access, higher levels of antiabortion sentiment or greater acceptance of teen motherhood.

The study did find, however, that across all of the focus countries, young people growing up in disadvantaged economic, familial and social circumstances are more likely than their better-off peers to engage in risky behavior and have a child during adolescence. It is true, therefore, that pregnancy and birth are more common among U.S. teens in part because the United States has a greater proportion of disadvantaged families. (While the United States has the highest per capita income of the study countries, it also has the highest percentage of its population who are poor.) However, at all socioeconomic levels, American teenagers are less likely than their peers in the other study countries to use contraceptives and more likely to have a child. For example, U.S. teenagers in the highest income subgroup have birthrates that are 14% higher than similar teenagers in Great Britain and rates that are higher than the overall teen birthrates in Sweden and France.

## LESSONS LEARNED

The AGI study also provides valuable insights into the reasons pregnancy and birth among teenagers are so much less common in other developed countries.

### Childbearing Regarded as Adult Behavior

There is a strong consensus in the European study countries as well as Canada that childbearing belongs in adulthood, generally considered to be when young people have completed their education, have become employed and independent from their parents and are living in stable relationships. The study concludes that in the United States, this attitude is much less strong and much more variable across groups and areas of the country.

### Clear Messages about Sexual Behavior

While adults in the other countries strongly encourage teens to wait until they have established themselves before having children, they are generally more accepting than American adults of teens having sex. In France and Sweden in particular, teen sexual expression is seen as normal and positive, but there is also widespread expectation that sexual intercourse will take place within committed relationships. (In fact, relationships among U.S. teens tend to be more sporadic and of shorter duration.) Equally strong is the expectation that young people who are having sex will take actions to protect themselves and their partners from pregnancy and sexually transmitted diseases. In keeping with this view, state or public schools in England and Wales, France and Sweden and in most of Canada teach sexuality education and provide comprehensive information about prevention. In addition, the media is used more frequently in government-sponsored campaigns for promoting responsible sexual behavior

("Promoting Contraceptive Use and Choice: France's Approach to Teen Pregnancy and Abortion," *TGR*, June 2000).

For adults in the United States, on the other hand, the fact that young people are having sex is more often considered to be, per se, the "problem." Because teens are often regarded and portrayed as being incapable of using contraception effectively, having sex is often equated with becoming pregnant and a teen parent; the slogan of one state's current teen pregnancy campaign is "You play, you pay." Moreover, the United States is the only country with formal policies directing state and federal funds toward educational programs that have as their sole purpose the promotion of abstinence. Over one-third (35%) of all local U.S. school districts that have policies on sexuality education require that abstinence be taught as the only appropriate option for unmarried people and that contraception either be presented as ineffective in preventing pregnancy or not be covered at all. Among school districts in the South— where birthrates are significantly higher than the national average—that proportion is 55%.

## Access to Family Planning Services

In countries that are more accepting of teenage sexual relationships, teenagers also have easier access to reproductive health services. In Canada, France, Great Britain and Sweden, contraceptive services are integrated into other types of primary care and are available free or at low cost for all teenagers. Generally, teens know where to obtain information and services and receive confidential and nonjudgmental care, the study reports.

In the United States, where attitudes about teenage sexual relationships are more conflicted, teens have a harder time obtaining contraceptive services. Many do not have health insurance or cannot get birth control as part of their basic health care. A high proportion turn to family planning clinics, where the cost of contraception is less and where, under current federal law, confidentiality is guaranteed. (There have been numerous attempts over many years to reverse this policy.) And even the guarantee of confidentiality may be a double-edged sword. It protects teens (research has shown that confidentiality is essential to many teens' willingness to come in for services), but because it is not necessarily the norm in more "mainstream," private-sector care, it may also reinforce the notion that by seeking services, teens are doing something "wrong."

## Youth Development

The study found that the other study countries are all committed, although to varying degrees, to the idea of the "welfare state," and several provide considerable assistance to young people across-the-board to ease the transition from adolescence to adulthood. France, Sweden and to some extent Great Britain and Canada seek to help all teens with vocational training and education and help in finding work and unemployment benefits. These supports, say researchers, increase teenagers' ability to plan for the future—and their motivation to delay pregnancy and childbearing.

The U.S. approach, on the other hand, emphasizes individual responsibility for one's own welfare. Education, training and employment are generally up to teens themselves, with the help of their families. In keeping with this tradition, government assistance for teens in the United States is targeted primarily to those who have already dropped out of school or otherwise "slipped through the cracks." These programs may be critical to the well-being and outlook for the future of small numbers of highly vulnerable teens, but they are unlikely to play much of a role, if any, in the reproductive behavior and decisions of U.S. teens generally.

## POLICY IMPLICATIONS

When reauthorization of the 1996 welfare law begins in earnest this year, as well as during the annual appropriations process, there will be loud debate over proposals, enthusiastically backed by the Bush administration, to launch new marriage promotion initiatives and to expand abstinence-only education programming. Many scholars as well as advocates, however, are uneasy with the notion of government as "marriage broker." And they question whether government effectively can—or even should—spend its capital on morality-based campaigns to convince people who are unmarried not to have sex. The research presented here, in fact, indicates that this approach is driven more by ideology than evidence. It strongly suggests that more-realistic attitudes about young people's sexuality and more-comprehensive responses to their needs, broadly defined, as they make the transition from adolescence to adulthood would be the more-appropriate approach.

Rep. Benjamin L. Cardin (D-MD) is one member of Congress who understands this. Cardin is ranking minority member of the Human Resources Subcommittee of the House Ways and Means Committee, which will play a key role in the welfare reauthorization process. At a November 2001 hearing on teenage pregnancy, Cardin articulated what he believes the government should be doing to build on the current progress: "I would say that we should continue our focus on personal responsibility; we should do a better job of not only funding local efforts to combat teen pregnancy, but also of highlighting successful programs; we should increase access to youth development and after-school programs that give teenagers productive activities to pursue; and we should promote the value of abstinence *without* undercutting our commitment to providing access to and information about contraception."

# 8

# Schools

## THE UNITED STATES CONTEXT

Public education in the United States has many problems. Foremost, schools are vastly unequal in resources because their finances depend largely on the local economy. This means, for example, that urban schools are poorly financed, yet they have the highest concentration of poor children, minority children, and children of recent immigrants. Educational policy, for the most part, is not a federal issue but rather divided into 50 state programs and 15,000 local district programs. Thus, there are wide differences in curricula, standards, and emphases depending on the locality. It is estimated that school districts need at least $100 billion to repair or replace deteriorating facilities. Many high school graduates are barely literate. Compared to their peers in other industrialized countries, U.S. students by the 12th grade do not fare well in mathematics and science. Latinos, the largest racial/ethnic minority in the United States, have a 30 percent dropout rate from high school, compared to 12 percent for African Americans and 9 percent for whites. Colleges and universities, the most important gatekeepers, are so expensive that they are becoming less available to the children of middle- and working-class parents and, obviously, the working poor and the poor. This leads, of course, to a two-tiered society.

As a result, educational performance in the United States varies by locality and the social and economic background of students. Most notably, the United States falls short on a number of indicators used to compare the industrialized nations on education (e.g., high school graduation rates, the gap between the highest and lowest performing students, per pupil expenditures as a percentage of income per person, early childhood education, and the number of days spent in school each year).

# 19

■■■

# Early Childhood Education and Care in Advanced Industrialized Countries

**Sheila B. Kamerman**

*Sheila B. Kamerman identifies three important trends in early childhood education found in various advanced industrial countries. She concentrates on the European and Nordic countries. How do U.S. policies compare?*

Whether in the OECD (Organisation for Economic Co-operation and Development) countries, the countries of the EU (European Union), the CIS (Commonwealth of Independent States) and Central and Eastern European countries, the ASEAN (Association of Southeast Asian Nations) countries, or others, interest in and attention to early care and education (ECE) is clearly growing. For the first time in about three decades, the OECD carried out a thematic review of ECE policies and programs in 20 of its 30 member countries, and UNESCO joined with the OECD in a subsequent review of ECE in four developing (or less-developed) countries, Brazil, Indonesia, Kenya, and Kazakhstan.

ECE is a policy priority throughout the EU countries in particular, even if curricula and rates of coverage vary. My focus here will be on three trends in ECE policy that have emerged in the EU and in selected OECD countries that are collectively referred to as "advanced industrialized countries."

Two factors have been especially important in bringing ECE to the forefront in these countries. First, increasing numbers of women have entered the labor force. Thus ECE services have become necessary to ensure that men and women have equal work opportunities and to facilitate the reconciliation of work and family life. Second, there has been a growing recognition that a posi-

*Source:* Sheila B. Kamerman, "Early Childhood Education and Care," *Phi Delta Kappan* 87 (November 2005) pp. 193–195. 2005. Reprinted by permission of Phi Delta Kappan and the author.

tive group experience enhances the cognitive, social, and emotional development of children and can help compensate for early disadvantages that many children experience.

## THREE POLICY TRENDS

Among the advanced industrialized countries, there have been three important recent developments in the area of ECE policy:

- specifying targets for achieving an expansion of ECE services, often by the year 2010;
- extending the duration of paid parental leaves, both to support the nurturing and caring role of parents and to reduce the need for out-of-home infant and toddler care; and
- changing the governance structure of ECE so that all policies and programs fall under the auspices of education, rather than being divided between education and health or social welfare.

## EXPANDING ECE SERVICES

Increasing the employment rate in the EU, especially the percentage of women in the labor force, is an explicit goal of the European employment strategy.[1] At its Lisbon summit in March 2000, the EU set a goal to increase the rate of female employment from 51% at that time to 57% by 2005 and 60% by 2010. Two years later, at the Barcelona summit, the EU took an important step toward achieving this goal by setting specific targets for the expansion of ECE services: at least 90% of children between age 3 and the age of compulsory school entry (age 5, 6, or 7) and at least 33% of children under age 3 are to be enrolled in ECE programs by 2010.

Although not binding, the Barcelona targets emphasize the importance of ECE for working parents, just as earlier the OECD had emphasized the importance of ECE for children's socialization and future school success.[2] The Barcelona targets for young children have not yet been achieved; however, access to ECE programs is clearly increasing. Nine of the 25 EU countries plus Norway and Iceland have already achieved the 90% goal for this age group, and half of the 16 remaining countries have 80% of this group enrolled. Among the OECD countries, Belgium, Denmark, Finland, France, Germany, Hungary, Iceland, Italy, Japan, Luxembourg, the Netherlands, Spain, Sweden, and the UK enroll around 90% of their children by the age of 4 in free (or very low-cost) early education services. Not all of the programs cover the full workday, but the school day in these countries is often significantly longer than the U.S. school day.

## EXTENDING PARENTAL LEAVE

Now we turn to the goal for the under-3s. While not all countries have a sufficient supply of services to cover one-third of the under-3s, some countries have established an alternative approach: paid and job-protected leaves from work to allow parents to care for a very young child at home.

There are several different types of parental leave plans that permit women, or men and women, to take time off from work at the time of childbirth or adoption or to meet other family needs. These plans are an essential element in reconciling work and family life and constitute the first component of an ECE system. Almost by definition, extended leaves following childbirth determine when out-of-home infant and toddler care services are needed.

The leave polices in the different countries vary in terms of their duration, benefit levels, eligibility criteria, and flexibility. Rather than set a target for the future implementation of leave policies, the EU has issued directives that member countries must provide at least 14 weeks of paid maternity leave (18 if the child is disabled) supplemented by at least 13 weeks of unpaid parental leave (18 if the child is disabled) for each parent.

The duration of these leaves is critical, as is the extent of the accompanying cash benefit, which will replace all or a significant part of the wages of an employed parent staying home to provide care and nurturing for a new baby. The Nordic countries provide a parental leave lasting about one year and a social insurance benefit that nearly replaces full wages, thus ensuring that a parent can provide infant care without significant loss of earnings. Several EU and Central and Eastern European countries provide extended parental or child-rearing leaves of two to three years, but with significantly less financial support.

The major trend in the 1980s and 1990s was to extend the various leave policies so as to create a real alternative to out-of-home infant care. Long leaves of up to three years may not be ideal for all parents and may have negative consequences for women's later wages and careers, but they do expand the care options for some.

## INTEGRATING CARE AND EDUCATION WITHIN THE EDUCATION SYSTEM

The Nordic countries made early care and education an explicit policy priority and stressed the integration of the two functions from the beginning of the movement in the 1970s. However, initially, the concept was to integrate the services under a free-standing social welfare system of care. In 1986, New Zealand became the first country to institute a dramatic and significant change in the delegation of policy responsibility, placing child care under the department of education.[3] Other countries subsequently transferred the responsibility for early care and education (for children of varying ages under the age of compulsory school entry) from social welfare or health ministries to education ministries. Sweden did so in 1996,[4] and similar developments occurred in some regions of northern Italy, in Spain, and then in England and Scotland in 1998.[5]

The reasoning in New Zealand was that moving child care to the department of education would facilitate the integration of care and education, improve the quality of child care, and increase the government's financial support for ECE.[6] A major theme in England and Scotland was that the integration of care and education—replacing a previously fragmented system divided between education and health—and the inclusion of child welfare services along with education and care in deprived areas in England and in all areas in Scotland would improve the situation of disadvantaged children especially. The reorganization in England and Scotland emerged in response to changes in welfare and social-assistance policies, the desire to increase employment among low-income single mothers, and a conviction that expanding the supply of early care and education services and placing them under education would help to reduce child poverty.

Sweden had already integrated care and education more than three decades before it put its education ministry in charge of those services. It had gone beyond a focus on the children of working parents and had a fully universal policy in place. The country also had very low rates of child poverty and social assistance. Thus in Sweden the focus became the simultaneous improvement of both ECE and primary schooling. The idea was for schools to adopt the greater emphasis on quality that characterized the ECE system and for the early childhood program to adopt educational principles.[7] At the same time, however, there was (and there continues to be) some anxiety about the possible "schoolification" of ECE.

## EARLY CARE AND EDUCATION AS A RIGHT

In this brief article, I have highlighted three important current trends in ECE policy: increasing the supply of services and expanding access, acknowledging the role of parental leave policies in reducing demand for out-of-home infant and toddler care, and integrating care and education within ministries or departments of education. Other trends appear to be emerging as well, if not quite as clearly as those discussed here. Among these are:

- a move to look beyond the kinds of quantitative goals set at Barcelona and to pay more attention to quality (group size, staff/child ratios, and staff qualifications) and affordability (including financing strategies);
- a growing awareness of the link between a decent-quality preschool experience and primary school readiness and performance; and
- a growing conviction that ECE should be an entitlement—that children should have the right to ECE just as they have the right to primary and secondary education now.

With regard to casting ECE as a right, although the European Commission does not have the authority to require member states to set national child-care policies based on the rights of children, these rights have already been recognized by the European Council of Ministers and are recognized in the proposed EU constitution and by many member states.[8] In Sweden, the reforms of 2001 and 2002 established preschool as a right for all children, regardless of the employment status of their parents; it is provided free to 4- and 5-year-olds and at a low cost to younger children.[9] And since New Zealand ratified the United Nations Convention on the Rights of the Child, children's rights have been emphasized as part of the rationale for that country's ECE policy as well.[10]

There is increasing discussion of the notion that all children have the right to free, high-quality early care and education. Acknowledging this right may become a major trend in the future.

## Notes

1. Janneke Plantenga and Melissa Siegel, "Child Care in a Changing World: European Child Care Strategies," paper presented at the Conference on Childcare in a Changing World, Groningen, Netherlands, 21–23 October 2005.
2. *Starting Strong: Early Childhood Education and Care* (Paris: OECD, 2001).
3. Anne Meade and Val Podmore, *Early Childhood Education Policy Co-ordination Under the Auspices of the Department/Ministry of Education: A Case Study of New Zealand* (Paris: UNESCO, Early Childhood and Family Policy Series, No. 1, 2002).
4. Hillevi Lenz Taguchi and Ingmarie Munkammar, *Consolidating Governmental Early Childhood Education and Care Services Under the Ministry of Education and Science: A Swedish Case Study* (Paris: UNESCO, Early Childhood and Family Policy Series, No. 6, 2003).
5. Bronwen Cohen et al., *A New Deal for Children? Reforming Education and Care in England, Scotland, and Sweden* (Bristol, England: Policy Press, 2004).
6. Meade and Podmore, op. cit.
7. Cohen et al., op. cit.; and idem, *Reforming Education and Care in England, Scotland, and Sweden* (Paris: UNESCO, Policy Brief on Early Childhood, 2003).
8. Plantenga and Siegel, op. cit.
9. Lenz Taguchi and Munkammar, op. cit.
10. Meade and Podmore, op. cit.

# 20

# Learning from South Korean Schools

**David J. Lynch**

*The United States ranks 18th in education among 36 nations examined by the OECD. South Korea, in contrast, ranks very high in graduation rates and other measures. This article provides some of the reasons for the success of the South Koreans and in doing so, provides some possible avenues for the United States to improve the education of its children.*

SEOUL—In any high school in the United States, it would be a routine question met with a routine answer. But here in South Korea, ask a principal for her school's dropout rate and then stand back:

"No one just drops out of school," says a disgusted Chung Chang Yong, principal of Ewha Girls' High School. "A student may transfer to another school, but no one just drops out. . . . To drop out of school is a major disaster, a catastrophe. It wouldn't happen unless it was unavoidable."

Maybe not in South Korea where 93% of all students graduate from high school on time. But in the United States, almost one-quarter of all students—more than 1.2 million individuals each year—fail to graduate. Once the world leader in secondary-school education, the United States now ranks a desultory 18th among 36 nations examined by the Organisation for Economic Co-operation and Development.

The U.S. also is one of only two countries, along with tiny Estonia, where the percentage of high school graduates is lower among younger workers than among their parents—stunning for a nation whose identity always has been defined by the expectation of better tomorrows. Educators and economists alike bemoan the nation's lost excellence, linking the failure to make better use of the

*Source:* David J. Lynch, "Learning from S. Korean Schools," *USA Today* (November 19, 2008), pp. B1–B2. Reprinted by permission.

nation's human capital to both rising income inequality and growing insecurity among the hard-hit middle class.

"The U.S. has rested on its laurels way too long. The Baby Boomers were the best-educated generation of any in the global workforce. Today's labor force entrants are not as lucky," says Jacob Funk Kirkegaard of the Peterson Institute for International Economics in Washington, D.C. "Other countries have increasingly caught up and surpassed the United States."

Stagnating educational attainment is just one of the warning signs that—even before the current financial crisis—stirred alarm about the competitiveness of the $14 trillion U.S. economy. Aging infrastructure and wasteful energy usage are among other national shortcomings that, to some, suggest the U.S. has lost a step to more nimble global rivals. "We've been asleep for a good number of years as a country," says Richard Freeman, economics professor at Harvard University. "It's not that we're doing so horrible. But the other guys are moving faster."

## LISTEN TO TEACHER

One of the fastest-moving is South Korea. In the early 1960s, this key U.S. ally had an economy equivalent to the least-developed countries in sub-Saharan Africa. In the next four decades, thanks to an increasingly educated workforce, it emerged as one of East Asia's tiger economies. Today, education remains the guiding principle of South Korean society, from affluent city dwellers to the poorest villagers.

"In a country so small, with no natural resources, the reason we can export cars and (information technology) is because of our human resources," Chung said.

While U.S. graduation rates have stagnated or even slid back, South Korea has shot ahead. In the U.S., the percentage of 55- to 64-year-olds who eventually get a high school degree, including a G.E.D., is exactly the same as those in the 25-to-34-year-old group, 87%. But South Korea has driven its rate from 37% to 97% for the younger group, the highest percentage of any of the 36 nations studied by the OECD.

With an ethic reminiscent of postwar America, parents here almost universally make their children's education the family's unquestioned priority. An experienced secondary-school teacher makes almost 25% more than a comparable American teacher, according to OECD data. As in all Confucian societies, students here are raised to revere teachers. An old saying has it that one should not dare step even on the shadow of a teacher.

Another sign of that commitment: National educational spending as a percentage of South Korea's $1 trillion economy, from both public and private sources, is higher than in the United States and higher than the OECD average.

As a percentage of the economy, South Korean families spend three times as much as Americans on education—except for college, where Americans spend fractionally more. What distinguishes South Korea is the $200 billion parents spend on private educational institutes, says Ryu Ji-Seong of the Samsung Economic Research Institute.

The South Korean formula combines fierce societal pressure, determined parents and students who study nearly round-the-clock. After a typical eight-hour school day, most students spend their remaining waking hours in private tutoring or reviewing schoolwork. "Society wants us to go to university and graduate," says Ewha student Yun Ji Lim, 18, who hopes to become an engineer.

Her mother, Baek So-Ae, 45, praises the school's science classes. But she spends about $8,000 annually on after-school tutors for her daughter in science and math. "I always have to reduce living expenses," she says. "We spend around one-third of our total income on education. That is definitely a burden."

But it's a burden willingly borne in status-conscious South Korea, where parents regard getting their children into the right university with a fervor that dwarfs even the most ardent Ivy League-crazed American mother or father.

"People say that university is not the end of everything, but it is one of the most important parts in life. Society wants professional people, and getting married is not the end for women these days," says Baek. "I think university is the best place to gain professionalism. It does not guarantee success, but it definitely raises the probability."

American missionaries founded Ewha Girls' High School in 1886 hoping to produce young women schooled in Christian values. Nestled in a leafy enclave in the center of Seoul, the spacious campus of modern brick buildings is equipped with the latest computers and high-tech gadgets.

In one classroom, about a dozen young girls wearing uniforms of pleated skirts and light-green V-necked sweaters or polo shirts cluster around a telescope held by a teacher. Down the hall, biology teacher Lee Sookyong wears a wireless headset microphone while lecturing.

One of the finest schools in the country, Ewha is a private institution, like more than half of all secondary schools here. The unusual public-private mix is a legacy of South Korea's deep poverty in the years following the 1950–53 Korean War. Imbued with a culture that revered learning but lacking the resources needed to build a nationwide education system, the government encouraged religious orders and wealthy intellectuals to start schools.

Ewha receives half of its annual budget from the central government; the rest comes from the school's private foundation and annual $2,000 tuition payments. Unlike private schools in the U.S., Ewha's students are selected by the government. Families who can't afford the tuition receive government subsidies.

The South Korean system also is notable for enforcing a national curriculum and for spreading resources far more evenly than does the U.S. Unlike students in poorer U.S. districts, which lack sufficient property tax receipts to fund quality instruction and account for a disproportionate share of dropouts, just about everyone here receives a decent education.

In the southern part of Seoul, Yeongdeungpo High School provides a glimpse of a more typical public institution. At midday, rambunctious boys play an intense game of soccer on an all-dirt field, a dusty contrast to Ewha's tony environs. Teachers are assigned here by a public board, while Ewha selects its instructors.

But the two schools share one characteristic: the fierce dedication of parents and children to completing their schooling. "Foreigners may think it's strange. I think the main difference between the Western and the Korean parents (is) their way of life is quite different from ordinary Westerners. They are ready to sacrifice themselves for their kids. Whereas ordinary Westerners are seeking their own happiness," says Seo Dong Mok, 64, the school's principal.

## BUILDING THE MIDDLE CLASS

For most of the 20th century, each generation of Americans received an average of two more years of schooling than their predecessors, and the supply of skilled workers rose faster than demand. But starting about 1980, that ceased to be the case, according to Lawrence Katz, an economist at Harvard University. The most recent generations have gained less than one extra year of education.

That change has driven a sharp rise in the wages that college-educated workers earn relative to the earnings of the less-educated. Demand for workers with the education to use computers and cope with an economy that can swiftly change course is outpacing the supply of those workers. And that makes it difficult to maintain the sort of broad-based middle class that characterized the U.S. for much of the last century.

Education "was a big part of the rise of the U.S. to economic dominance and creation of a broad middle class. . . . If education doesn't keep up, it impacts not only growth, but also inequality," says Katz.

While there are many elements of the South Korean system that no one suggests are worth replicating, including a conformist regimen and grinding workload, its success isn't limited to high graduation rates. South Korean students also routinely best their American counterparts in standardized tests. In 2006, for example, South Koreans ranked second on the Program for International Student Assessment (PISA) math test. American kids finished 25th of 30 countries on the exam, which is administered to 400,000 15-year-olds every three years.

The best U.S. high schools remain superlative, and the nation's universities are regarded internationally as the best in the world. The problem is that the performance of U.S. high schools is uneven. Some systems, such as Fairfax County, Va., are top-notch, while other poor-performing school systems are what experts at Johns Hopkins University call "dropout factories." Students in Detroit, for example, have just a 37.5% chance of graduating, according to the Alliance for Excellent Education.

Globalization also has raised the bar on what is acceptable. Whereas the dropouts of an earlier era could count on landing well-paying factory jobs in the American heartland, today's dropouts confront a reordered globalized economy where unskilled work increasingly is migrating to low-wage nations in Asia or Latin America.

"It's not just Brooklyn and Boise anymore. (American students) are competing with Bangalore and Beijing," says Bob Wise, president of the nonpartisan Alliance for Excellent Education. "There's an international standard being set every day. It's called the international market. We can't shield our students from its demands."

Still, the South Korean approach is not without serious flaws, as parents and educators here are quick to note. The emphasis on endless study produces students who perform well on tests but often fall short in creativity. Classes also are far larger than a typical American high school, with about 40 students in each Ewha classroom.

The government plans to address some of these shortcomings. It hasn't gone unnoticed that so many parents yearn for their kids to study abroad. The country has only a relative handful of top-shelf universities, not nearly enough for the avalanche of eager graduates its high schools produce. And educators recognize the need to adapt schools to produce creative, flexible workers for today's jobs rather than churn out more or less identical industrial-age drones. "It's not obvious what the right mechanism is," says Harvard's Freeman. "Probably some mix between the Korean and American ways would be ideal."

# 21

# A World Transformed: How Other Countries Are Preparing Students for the Interconnected World of the 21st Century

**Vivien Stewart**

*This essay assesses how the United States compares with other countries in preparing students for life in the global era.*

Globalization is the central feature of our time. As global networks expand, countries in every corner of the Earth are affected. Major forces are driving change at an accelerated pace, creating new challenges for education systems worldwide. The globalization of economies has meant that an increasing proportion of jobs is tied to international trade. New discoveries in science and the rapid spread of new technologies are "flattening the world" and organizing work in virtual, not just physical, communities.[1] Demographic movements are increasing student diversity in schools in many nations worldwide. Changing opportunities—such as increasing access to education and health services for all—and changing threats to human security—ranging from environmental degradation and climate change to global diseases, terrorism, and weapons proliferation—are driving international cooperation across a wider range of occupations than ever before.

Do American students have the knowledge and skills to function effectively and be leaders in this increasingly interconnected world? Last year, Harvard University released the report of its first major review of the undergraduate curriculum in almost 30 years. The study concluded that, in a fast-changing world, students urgently need a deeper understanding of the principles of science and a

*Source:* Vivien Stewart, "A World Transformed: How Other Countries Are Preparing Students for the Interconnected World of the 21st Century," *Phi Delta Kappan* 87 (November 2005), pp. 229–232. Reprinted by permission of Asia Society.

far greater grasp of international affairs. It recommended significant reforms of the undergraduate curriculum to ensure more substantial international knowledge and experience and stronger foreign language skills for graduates, who will need to be "globally competent."[2]

However, while U.S. higher education is moving to internationalize its curriculum, K–12 education trails far behind. Studies by the Asia Society and the National Geographic Society have identified a huge gap in most American students' knowledge about Asia and other regions of the world that are vital to our nation's economic prosperity and national security. When compared to students in eight other industrial countries, young Americans are next to last in their knowledge of geography and current affairs.[3] And the U.S. has very little capacity in Asian languages.

How are other countries addressing the need for "global competence and global citizenship"? Of the many approaches to teaching about the world, world geography, world history, foreign languages, citizenship education, and global or development education are the most common. However, science, literature, and the arts can all incorporate international content and perspectives. Unlike other, more traditional areas of educational discourse—literacy, math, and science, for example—there is very little systematic research on this emerging issue. No comprehensive account of what other countries are doing exists, nor is there even agreement on definitions. However, I will highlight here some trends and innovative efforts from around the world and the different forces that are driving them.

## EUROPE

According to a recent study by the IEA (International Association for the Evaluation of Educational Achievement), rapid economic and political change in Europe—the transition to market economies and democratic structures in Eastern Europe and the creation of a new supranational structure, the European Union—is focusing educators' attention on preparing students for changing political and economic realities.[4] At the same time, there are efforts to align education with the economic development and international relations goals of governments—goals which have grown increasingly global.

In the United Kingdom, for example, the Department of Education and Skills has set out a vision: "The people of the U.K. should have the knowledge, skills, and understanding they need to live in and contribute effectively to a global society and to work in a competitive global economy."[5] This vision includes incorporating a global dimension into the learning experiences of all children; beginning foreign language instruction earlier (age 7) and ensuring that, by 2010, all students will have the chance to learn at least one other language; establishing an International School Award program to encourage schools to integrate international content into their curriculum; and creating partnerships with schools in other countries through the Global Gateway website. Simultaneously, the U.K. Department for International Development is encouraging education about economic development by disseminating and providing teacher training for a curriculum that focuses on the Millennium Development Goals of the U.N.

Sweden, Finland, and Holland, all countries with strong education systems as measured by international assessments, are increasing their emphasis on development/global education, languages, and world geography. In France and Italy, world geography and world history are mandatory subjects of study, beginning in the early grades. Of great importance, most European countries start a first foreign language in the elementary grades, and many are raising their requirements for second foreign languages. Another recent initiative is the European Strategy Framework for Improving Global Education, which was created at a conference in Maastricht, Netherlands, in 2002, under the auspices of the Council of Europe.[6] As in the U.K., global/development education is promoted primarily by international development agencies (both governmental and nongovernmental) and is not yet in the mainstream of education. In Eastern Europe and the former Soviet Union, on the other hand, the dominant focus has been on introducing international economics education and Western approaches to social science.

## AUSTRALIA

In the early 1990s, the Australian government decided to engage more deeply with Asia for economic, demographic, and security reasons. In an examination of their system, Australian educators found that the schools' instruction on Asia was very basic and shot through with exotic stereotypes. Accordingly, the government established and funded the Asia Education Foundation as a national organization to promote the study of Asia and Asian languages in Australian schools. Over a 10-year period, the foundation produced materials to help teachers infuse the study of Asia into different curriculum areas, provided professional development to 100,000 teachers, helped 900 teachers take postgraduate programs in teaching Asian studies, and enabled 2,000 teachers to participate in study tours in the region.

Today, about half of Australian schools teach about Asia in a sustained and systematic way, and another quarter do it somewhat superficially. In addition, between 1994 and 2000, the learning of Asian languages increased significantly, and 23% of students now study one of the four languages identified as priorities—Japanese, Bahasa-Indonesian, Chinese, and Korean.[7] Increasing students' ability to navigate the thriving Asian economies clearly will provide economic benefits to Australia, and growing numbers of Asian students also see Australia as an attractive alternative to the U.S. for university study.

## ASIA

As part of the dramatic modernization of its education system, the People's Republic of China is developing an increasingly international focus in its schools.

English is now the second language of China and will be taught to all students from third grade on. China's schools are teaching world history and world geography, and the Project on Education for International Understanding is updating textbooks through the addition of more international content. Schools are encouraged to host visiting international teachers, especially from English-speaking countries. Teachers are encouraged to study abroad, and schools are strongly encouraged to form sister-school partnerships with schools in other countries. While these changes have not yet extended to its vast rural areas, where basic education is still underdeveloped, China's intention is clearly to prepare young people to be able to function in an increasingly complex and interconnected world.

After World War II, the education system in Japan was changed dramatically to include the teaching of English and an emphasis on international exchange. In the 1980s and 1990s, corporations pressed for more international curricula to keep the country globally competitive. Multicultural and human-rights education were also popular, partly in response to the increasing numbers of Koreans living in Japan. And Mandarin is now being introduced as an important language of study. However, as in most countries around the world, schooling is still seen as a major force in the building of national loyalties, despite the addition of some international elements described above.

South Korea, Singapore, and Taiwan have focused on the adoption of master plans to put high-speed computers in schools as a means of connecting their students to world knowledge. In this way, these nations are also encouraging more student-directed work to supplement the traditional teacher-directed approaches.

## MEDIA, TECHNOLOGY, AND INTERNATIONAL EXCHANGE

In addition to updating and "internationalizing" their school curricula, countries can take advantage of the vast new media and information-technology resources to teach their students about the world. Since studies of children's television use in more than 23 countries have found that 12-year-olds tend to watch about three hours of television a day no matter where they live, and since access to computer and information technology is rapidly increasing around the world, it is arguably the case that these are the most significant instruments of international education in most countries. Unfortunately, the content of television leaves much to be desired for such purposes, although there are outstanding examples of explicit use of "edutainment" to promote cross-cultural understanding and overcome past hatreds.[8]

Information technology is increasingly being harnessed by educators in many countries to teach about the world. Whether by accessing newspapers from different countries, taking part in global data-collection projects in science, or linking classrooms for language or cultural exchange purposes, schools in many countries are being encouraged to use technology to help students learn "with" and not just "about" their peers in other nations. Although there are no systematic data on the numbers of such "virtual" school-linkage projects, data from iEARN, one of the largest organizations facilitating such linkages, suggest that, despite the scale of technology available in U.S. schools, only 1,500 of the more than 20,000 classrooms participating in iEARN projects are in the U.S.[9]

With international travel far easier than ever before, there is an increasing emphasis on studying abroad as a means of exposing students in a powerful way to other cultures. The number of U.S. students who study abroad is increasing but remains low compared with the figures for other countries. Less than 0.5% of U.S. students studied abroad in 2000, compared with 3% for France and China, 16% for Ireland, and 30% for Singapore.

## HOW DOES THE U.S. COMPARE WITH OTHER COUNTRIES?

In the U.S. there is considerable ferment with regard to these issues. As the November 2004 special section of the *Kappan* pointed out, local schools have launched hundreds of grassroots efforts to try to prepare students for a more global world.[10] States are taking steps to prepare a more globally sophisticated work force through creating new policy frameworks and new curricular and professional development initiatives, using distance education and online courses, encouraging partnerships with schools in other countries, and creating internationally themed schools as part of their high school redesign efforts. There is also clear and growing interest among students in more international content and in opportunities to learn world languages, especially Chinese.

However, these innovations are small in scale, lack the funding to reach significant numbers of students, and are not yet part of the assessment and teacher preparation systems. Moreover, despite persistent calls from the U.S. State Department, the U.S. Defense Department, and the business community to expand the nation's capacity in a wider range of major world languages, there has been no significant national initiative to address the issue. While there are vehicles for structured interaction between countries on such subjects as science, math, and technology, there is also a need for more systematic research on the effectiveness of different approaches to global education and for cross-national sharing of best practices as educators strive to give their students new international skills for a new Global Age.[11]

## Notes

1. Thomas L. Friedman, *The World Is Flat: A Brief History of the Twenty-First Century* (New York: Farrar, Straus & Giroux, 2005).
2. *A Report of the Harvard College Curricular Review* (Cambridge, Mass.: Harvard University Faculty of Arts and Sciences, April 2004).
3. National Commission on Asia in the Schools, *Asia in the Schools: Preparing Young Americans for Today's Interconnected World* (New York: Asia Society, 2001); and

"National Geographic/Roper 2002 Global Geographic Literacy Survey," November 2002, www.nationalgeographic.com (search on the title).

4.  Judith Torney-Purta et al., *Citizenship and Education in Twenty-Eight Countries: Civic Knowledge and Engagement at Age Fourteen* (Amsterdam: IEA, 2001).

5.  *Putting the World into World-Class Education* (London: Department for Education and Skills, 2004), p. 1.

6.  Ida McDonnell, Henri-Bernard Solignac Lecomte, and Liam Wegimont, *Public Opinion Research, Global Education and Development Cooperation Reform: In Search of a Virtuous Circle* (Maastricht: Europe-Wide Global Education Congress, 15–17 November 2002).

7.  *States Institute on International Education in the Schools Report* (New York: Asia Society, 2003), p. 26.

8.  Ellen Wartella and Gary E. Knell, "Raising a World-Wise Child and the Power of Media," *Phi Delta Kappan*, November 2004, pp. 222–24.

9.  Linda G. Roberts, "Harnessing Information Technology for International Education," *Phi Delta Kappan*, November 2004, pp. 225–28.

10. Emily Sachar, *Schools for the Global Age* (New York: Asia Society, 2004).

11. Kenneth A. Tye, *Global Education: A Worldwide Movement* (Orange, Calif.: Interdependence Press, 1999); and *Building National Capacity in Chinese* (New York: Asia Society, 2005).

# 9

∎ ∎ ∎

# Work

## THE UNITED STATES CONTEXT

As noted elsewhere in this text, pay for work in the United States is highly skewed, with chief executive officers at large corporations making as much as 500 times the pay of the average blue-collar worker. This gap is actually understated because it does not include stock options, paid insurance, travel subsidies, country club memberships, huge retirement settlements, and other perquisites that are commonly provided to corporate executives but not to their workers. The gap between the pay and benefits of corporate executives and their workers is much higher in the United States than in any other industrialized nation.

Public policy in the United States actually accentuates the gap between the rich and the poor. For example, blue-collar workers cannot write off their lunches at work but executives get a tax break for their business meals. The tax code also gives tax breaks for "business travel" and even for owning second homes, advantages only to those in the upper tier. Moreover, while wages are taxed fully, profits made from the sale of stocks, bonds, land, houses, and other property are taxed at a lower rate. Also, Congress recently made it easier to pass wealth on to heirs by increasing the amount exempt from estate taxes. At the same time, Congress has chosen not to provide universal health insurance, a living wage, subsidized child care, universal preschool for four- and five-year-olds, and free public education through college as found in other industrialized nations.

A major difference between the United States and other industrialized nations is that the United States has a relatively weak and declining labor union movement. The proportion of workers in unions fell from 27 percent in 1978 to 13 percent in 2009. This erosion in the numbers of union workers, coupled with the rise of international competition and accelerated capital mobility, has weakened their bargaining power.

Summarizing the situation of U.S. workers, Larry Williams and Mary Otto say:

Americans are working longer hours than their counterparts in any other industrialized nation; a growing share of the workforce has no pension and health benefits; and the income gap between the rich and rest of society continues to widen. From these crosscurrents emerges a snapshot of a divided society in which the middle class is running harder and harder to support a bountiful lifestyle while the wealthiest can afford unimaginable luxuries and the poor find work but little security in a world that appears to be leaving them behind. (Williams and Otto, 1999:1E)

## Reference

Williams, Larry, and Mary Otto. 1999. "Mild Unrest Marks Modern Labor Day." *Denver Post* (September 6):1E, 5E.

# 22

■ ■ ■

# The Vanishing American Vacation

### Don Monkerud

> *Compared to people in other developed countries, Americans*
> *work more hours per week, have less vacation time, and when*
> *provided vacation time, they are less inclined to take it. Why?*

In 1882, New York clamored for an appearance by the champion of laissez-faire capitalism, Herbert Spencer, who provided Charles Darwin with the phrase, "Survival of the fittest."

Spencer agreed to meet the captains of American industry, but his appearance was a disaster. Spencer told the assembly they didn't understand his ideas, for he disapproved of American capitalism. Americans, he claimed, are pathologically obsessed with work.

Overwork risks their mental and physical health and they need a "revised ideal of life" that includes relaxation. "Life is not for learning, nor is life for working," said Spencer, "but learning and working are for life."

Almost 125 years later, Americans still haven't gotten the message. Compared to people in other developed countries, Americans don't ask for more vacation time, don't take all the vacation time their employers give them, and continue to work while they are on vacation.

There are a number of theories about why Americans don't demand more vacation time: fear of leaving work that will pile up in their absence; fear that other employees will show more devotion to the job and get promoted above them; a distaste for relating to a mate and children outside of their tightly structured lives; and they've been convinced that economic success depends on subservience to employers who control their work lives. Consider that:

- Some 88 percent of Americans carry electronic devices while on vacation to communicate with work, and 40 percent log-on to check their work email.

*Source:* Don Monkerud, "The Vanishing American Vacation," *AlterNet* (September 3, 2007). Online: www.alternet.org/story/61122. Reprinted with permission from AlterNet.org, a project of the Independent Media Institute.

- A third of all Americans don't take their allotted vacation and 37 percent never take more than a week at a time.

Many employees have no choice because they are at the bottom of the pay scale and are forced to work to make ends meet. A third of all women and a quarter of all men receive no paid vacation. We've been globalized, downsized and privatized until we are little more than production units.

The U.S. remains the only industrialized country in the world that has no legally mandated annual leave. France leads the world with 30 days off a year. Employees in Britain, German, Australia, Spain and Sweden have 20 or more days off a year, and Canada and Japan have 10 days off, about the same as some American corporations allow their workers. The Chinese get three weeks off a year, and this is only the legally mandated vacation time. Many employees in other countries take six or more weeks off a year (the French average 39 days and the English 24).

Meanwhile, those who profit from our labor amass wealth. For the fifth consecutive year in a row—a Bush record—the average American's income remained below what it was in 2000. Those making over $1 million a year (less than a quarter of one percent of all taxpayers) increased their income 26 percent, and 62 percent of that increase came from Bush tax cuts on investments: capital gains and dividends.

Our mythology claims the work ethic makes America great, but does it? We have the highest productivity in the world because we work more overtime— 40 percent of Americans work 50 hours a week and some workweeks typically run 60 to 70 hours.

Workers in France, Ireland, Norway and Holland are more productive than American workers: Germany and Britain lag slightly behind, and all of them have more vacation time than we do.

It's not like we don't need vacations. One in three American workers are chronically overworked and report job stress. We are working longer hours, our jobs are more demanding, and we have more tasks to perform. 40 percent of parents with teenage children report high stress levels, and those making over $50,000 a year report the highest levels of stress.

We can't expect to wait until retirement to have more time off, either. For the first time in history—another Bush record—four generations of Americans are now working. After decades of decline, the number of workers 55 and over has increased. Today 6.4 percent of those 75 and older work. The number of those receiving pensions decreased by half since 1980 and the age to receive full Social Security benefits increased to 67. Over 60 percent of those between 55 and 64 in California are working, an increase of 7.4 percent since 1980.

Whether it's greed, an ingrained protestant work ethic, economic necessity or some other reason, there's no excuse for not having mandated vacation time.

No one is ever taken advantage of without their agreement, so perhaps Americans live to work. If not, it's time for Americans to take Herbert Spencer's advice, demand more vacation time, relax and enjoy your life.

# 23

# A New WPA?

## Ryan A. Dodd

*At the beginning of the Obama presidency, the United States
faced an economic crisis, most fundamentally a crisis of job loss
and job security. Can the government, acting as an employer of
last resort, guarantee full employment? This essay describes Argentina's economic crisis in 2001 and how that experience might
guide direct government job creation in the United States.*

Dark clouds are now looming over America's economic future. As first the
stock market boom and then the housing boom have come to an end, along
with the fountains of cheap credit that were their mainspring, the perennial
gale of unemployment is blowing in. The president and Congress have addressed the downturn with tax rebates and talk of "debt relief." Meanwhile,
public infrastructure is crumbling. Workers' wages are stagnating while their
work hours are rising. Health insurance is becoming less and less affordable for
the typical family. And as U.S. military spending escalates, government spending on essential services is drastically reduced.

All of these facts serve to remind us that capitalist economies are inherently unstable and structurally incapable of creating full employment at decent
wages and benefits. While tax rebates and debt relief may provide some minor
protection from the coming economic storm, these measures are temporary—
and inadequate—responses to a perpetual problem. As an alternative to these
ad hoc policies or, worse yet, the free-market fundamentalism still widely
preached in Washington, some economists and policymakers, in the United
States and abroad, are touting a policy that seeks to end unemployment via a
government promise to provide a job to anyone ready, willing, and able to
work.

*Source:* Ryan A. Dodd, "A New WPA?" *Dollars & Sense*, number 275 (March/April 2008), pp. 12–17.
Reprinted by permission of *Dollars & Sense*, a progressive economics magazine www.dollarsand
sense.org.

## ARGENTINA'S EXPERIMENT IN DIRECT JOB CREATION

In early December 2001, following nearly two decades of neoliberal restructuring, the Argentine economy collapsed. Apparently, two decades of privatization, liberalization, and government austerity, ushered in by Argentina's brutal military junta (in power from 1976 to 1983), were not enough to sate the appetites of global financial capital: earlier that year the International Monetary Fund had withheld $1.3 billion in loans the country needed to service its $142 billion external debt. In response to the IMF's action, the government froze all bank accounts (although many wealthy Argentines managed to relocate their funds abroad before the freeze) and drastically cut government spending. As a consequence, the economy experienced a severe depression as incomes and expenditures fell through the floor. The unemployment rate shot up to a record 21.5% by May 2002, with over 50% of the population living in poverty.

The popular response to the crisis was massive. Protests and demonstrations erupted throughout the country. The government went through five presidents in the course of a month. Workers eventually reclaimed dozens of abandoned factories and created democratically run cooperative enterprises, many of which are still in operation today and are part of a growing co-op movement.

Reclaiming factories was a lengthy and difficult process, however, and the immediate problem of unemployment remained. In response, in April 2002 the Argentine government put into place a direct job creation program known as *Plan Jefes de Hogar* ("Heads-of-Household Plan"), which promised a job to all heads of households satisfying certain requirements. In order to qualify, a household had to include a child under the age of 18, a person with a disability, or a pregnant woman; the household head had to be unemployed; and each household was generally limited to only one participant in the program. The program provided households with 150 pesos a month for four hours of work a day, five days a week. Program participants mainly engaged in the provision of community services and/or participated in worker training programs administered by local nonprofits.

While limited in scope and viewed by many in the government as an emergency measure, the program was incredibly successful and popular with its workers. It provided jobs and incomes to roughly 2 million workers, or 13% of Argentina's labor force, as well as desperately needed goods and services—from community gardens to small construction projects—to severely depressed neighborhoods. The entry of many women into the program, while their husbands continued to look for jobs in the private sector, had a liberating effect on traditional family structures. And by some accounts, the program helped facilitate the cooperative movement that subsequently emerged with the takeover of abandoned factories. Not surprisingly, as Argentina's economy has recovered from the depths of the crisis, the government has recently made moves to discontinue this critical experiment in direct job creation.

## "EMPLOYER OF LAST RESORT"

The Argentine experience with direct job creation represents a real-world example of what is often referred to as the *employer of last resort* (ELR) proposal by a number of left academics and public policy advocates. Developed over the course of the past two decades, the ELR proposal is based on a rather simple idea. In a capitalist economy, with most people dependent on private employment for their livelihoods, the government has a unique responsibility to guarantee full employment. This responsibility has been affirmed in the U.N. Universal Declaration of Human Rights, which includes a right to employment. A commitment to full employment is also official U.S. government policy as codified in the Employment Act of 1946 and the Humphrey-Hawkins Act of 1976.

Although many versions of the ELR proposal have been put forward, they all revolve around the idea that national governments could guarantee full employment by providing a job to anyone ready, willing, and able to work. The various proposals differ mainly on the wage and benefit packages they would provide to participants. The most common proposal calls for paying all participants a universal basic wage and benefit package, regardless of skills, work experience, or prior earnings. This wage and benefit package would then form the effective minimum for both the public and private sectors of the economy. After fixing a wage and benefit package, the government would allow the quantity of workers in the program to float, rising and falling in response to cyclical fluctuations in private-sector employment.

As with Argentina's program, ELR proposals typically call for participants to work in projects to improve their local communities—everything from basic infrastructure projects to a Green Jobs Corps. Most ELR proponents also advocate a decentralized approach similar to Argentina's, with local public or nonprofit institutions planning and administering the projects, though it is essential that the program be funded at the national level.

This raises an important question: How will governments pay for such a large-scale program? Wouldn't an ELR program require significantly raising taxes or else result in exploding budget deficits? Can governments really afford to employ everyone who wants a job but cannot find one in the private economy? Advocates of ELR address the issue of affordability in different ways, but all agree that the benefits to society vastly outweigh the expense. Many ELR advocates go even further, arguing that any talk of "costs" to society misrepresents the nature of the problem of unemployment. The existence of unemployed workers represents a net cost to society, in terms of lost income and production as well as the psychological and social stresses that result from long spells of unemployment. Employing them represents a net benefit, in terms of increased incomes *and* enhanced individual and social wellbeing. The real burden of an ELR program, from the perspective of society, is thus effectively zero.

Most estimates of the direct cost of an ELR program are in the range of less than 1% of GDP per year. For the United States, this was less than $132 billion in 2006, or about 5% of the federal budget. (By way of comparison, in 2006 the U.S.

government spent over $120 billion on the wars in Iraq and Afghanistan—and that figure does not include the cost of lives lost or ruined or the future costs incurred, for example, for veterans' health care.) Furthermore, an ELR program provides benefits to society in the form of worker retraining, enhanced public infrastructure, and increased social output (e.g., cleaner parks and cities, free child care, public performances, etc.). By increasing the productivity of those participants who attend education or training programs, an ELR program would also decrease real costs throughout the economy. Estimates of program costs take into account a reduction in other forms of social assistance such as food stamps, cash assistance, and unemployment insurance, which would instead be provided to ELR participants in the form of a wage and benefit package. Of course, those who cannot work would still be eligible for these and other forms of assistance.

Today, the ELR idea is mostly confined to academic journals and conferences. Still, proponents can point to a number of little known real-world examples their discussions have helped to shape. For example, the Argentine government explicitly based its *Jefes de Hogar* program on the work of economists associated with the Center for Full Employment and Price Stability (CFEPS) at the University of Missouri-Kansas City. Daniel Kostzer, an economist at the Argentine Ministry of Labor and one of the main architects of the program, had become familiar with the CFEPS proposal and was attempting to create such a program in Argentina a few years before the collapse provided him with the necessary political support. Similar experiments are being considered or are currently underway in India, France, and Bolivia. Advocates of ELR proposals can also be found at the Levy Economics Institute (U.S.), the Center for Full Employment and Equity (Australia), and the National Jobs for All Coalition (U.S.).

## THE CASE FOR DIRECT JOB CREATION

Involuntary unemployment is a fundamental and inherent feature of a capitalist economy left to its own devices. In a society where most people depend on employment in the private sector for their livelihood, the inability of a capitalist economy to consistently create enough jobs for all who seek work is deeply troubling, pointing to the need for intervention from outside of the private sector. ELR advocates view national governments—with their unique spending ability, and with their role as, in principle, democratically accountable social institutions—as the most logical institutions for collective action to bring about full employment. In addition, government job creation is viewed as the simplest and most direct means for overcoming the problem of involuntary unemployment in a capitalist economy.

The standard mainstream response to the problem of unemployment is to blame the victims of capitalism for lacking the necessary talents, skills, and effort to get and keep a job. Hence, the mainstream prescription is to promote policies aimed at enhancing the "human capital" of workers in order to make them more "competitive" in a rapidly globalizing economy. The response of

ELR advocates is that such policies, if they accomplish anything at all, simply redistribute unemployment and poverty more equitably. For example, according to the Bureau of Labor Statistics, the number of unemployed workers (including so-called "discouraged" and "underemployed" workers) in August 2007 was 16.4 million, while the number of job vacancies was 4.1 million. No amount of investment in human capital is going to change the fact that there simply aren't enough jobs to go around.

Advocates of ELR also consistently reject the Keynesian rubric, with its focus on demand-management strategies—that is, policies aimed at increasing aggregate demand for the output of the economy. This approach has been pursued either directly, through government spending on goods and services (including transfer payments to households), or indirectly, largely through policies intended to increase private investment. Such an approach exacerbates inequality by biasing policy in favor of the already well-to-do, through tax cuts and investment credits to wealthy individuals and powerful corporations. These policies also tend to privilege the more highly skilled and better-paid workers found in the industries that generally benefit from the government's largesse (often arms manufacturers and other military-related companies). For example, much of the increase in government spending during the Cold War era went into the high-tech, capital-intensive, and oligopolized sectors of the economy. Capital-intensive industries require relatively small amounts of labor, and, thus, produce little employment growth per dollar of government expenditure. Under this policy approach, the most that lower-paid or unemployed workers could hope for would be to snatch a few crumbs from the great corporate feast as the economy expanded over time.

In contrast to both the human-capital and demand-management approaches, ELR provides a means for rapidly achieving zero involuntary unemployment. By definition, anyone who is unemployed and chooses not to accept the ELR offer would be considered voluntarily unemployed. Many individuals with sufficient savings and decent job prospects may forgo the opportunity to participate in the ELR program, but ELR always provides them with a backup option.

In addition to the immediate effects of ELR on employment, the program acts as an "automatic stabilizer" in the face of cyclical fluctuations in the private sector of the economy. During a recession, the number of participants in the program can be expected to grow as people are laid off and/or find it increasingly difficult to find private-sector employment. The opposite happens during the recovery phase of the business cycle, as people find it easier to find private-sector employment at wages above the ELR minimum. As a result, ELR advocates argue, the existence of such a program would dampen fluctuations in private-sector activity by setting a floor to the decline in incomes and employment.

A final and less discussed benefit of the program is its socializing effect. The example of Argentina is instructive in this respect. The nature of employment in the *Jefes* program, oriented as it was toward community rather than market imperatives, created a sense of public involvement and responsibility. Participants reported increases in morale and often continued to work beyond the four hours a day for which they were getting paid; they appreciated the cooperative nature of most of the enterprises and their focus on meeting essential community needs as opposed to quarterly profit targets. By expanding the public sphere, the *Jefes* program created a spirit of democratic participation in the affairs of the community, unmediated by the impersonal relations of market exchange. These are the kinds of experiences that are essential if capitalist societies are to move beyond the tyranny of the market and toward more cooperative and democratic forms of social organization.

Some economists and advocates have pressed for a similar proposal, the *basic income guarantee* (BIG). Instead of guaranteeing jobs, under this proposal the government would guarantee a minimum income to everyone by simply giving cash assistance to anyone earning below that level, in an amount equal to the gap between his or her actual income and the established basic income. (Hence this proposal is sometimes referred to as a "negative income tax.") BIG is an important idea deserving wider discussion than it has so far received. But ELR advocates have a number of concerns. One is that a BIG program is inherently inflationary: by providing income without putting people to work, it creates an additional claim on output without directly increasing the production of that output. Another is that BIG programs are less politically palatable—and hence less sustainable—than ELR schemes, which benefit society at large through the provision of public works and other social goods, and which avoid the stigma attached to "welfare" programs. Finally, a job offers social and psychological benefits that an income payment alone does not: maintaining and enhancing work skills, keeping in contact with others, and having the satisfaction of contributing to society. When, for instance, participants in Argentina's *Jefes* program were offered an income in place of a job, most refused; they preferred to work. Consequently, ELR programs meet the same objectives as basic income guarantee schemes and more, without the negative side effects of inflation and stigmatization. Nonetheless, a BIG program may be appropriate for those who should not be expected to work.

## LEARNING FROM THE PAST

The idea that the government in a capitalist economy should provide jobs for the unemployed is not new. In the United States, the various New Deal agencies created during the Great Depression of the 1930s offer a well-known example. Organizations such as the Works Progress Administration and the Civilian Conservation Corps were designed to deal with the massive unemployment of that period. Unemployment peaked at almost 25% of the civilian labor force in 1933 and averaged over 17% for the entire decade. These programs were woefully inadequate, largely due to their limited scale. It ultimately took the massive increases in government expenditure precipitated by the Second World War to pull the U.S. economy out of depression.

The onset of the postwar "Golden Age" and the dominance of Keynesian economics sounded the death knell of direct job creation as a solution to unemployment. The interwar public employment strategy was replaced with a "demand-management" strategy—essentially a sort of trickle-down economics in which various tax incentives and government expenditure programs, mainly military spending, were used to stimulate private investment. Policymakers believed that this would spur economic growth. The twin problems of poverty and unemployment would then be eliminated since, according to President Kennedy's famous aphorism, "a rising tide lifts all boats."

In the mid-1960s, the civil rights movement revived the idea of direct job creation as a solution to the problems of poverty and unemployment. Although the Kennedy and Johnson administrations had declared a so-called War on Poverty, the movement's call for direct job creation fell on deaf ears as the Johnson administration, at the behest of its Council of Economic Advisers, pursued a more conservative approach based on the standard combination of supply-side incentives to increase private investment and assorted strategies to "improve" workers' "human capital" so as to make them more attractive to private employers.

The rise to dominance of neoliberalism since the mid-1970s has resulted in a full-scale retreat from even the mildly social democratic policies of the early postwar period. While a commitment to full employment remains official U.S. economic policy, the concerns of central bankers and financial capitalists now rule the roost in government circles. This translates into a single-minded obsession with fighting inflation at the expense of all other economic and social objectives. Not only is fighting inflation seemingly the only concern of economic policy, it is seen to be in direct conflict with the goal of full employment (witness the widespread acceptance among economists and policymakers of the NAIRU, or "non-accelerating inflation rate of unemployment" theory, which posits that the economy has a set-point for unemployment, well above zero, below which rapidly rising inflation must occur). Whenever falling unemployment leads to concerns about "excessive" wage growth, central banks are expected to raise interest rates in an attempt to force slack on the economy and thereby decrease inflationary pressures. The resulting unemployment acts as a kind of discipline, tempering the demands of working-class people for higher wages or better working conditions in favor of the interests of large commercial and financial institutions. The postwar commitment to full employment has finally been sacrificed on the altar of price stability.

## ELR AND CAPITALISM

As demonstrated by the history of public employment programs in the United States and the example of Argentina, direct job-creation programs do not happen absent significant political pressure from below. This is the case whether or not those calling for change explicitly demand an ELR program. Given the hegemonic position of neoliberal ideology, there are many powerful forces today that would be hostile to the idea of governments directly creating jobs for the unemployed. These forces represent a critical barrier to the implementation of an ELR program. In fact, these forces represent a critical barrier to virtually any project for greater social and economic justice. The purpose of initiating a wider discussion of ELR proposals is to build them into more comprehensive programs for social and economic justice. As is always the case, this requires the building of mass-based social movements advocating for these and other progressive policies.

A significant objection to the ELR proposal remains: it's capitalism, stupid. If you don't like unemployment, poverty, and inequality—not to mention war, environmental destruction, and alienating and exploitative work—then you don't like capitalism, and you should seek alternatives instead of reformist employment policies. ELR advocates would not disagree. In the face of the overlapping and myriad problems afflicting a capitalist economy, the achievements of even a full-scale ELR program would be limited. The political difficulties involved in establishing an ELR program in the first place, in the face of opposition from powerful elements of society, would be immense. And certainly, the many experiments in non-capitalist forms of economic and social organization currently being carried out, for example, in the factories of Argentina and elsewhere, should be championed. But it is fair to ask: shouldn't we also champion living wage laws, a stronger social safety net for those who cannot or should not be expected to work, and universal health care—as well as an end to imperialist wars of aggression, environmentally unsustainable practices, and the degradation of work? In sum, shouldn't we seek to alleviate the symptoms of capitalism, even as we work toward a better economic system?

## Sources

Joseph Halevi, "The Argentine Crisis," *Monthly Review,* (April 2002); Pavlina Tcherneva, "Macroeconomic Stabilization Policy in Argentina: A Case Study of the 2002 Currency Collapse and Crisis Resolution through Job Creation" (Bard College Working Paper, 2007); L. Randall Wray, *Understanding Modern Money: The Key to Full Employment and Price Stability* (Edward Elgar, 1998); Congressional Research Service, "The Cost of Iraq, Afghanistan and Other Global War on Terror Operations Since 9/11," (www.fas.org/sgp/crs/natsec/RL33110.pdf, update 7/07); National Jobs for All Coalition, "September 2007 Unemployment Data," (www.njifac.org/jobnews/html); Nancy Rose, "Historicizing Government Work Programs: A Spectrum from Workfare to Fair Work" (Center for Full Employment and Price Stability, Seminar Paper No. 2, March 2000); Judith Russell, *Economics, Bureaucracy and Race: How Keynesians Misguided the War on Poverty* (Columbia Univ. Press, 2004); Fadhel Kaboub, "Employment Guarantee Programs: A Survey of Theories and Policy Experiences" (Levy Econ. Inst., Working Paper No. 498, May 2007).

# 10

# Health Care
# and Delivery

## THE UNITED STATES CONTEXT

The United States spends more for health care, both in total dollars and percentage of gross domestic product, than any other industrialized nation. (The following is taken from Eitzen and Baca Zinn, 2009.) It also has the most technologically sophisticated health care with the best trained practitioners. Why, then, when compared to other advanced industrial societies, does the United States have a relatively high infant mortality rate, the highest percentage of low-birth-weight babies, and rank lower in life expectancy? The answer to this contradiction is that health care in the United States is rationed on the basis of ability to pay; the system is superb for people who can afford it but falls woefully short for those who cannot. For those with adequate health insurance, the system works. But many are left out. The U.S. system left approximately 45.7 million uninsured (17.5 percent of whom worked full-time) in 2007, including 8.1 million children (U.S. Census Bureau, 2008). Another 50 million are underinsured, which leaves them exposed to large financial risks or excludes coverage for certain medical problems.

This has serious consequences, endangering the lives of millions of adults and children on the economic margins. They are more likely to delay needed health care, receive less preventive and primary care, and have illnesses in more advanced stages, all of which result in higher mortality rates (Miringoff and Miringoff, 1999:93).

The problem of inadequate or nonexistent health insurance is increasing. Over the past two and a half decades the proportion of Americans without health insurance has risen from 11 percent in 1976 to 16 percent in 2003. This increase in the uninsured results from our reliance on obtaining insurance through employment. The problem is that fewer employers are providing coverage for their employees or are limiting their coverage in order to increase or maintain their profits. Also, when workers change jobs their previous insurance generally is not portable. Of course, workers who are laid off lose their health insurance. Economist Robert Kuttner argues that the United States must change its health care system, in line with what other industrialized nations have done:

> The only way to cut through this mess is, of course, to have universal health insurance. All insurance is a kind of cross-subsidy. The young, who on average need little care, subsidize the old. The well subsidize the sick.
>
> With a universal system, there is no private insurance industry spending billions of dollars trying to target the well and avoid the sick, because everyone is in the same system. There is no worry about "portability" when you change jobs, because everyone is in the same system. And there are no problems choosing your preferred doctor or hospital, because everyone is in the same system. (Kuttner, 1998:27)

## References

Eitzen, D. Stanley, and Maxine Baca Zinn. 2009. *Social Problems,* 10th ed. Boston: Allyn and Bacon.

Kuttner, Robert. 1998. "Toward Universal Coverage." *Washington Post National Weekly Edition* (July 20):27.

Miringoff, Marc, and Marque-Luisa Miringoff. 1999. *The Social Health of the Nation: How America is Really Doing.* New York: Oxford University Press.

U.S. Bureau of the Census. 2008. "Income, Poverty, and Health Insurance Coverage in the United States: 2007." *Current Population Reports,* P60–235 (August).

# 24

■ ■ ■

# International
# Health Systems

**Physicians for a National Health Program**

> *A study of major health care systems around the world may
> help Americans find solutions to our current crisis. This article
> summarizes the single-payer systems of Canada, Denmark,
> Norway, and Sweden, as well as the national health care service
> programs of Britain and Spain. Universal health insurance, of
> the variety found in Germany and France, rounds out this
> survey of health care system alternatives.*

Learning about other health care systems in the world not only expands our
knowledge and understanding of them; it also helps us discover new perspectives on how to improve upon our own. Health care systems in the Organization for Economic Cooperation and Development (OECD) countries primarily
reflect three types of programs.

- In a single-payer national health insurance system, as demonstrated by
  Canada, Denmark, Norway, and Sweden, health insurance is publicly administered and most physicians are in private practice.
- Great Britain and Spain are among the OECD countries with national
  health services, in which salaried physicians predominate and hospitals
  are publicly owned and operated.
- Highly regulated, universal, multi-payer health insurance systems are il-
  lustrated by countries like Germany and France, which have universal
  health insurance via sickness funds. The sickness funds pay physicians
  and hospitals uniform rates that are negotiated annually (also known as
  an "all-payer" system).

*Source:* Physicians for a National Health Program, 2000. PNHP website publication. www.pnhp.org.
Reprinted by permission.

## AUSTRALIA

Australia's population size of 19 million people is roughly the same as that of Texas. Its infant mortality rate is 5 per 1,000 live births, and life expectancy at birth is 75.9 years for men and 81.5 years for women. In 1941, the beginnings of Australia's universal health care system emerged. Australia spends 8.5% of its GDP on health care, and its 1998 per capita expense was $2,043-US.

The government administers the compulsory national health insurance program (Medicare). National health insurance is funded by a mixture of general tax revenue, a 1.5% levy on taxable income (which accounts for 18.5% of federal outlays on health), state revenue, and fees paid by patients. The government funds 68% of health expenditures (45% federal and 23% state) and has control over hospital benefits, pharmaceuticals, and medical services. States are charged with operating public hospitals and regulating all hospitals, nursing homes, and community based general services. Additionally, the states pay for the public hospitals with federal government assistance negotiated via five yearly agreements. Mainly not-for-profit mutual insurers (private insurance) cover the gap between Medicare benefits and schedule fees for inpatient services. Private insurance covers 1/3 of the population and accounts for 11% of health expenditures.

Patients are free to choose their GP. Primary care physicians act as gatekeepers, and physicians are generally reimbursed by a fee-for-service system. The government sets the fee schedules, but physicians are free to charge above the scheduled fee or they may directly bill the government when there is no patient charge. Prescription pharmaceuticals have a patient co-payment, and out-of-pocket payments account for 19% of health expenditures. Physicians in public outpatient hospitals are either salaried or paid on a per-session basis.

## AUSTRIA

Austria is home to 7.6 million people, approximately the same number that live in North Carolina. The country has universal access to health care through a compulsory system of social insurance. A system of private insurance also exists. About 8.2% of Austria's GDP is spent on health care, and the 1998 per capita expense was $1,968-US.

Private doctors with contracts to the social insurance funds are paid on a fee-for-service system with expenditure limits based on the case and per doctor per pay period. Hospital physicians are salaried. Approximately 50% of the health expenditures are funded by progressive payroll taxes, 25% are financed by non-specific taxes, and the rest is funded directly out-of-pocket or through private insurance companies. The contributions to the health insurance funds (payroll taxes) are split between employers and employees on a parity basis.

Patients are free to choose their physicians, as long as the physician has a contract with the insurer. Benefits and prices of services are fixed in agreements between representatives of the insured and representatives of the providers. All medical and nursing education is free. The infant mortality rate in Austria is 4.9

per 1,000 live births, and life expectancy at birth is at 74.7 years for men and 80.9 years for women.

## BELGIUM

Belgium is home to about 10.2 million people, almost the same number of people who live in the state of Ohio. Its infant mortality rate is 6 per 1,000 live births, and its life expectancy at birth is 74.8 years for men and 81.1 years for women. Today, Belgium spends 8.8% of its GDP on health care, and the 1998 per capita expense was $2,081-US.

The health care system is funded primarily through sickness funds. Belgium's health insurance program operates at four distinct levels: the central government, national associations, federations of local societies, and local mutual aid societies. The general attitude in Belgium is that the pluralism of the health insurance system stimulates each local fund to work hard to attract and satisfy its members.

Patients have their free choice of any doctor. Primary care physicians are paid via fee-for-service, directly from the patient, or partially reimbursed, except with low-income patients who are exempt from pay. They are reimbursed with a negotiated fee, but extra billing is allowed. Specialists are paid via fee-for-service and are not restricted to hospitals.

## CANADA

Canada's population size of 30.5 million people is roughly the same as that of California. Its infant mortality rate is 5.5 per 1,000 live births, and its life expectancy at birth is 75.8 years for men and 81.4 years for women. National health insurance had been discussed in Canada at the federal level since 1919, but no real action was taken until 1944. Today, Canada's health system is characterized by single-payer national health insurance, and the federal government requires that insurance cover "all medically necessary services." Canada spends 9.5% of GDP towards health care, and the 1998 per capita expense was $2,312-US.

National health insurance (Medicare) is a public program administered by the provinces and overseen by the federal government. Medicare is funded by general tax revenues. Federal contributions are tied to population and provincial economic conditions, and provinces pay the remainder. Medicare accounts for 72% of health expenditures. In addition, the majority of Canadians have supplemental private insurance coverage through group plans, which extends the range of insured services, such as dental care, rehabilitation, prescription drugs, and private care nursing. The private sector (private insurance and out-of-pocket payments) accounts for 28% of health expenditures.

Most physicians in Canada are in private practice and accept fee-for-service Medicare payment rates set by the government. Provincial medical associations negotiate insured fee-for-service schedules with provincial health ministries.

Some physicians set their own rates but are not reimbursed by the public system. Hospitals are mainly non-profit and operate under global institution-specific or regional budgets with some fee-for-service payment. Less than 5% of all Canadian hospitals are privately owned.

## FINLAND

Finland has a population size of 5 million people, which is about the same number of people who live in the state of Maryland. Finland has an infant mortality rate of 4.2 per 1,000 live births and its life expectancy at birth is 73.5 years for men and 80.6 years for women. The country spends 6.9% of GDP on health care, and its 1998 per capita expense was $1,502-US. In 1964, national health insurance was enacted in Finland.

The Finnish health system is primarily funded (80%) by general tax revenues collected by the local and national governments. The basic administrative levels in Finland are divided into communes and municipalities. The local authorities in Finland number 445, averaging about 10,000 people each.

GP's practice mostly in health centers. They are salaried, but many are paid fee-for-service for overtime. Hospital physicians, who must be specialists, are salaried.

## DENMARK

Denmark, a small country, is home to 5.3 million people—the same number as in the state of Wisconsin. Its infant mortality rate is 4.7 per 1,000 live births, and its life expectancy at birth is 73.7 years for men and 78.6 years for women. Denmark has had a single-payer national health system since 1961. Approximately 8.3% of GDP is spent on health care, and the 1998 per capita expense was $2,133-US.

The Danish health care system is funded by progressive income taxes, and is publicly administered. Hospitals are run by the 14 counties and the City of Copenhagen. Physicians who work with the hospitals receive salaries, which are determined by negotiation between government and doctor's unions. GP's are 40% per capita fee, and 60% fee-for-service. Specialists are mostly fee-for-service. All medical and nursing education is free.

There is strong incentive for patients to choose a GP in their immediate area of residence. GP's will then make referrals to specialists. There are no co-pays for physician or hospital care, but patients do pay a share of drug costs—usually between 25 and 50%. Private insurance, held by approximately 27% of the population, is used mainly for medications and dental expenses.

## FRANCE

France has a population close to that of the entire Midwest—60.9 million people. France has an infant mortality rate of 4.7 per 1,000 live births and a life expectancy at birth of 74.6 years for men and 82.2 years for women. The country has had a national health insurance system since 1928, but universal coverage did not occur until 1978. Approximately 9.6% of France's GDP is spent on health care, and its 1998 per capita expense was $2,077-US.

The French health care system is primarily funded by Sickness Insurance Funds (SIF's), which are autonomous, not-for-profit, government-regulated bodies with national headquarters and regional networks. They are financed by compulsory payroll contributions (13% of wage), of employers (70% of contributions) and employees (30% of contributions). SIF's cover 99% of the population and account for 75% of health expenditures. The 3 main SIF's (CNAMTS, MSA, and CANAM) cover about 95% of the population, and the remaining 5% of the insured population are covered under 11 smaller schemes. The remainder of health expenditures is covered by the central government, by patients' out-of-pocket payments, and by Mutual Insurance Funds (MIF's), which provide supplemental and voluntary private insurance to cover cost-sharing arrangements and extra billings. MIF's cover 80% of the population and account for 6% of health expenditures. The major public authority in the French health system is the Ministry of Health. Below this are 21 regional health offices that regulate each of the 95 provinces.

Patients are free to choose their providers and have no limits on the number of services covered. GP's have no formal gatekeeper function. Private physicians are paid on a fee-for-service basis and patients subsequently receive partial or full reimbursement from their health insurance funds. The average charge for an office visit to a GP and a specialist are $18 and $25, respectively. Private hospitals are profit-making and non-profit making, usually with fee-for-service physicians. Public hospitals employ salaried physicians, who make up 1/3 of all GP's in France. All medical and nursing education is free.

## GERMANY

Germany is home to approximately 82 million people, nearly 1/3 of the U.S. population. Germany's infant mortality rate is 4.7 per 1,000 live births, and its life expectancy at birth is 74.5 years for men and 80.5 years for women. In 1883, Germany was the first country to establish the foundations of a national health insurance system and has since gradually expanded coverage to over 92% of the population. Today, Germany spends 10.6% of its GDP on health care, and the 1998 per capita expense was $2,424-US.

Everyone in Germany is eligible for health insurance, and individuals above a determined income level have the right to obtain private coverage. The German health care system is predominantly characterized by Sickness Insurance Funds (SIF's), which are funded by compulsory payroll contributions (14% of wage), equally shared by employers and employees. SIF's cover 92% of the population and account for 81% of health expenditures. The rest of the population (the affluent, self-employed, and civil servants) is covered by private insurance, which is based on voluntary, individual contributions. Private insurance accounts for 8% of health expenditures.

GP's have no formal gatekeeper function. Private physicians, over half of which are specialists, are paid on a fee-for-service basis. Representatives of the sickness funds negotiate with the regional associations of physicians to determine aggregate payments. Physicians who work in hospitals are full-time salaried specialists, whose work is entirely devoted to in-patients. All medical and nursing education is free.

## JAPAN

Japan has a population of 122 million people, nearly half that of the United States. The infant mortality rate in Japan is 3.6 per 1,000 live births, and life expectancy at birth is at 77.2 years for men and 84 years for women. Approximately 7.6% of GDP is spent on health care, and the 1998 per capita expense was $1,822-US. Japan's current system of universal health care was initiated in 1958.

The Employee's Health Insurance System is financed by compulsory payroll contributions (8% of wage), equally shared by employers and employees, and covers employees and their dependents. The National Health Insurance System covers the self-employed, pensioners, their dependents, and members of the same occupation. The local governments act as insurers, and premiums are calculated on the basis of income, the number of individuals in the insured household, and assets. Premiums account for 57% of health expenditures. The federal government contributes 24% to medical care expenditures and local governments contribute 7%.

About 80% of hospitals and 94% of private clinics are privately owned and operated. While some public not-for-profit hospitals exist, investor-owned for-profit hospitals are prohibited in Japan. Patients are free to choose their ambulatory care physicians, who are reimbursed on the basis of a negotiated, uniform fee-for-service schedule. Physicians have no formal gatekeeper function. Due to the combination of medical and pharmaceutical practices a large part of a physician's income is derived from prescriptions. Hospital physicians have fixed salaries.

## NETHERLANDS

The Netherlands has a population of 15.8 million, which is approximately the same number of people who live in the state of Florida. In 1997, 72% of the population had government-assured health insurance coverage. The infant mortality rate is 5.2 per 1,000 live births and life expectancy is at 75.2 years for men and 80.7 years for women. The Netherlands spend 8.6% of its GDP on health care, and the 1998 per capita expense was $2,070-US.

The health care system in the Netherlands is very similar to that in Belgium; health care is primarily financed by employer-employee social insurance. Health care is provided by private not-for-profit institutions, and the compulsory health insurance system is financed through sickness funds. 70% of the population is in the public health care system. 30% of the population (mostly civil servants and high-income groups) has private insurance, because they are not eligible for social health insurance. There are currently plans to convert the entire system to a tax-based one.

Most primary care physicians are in a solo office practice (54%) or practice in small groups. Reimbursement is by capitation for "public patients" (2/3) and via fee-for-service (1/3). Specialists are salaried and are restricted to hospitals.

## NEW ZEALAND

New Zealand has a population size close to that of Atlanta, Georgia—3.5 million people. In 1941, it achieved universal coverage and was the first country with a free-market economy to do so. Radical health sector restructuring occurred in 1993, which introduced a set of market-oriented ideas. However, the new system performed poorly and was thus restructured 3 years later. Today, New Zealand spends 8.1% of its GDP on health care and the 1998 per capita expense was $1,424-U.S. The infant mortality rate is 6.8 per 1,000 live births and life expectancy is at 75.2 years for men and 80.4 years for men.

The health system is funded through taxation and administered by a national purchasing agent, the Health Funding Authority (HFA). Health care is provided by 23 hospital provider organizations (Hospital and Health Services), GP's (most of whom are grouped as independent Practitioner Associations, IPA's), and other noncrown providers of child care, disability support services, etc. These parties compete for the provision of health services. Public funding accounts for 76% of health expenditures. Complementary, non-profit, private insurance, on the other hand, covers about 1/3 of the population and accounts for 7% of health expenditures. It is most commonly used to cover cost-sharing requirements, elective surgery in private hospitals, and specialist outpatient consultations. New Zealand's government is a purchaser and provider of health care and retains the responsibility for legislation and general policy matters.

Health care is free for children, and all patients have their free choice of GP. Out-of-pocket payments account for 17% of health expenditures. GP's act as gatekeepers and are independent, self-employed providers. They are paid via fee-for-service, partial government subsidy, and negotiated contracts with HFA through IPA's. The payment system is currently moving from fee-for-service to capitation. Private insurance and out-of-pocket contributions pay the remainder. Hospitals are mostly semiautonomous, government-owned companies that contract with the HFA. Specialists are commonly salaried, but may supplement their salaries through treatment of private patients.

## NORWAY

Norway is home to approximately 4.4 million people, about the same number that live in Washington DC. Norway has had a single-payer national health insurance system since 1966. The National Insurance Act guaranteed citizens universal access to all forms of medical care. Norway's health system is funded by progressive income tax, and from block grants from central government, with 8.96 of GDP being spent on health care, and in 1998 the per capita expense was $2,425-US.

Patients are free to choose their own physician and hospital, however, registration with local GP's who act as gatekeeper, will begin in 2001. Patients are responsible for co-pays for some physician visits, approximately $15. Patients are also responsible for co-pays for prescription drugs, up to $216 per year. Once that level of expense has been reached, prescription drugs are covered at 100%. All hospital care is covered at 100%.

Hospital physicians have fixed salaries. GP's have either fixed salaries or fee-for-service agreements. All medical and nursing education is free. The infant mortality rate in Norway is 4 per 1,000 live births, and life expectancy at birth is at 75.5 years for men and 81.3 years for women.

## SPAIN

Spain's population size is close to that of Texas and New York combined—about 39.1 million people. The country has had a comprehensive, single-payer national health service since 1978. The Constitution of 1978 explicitly affirms everyone's right to health care. Spain spends 7.1% of its GDP on health care, and its 1998 per capita expense was $1,218-US.

The Spanish health care system is funded by payroll taxes through the National Institute of Health program (INSALUD), which in 1984 was 75% financed by employers and 25% financed by employees. Those with higher incomes have the option of obtaining private medical care. Public hospitals are run by one of the provinces or municipalities. The INSALUD program operates a large network of hospitals and ambulatory care clinics. Hospital physicians are on full-time salaries.

All medical and nursing education is free. The infant mortality rate in Spain is 5 per 1,000 live births, and its life expectancy at birth is 74.8 years for men and 82.2 years for women.

## SWEDEN

Sweden has a population close to that of New York City—8.8 million people. The country has an infant mortality rate of 3.6 per 1,000 live births and a life expectancy at birth of 76.9 years for men and 81.9 years for women. Sweden spends 8.4% of its GDP on health care, the 1998 per capita expense was $1,746. Sweden has had its current universal health care system since 1962. Tuition for medical and nursing education is free, and students generally take loans for living expenses of around $9,000-U.S. per year.

The Swedish health care system is financed by both incomes and patient fees. County councils own and operate hospitals, employ physicians and run the majority of general practices and outpatient facilities. Other physicians work in private practice and are paid by the counties on a fee-for-service basis.

Co-pays, which were mandated in 1970, are capped, with limits on how much a person is required to contribute annually. For example, patients over age 16 pay $9 per day for hospitalization. The maximum individual expense for hospital and physician services is approximately $108 per year. The maximum individual expense for prescription drugs is $156 per year. Once these sums are met, care is covered at 100%.

## UNITED KINGDOM

Britain has a population size of 57 million, nearly three times the number of people in Texas. The infant mortality rate in the United Kingdom is 5.7 per 1,000 live births, and life expectancy at birth is 74.6 years for men and 79.7 years for women. Britain has had a National Health Service (NHS) since 1948. 6.7% of GDP goes towards health expenditures, and the 1998 per capita expense was $1,461-US.

The British government is a purchaser and provider of health care and retains responsibility for legislation and general policy matters. The government decides on an annual budget for the NHS, which is administered by the NHS executive, regional, and district health authorities. The NHS is funded by general taxation and national insurance contributions and accounts for 88% of health expenditures. Complementary private insurance, which involves both for-profit and not-for-profit insurers, covers 12% of the population and accounts for 4% of health expenditures.

Physicians are paid directly by the government via salary, capitation, and fee-for-service. GP's act as gatekeepers. Private providers set their own fee-for-service rates but are not generally reimbursed by the public system. Specialists may supplement their salary by treating private patients. Hospitals are mainly semi-autonomous, self-governing public trusts that contract with groups of purchasers on a long-term basis.

The British government this year has announced a huge funding increase for the NHS. Specifically, it will receive 6.2% more in funding every year until 2004. Current plans to improve the system over the next five years include hiring 7,500 more specialists, 2,000 GP's and 20,000 nurses; providing 7,000 more acute beds in existing hospitals and building 100 new hospitals by 2010; demanding that GPs see a patient within 48 hours of an appointment; and finally, guaranteeing that patients wait no more than three months for their first outpatient appointment with a specialist and no more than six months after that appointment for an operation.

## Bibliography

### Multiple Country References

1. OECD Health Data 2000. Available at www.oecd.org.
2. National health systems of the world, Volume 1: The countries, Roemer, MI, 1991, New York: Oxford University Press.
3. Multinational comparisons of health care: Expenditures, coverage, and outcomes, Anderson, G (with Axel Wiest), Oct. 1998, The Commonwealth Fund.

4. Primary care: Balancing health needs, services, and technology, Starfield, B, 1998, New York: Oxford University Press.

## Single Country References

1. Austria: "Questionnaire on the Austrian health system," Widder, Joachim, MD, PhD, Vienna University General Hospital Department of Radiotherapy and Radiobiology, 2000.

   "Questionnaire on the Austrian health system," Theurl, E, Austria University, Institut fur Finanzwissenschaft der Universitat Innsbruck, A-6020 Innsbruch, 2000.

2. Belgium and the Netherlands: "Belgium and the Netherlands revisited," Van Doorslaer, E & Schut, FT, Journal of Health Politics, Policy and Law, Oct. 2000.

3. Denmark: Health care in Denmark, published by The Ministry of Health, 1997.

4. France: "Health care under French national health insurance," Rodwin, VG & Sandier, S, Health Affairs, Fall 1993.

5. Germany: "The German health system: Lessons for reform in the United States," Jackson, JL, Archival of Internal Medicine, 1997.

   "The German health-care system," Wahner-Roedler, DL, Knuth, P & Juchems, RH, Mayo Clinical Proc, 1997.

6. Japan: "Japanese health care: Low cost through regulated fees," Ikegami, N, Health Affairs, Fall 1991.

7. Sweden: "The health care system in Sweden," published by The Swedish Institute, May 1999.

   "The Health and Medical Services Act," promulgated June 30, 1982.

8. United Kingdom: "Britain's health care, and ours," Sidel, VW, Letter to the Editor, *The New York Times*, Feb. 14, 2000.

# 25

■■■

# Has Canada Got the Cure?

## Holly Dressel

*This essay compares the Canadian and U.S. health care systems and finds that the Canadian system is better. The author concludes: "Like it or not, believe it makes sense or not, publicly funded, universally available health care is simply the most powerful contributing factor to the overall health of the people who live in any country."*

Should the United States implement a more inclusive, publicly funded health care system? That's a big debate throughout the country. But even as it rages, most Americans are unaware that the United States is the only country in the developed world that doesn't already have a fundamentally public—that is, tax-supported—health care system.

That means that the United States has been the unwitting control subject in a 30-year, worldwide experiment comparing the merits of private versus public health care funding. For the people living in the United States, the results of this experiment with privately funded health care have been grim. The United States now has the most expensive health care system on earth and, despite remarkable technology, the general health of the U.S. population is lower than in most industrialized countries. Worse, Americans' mortality rates—both general and infant—are shockingly high (Figure 25.1).

## DIFFERENT PATHS

Beginning in the 1930s, both the Americans and the Canadians tried to alleviate health care gaps by increasing use of employment-based insurance plans. Both

*Source:* Holly Dressel, "Has Canada Got the Cure?" *YES! Magazine* (Fall 2006). YES! is a nonprofit, ad free national publication that offers positive solutions for creating a just and sustainable world. To subscribe, visit www.yesmagazine.org/subscribe or call (800) 937-4451.

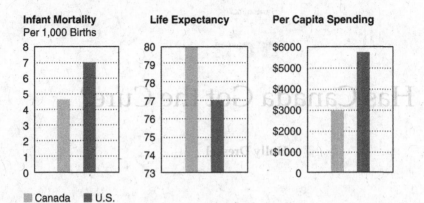

**FIGURE 25.1**   Side-by-Side: No Comparison
Canada and the U.S. used to be twins on public-health measurements. Here's how it looks after 35 years of Canadian universal health care.

*Source:* World Health Organization *CIA World Fact Book*, Centers for Disease Control.

countries encouraged nonprofit private insurance plans like Blue Cross, as well as for-profit insurance plans. The difference between the United States and Canada is that Americans are still doing this, ignoring decades of international statistics that show that this type of funding inevitably leads to poorer public health.

Meanwhile, according to author Terry Boychuk, the rest of the industrialized world, including many developing countries like Mexico, Korea, and India, viscerally understood that "private insurance would [never be able to] cover all necessary hospital procedures and services; and that even minimal protection [is] beyond the reach of the poor, the working poor, and those with the most serious health problems."[1] Today, over half the family bankruptcies filed every year in the United States are directly related to medical expenses, and a recent study shows that 75 percent of those are filed by people with health insurance.[2]

The United States spends far more per capita on health care than any comparable country. In fact, the gap is so enormous that a recent University of California, San Francisco, study estimates that the United States would save over $161 billion every year in paperwork alone if it switched to a [single-payer] system like Canada's.[3] These billions of dollars are not abstract amounts deducted from government budgets; they come directly out of the pockets of people who are sick.

The year 2000 marked the beginning of a crucial period, when international trade rules, economic theory, and political action had begun to fully reflect the belief in the superiority of private, as opposed to public, management, especially in the United States. By that year the U.S. health care system had undergone what has been called "the health management organization revolution." U.S. government figures show that medical care costs have spiked since 2000, with total spending on prescriptions nearly doubling.[4]

## CUTTING COSTS, CUTTING CARE

There are two criteria used to judge a country's health care system: the overall success of creating and sustaining health in the population, and the ability to control costs while doing so. One recent study published in the Canadian Medical Association Journal compares mortality rates in private forprofit and nonprofit hospitals in the United States. Research on 38 million adult patients in 26,000 U.S. hospitals revealed that death rates in for-profit hospitals are significantly higher than in nonprofit hospitals: for-profit patients have a 2 percent higher chance of dying in the hospital or within 30 days of discharge. The increased death rates were clearly linked to "the corners that for-profit hospitals must cut in order to achieve a profit margin for investors, as well as to pay high salaries for administrators."[5]

"To ease cost pressures, administrators tend to hire less highly skilled personnel, including doctors, nurses, and pharmacists . . . ," wrote P. J. Devereaux, a cardiologist at McMaster University and the lead researcher. "The U.S. statistics clearly show that when the need for profits drives hospital decisionmaking, more patients die."

## THE VALUE OF CARE FOR ALL

Historically, one of the cruelest aspects of unequal income distribution is that poor people not only experience material want all their lives, they also suffer more illness and die younger. But in Canada there is no association between income inequality and mortality rates—none whatsoever.

In a massive study undertaken by Statistics Canada in the early 1990s, income and mortality census data were analyzed from all Canadian provinces and all U.S. states, as well as 53 Canadian and 282 American metropolitan areas.[6] The study concluded that "the relationship between income inequality and mortality is not universal, but instead depends on social and political characteristics specific to place." In other words, government health policies have an effect.

"Income inequality is strongly associated with mortality in the United States and in North America as a whole," the study found, "but there is no relation within Canada at either the province or metropolitan area level—between income inequality and mortality."

The same study revealed that among the poorest people in the United States, even a one percent increase in income resulted in a mortality decline of nearly 22 out of 100,000.

What makes this study so interesting is that Canada used to have statistics that mirrored those in the United States. In 1970, U.S. and Canadian mortality rates calculated along income lines were virtually identical. But 1970 also marked the introduction of Medicare in Canada—universal, [single-payer] coverage. The simple explanation for how Canadians have all become equally healthy, regardless of income, most likely lies in the fact that they have a publicly funded, single-payer health system and the control group, the United States, does not.

## INFANT MORTALITY

Infant mortality rates, which reflect the health of the mother and her access to prenatal and postnatal care, are considered one of the most reliable measures of the general health of a population. Today, U.S. government statistics rank Canada's infant mortality rate of 4.7 per thousand 23rd out of 225 countries, in the company of the Netherlands, Luxembourg, Australia, and Denmark. The U.S. is 43rd—in the company of Croatia and Lithuania, below Taiwan and Cuba.

All the countries surrounding Canada or above it in the rankings have tax-supported health care systems. The countries surrounding the United States and below have mixed systems or are, in general, extremely poor in comparison to the United States and the other G8 industrial powerhouses.

There are no major industrialized countries near the United States in the rankings. The closest is Italy, at 5.83 infants dying per thousand, but it is still ranked five places higher.[7]

In the United States, infant mortality rates are 7.1 per 1,000, the highest in the industrialized world—much higher than some of the poorer states in India, for example, which have public health systems in place, at least for mothers and infants. Among the inner-city poor in the United States, more than 8 percent of mothers receive no prenatal care at all before giving birth.

## OVERALL U.S. MORTALITY

We would have expected to see steady decreases in deaths per thousand in the mid-twentieth century, because so many new drugs and procedures were becoming available. But neither the Canadian nor the American mortality rate declined much; in fact, Canada's leveled off for an entire decade, throughout the 1960s. This was a period in which private care was increasing in Canadian hospitals, and the steady mortality rates reflect the fact that most people simply couldn't afford the new therapies that were being offered. However, beginning in 1971, the same year that Canada's Medicare was fully applied, official statistics show that death rates suddenly plummeted, maintaining a steep decline to their present rate.

In the United States, during the same period, overall mortality rates also dropped, reflecting medical advances. But they did not drop nearly so precipitously as those in Canada after 1971. But given that the United States is the richest country on earth, today's overall mortality rates are shockingly high, at 8.4 per thousand, compared to Canada's 6.5.

## RICH AND POOR

It has become increasingly apparent, as data accumulate, that the overall improvement in health in a society with tax-supported health care translates to better health even for the rich, the group assumed to be the main beneficiaries of the American-style private system. If we look just at the 5.7 deaths per thousand among presumably richer, white babies in the United States, Canada still does better at 4.7, even though the Canadian figure includes all ethnic groups and all income levels. Perhaps a one-per-thousand difference doesn't sound like much. But when measuring mortality, it's huge. If the U.S. infant mortality rate were the same as Canada's, almost 15,000 more babies would survive in the United States every year.

If we consider the statistics for the poor, which in the United States have been classified by race, we find that in 2001, infants born of black mothers were dying at a rate of 14.2 per thousand. That's a Third World figure, comparable to Russia's.[8]

But now that the United States has begun to do studies based on income levels instead of race, these "cultural" and genetic explanations are turning out to be baseless. Infant mortality is highest among the poor, regardless of race.

Vive la différence! Genetically, Canadians and Americans are quite similar. Our health habits, too, are very much alike—people in both countries eat too much and exercise too little. And, like the United States, there is plenty of inequality in Canada, too. In terms of health care, that inequality falls primarily on Canadians in isolated communities, particularly Native groups, who have poorer access to medical care and are exposed to greater environmental contamination. The only major difference between the two countries that could account for the remarkable disparity in their infant and adult mortality rates, as well as the amount they spend on health care, is how they manage their health care systems.

The facts are clear: Before 1971, when both countries had similar, largely privately funded health care systems, overall survival and mortality rates were almost identical. The divergence appeared with the introduction of the single-payer health system in Canada.

The solid statistics amassed since the 1970s point to only one conclusion: like it or not, believe it makes sense or not, publicly funded, universally available health care is simply the most powerful contributing factor to the overall health of the people who live in any country. And in the United States, we have got the bodies to prove it.

## Notes

1. Terry Boychuk. *The Making and Meaning of Hospital Policy in the United States and Canada.* University of Michigan Press, Ann Arbor: 1999.
2. David U. Himmelstein, et al. Health Affairs, Jan.–June 2005, http://content.health affairs.org/cgi/reprint/hlthaff.w5.63v1

3. Professor James Kahn, UCSF, quoted in Harper's Magazine, "Harper's List," Feb. 2006.

4. National Health Expenditure Data, www.cms.hhs.gov/NationalHealthExpendData/downloads/tables.pdf.

5. Devereaux, Dr. P.J., et al. "A Systematic Review and Meta-Analysis of Studies Comparing Mortality between Private For-Profit and Private Not-For-Profit Hospitals," Canadian Medical Association Journal, May 2002.

6. Nancy A. Ross et al. "Relation between Income Inequality and Mortality in Canada and in the United States: Cross Sectional Assessment Using Census Data and Vital Statistics," Statistics Canada, reprinted in Health Geography, GEOG-303, ed. Nancy Ross, McGill University, 2005, pp. 109–117.

7. CIA World Fact Book. www.cia.gov/cia/publications/factbook/rankorder/2091rank.html

8. See, among many studies blaming race, Child Health USA 2003, Health Status—Infants; HRSA, with graphs such as "Breastfeeding Rates by Race/Ethnicity, 2001"; "Very Low Birth Weight Among Infants, by Race/Ethnicity 1985–2001"; www.mchb.hrsa.gov/chusa03.

# Problems of People, Resources, and Place

# Cities

## THE UNITED STATES CONTEXT

There were two dramatic population movements in the United States during the twentieth century—from rural areas and small towns to the cities and then outward from the central cities to the suburbs. The latter represents an exodus by predominantly young and middle-aged upper-middle-class and middle-class whites as well as business and industry to the outer rings of metropolitan areas. This movement of people and jobs to the suburbs has resulted in many urban problems.

First, the central cities are faced with shrinking economic resources schools, infrastructure, and other essential services (e.g., recreation, libraries, crime control, and fire protection). This is the result of the loss of their tax base to the suburbs. The suburbs, then, can generally afford better schools, parks, and police protection than found in the cities.

Second, the predominantly white flight to the suburbs leaves the central cities with a disproportionate concentration of minorities (including recent immigrants), elderly, and poor people. Thus, suburbanization has meant the geographic separation of the social classes and races.

Third, the move of warehouses, factories, and other businesses to the suburbs has left inner city residents with fewer job opportunities. The resulting high unemployment and hopelessness has led to a social deterioration of ghetto neighborhoods that were once stable.

Fourth, and related to job loss, is disinvestment in urban centers as banks, savings and loans, and insurance companies have redlined certain areas in metropolitan areas (*redlining* is the practice of not providing loans or insurance in what are defined as undesirable areas). These "undesirable areas" are almost always highly concentrated with racial minorities and located in the central cities. This practice, technically outlawed by federal law but commonly used, results in a self-fulfilling prophecy—individuals and businesses in the "undesirable areas" do not receive loans and insurance, which results in failed businesses, business relocation, and further social disruptions, thus "proving" the negative label by banks and insurance companies.

Fifth, policies by the federal government have further caused the deterioration of central cities. Federal aid to cities has declined ever since the Reagan administration, including funds for mass transit, infrastructure maintenance, and grants for subsidized housing.

Finally, the spreading out of metropolitan areas (urban sprawl) has led to (1) greater reliance on the automobile, (2) environmental problems such as housing and asphalt replacing farmland and wildlife habitats, as well as air pollution, and (3) highly congested traffic and long commuting times.

# 26

### ■ ■ ■

# New Lessons from the Old World: The European Model for Falling in Love with Your Hometown

**Jay Walljasper**

*Walljasper asks why European cities are devoid of suburban sprawl, so alive in street culture, and mostly lacking in slums. The answer is an active social policy dedicated to maintaining the vitality of cities by reducing pollution, protecting historic neighborhoods, improving public transportation, expanding pedestrian zones, preserving green spaces, installing bike lanes, and enacting guidelines to halt sprawl.*

My infatuation with cities began on a college-vacation visit to Montreal, where I was enchanted by picturesque squares, sleek subway trains and the intoxicating urbaneness all around. Sitting up most of the night in sidewalk cafés along rue St. Denis, I marveled at how different this city felt from the places I had known growing up in Illinois. Street life, in the experience of my childhood, was what happened in the few steps between a parking lot and your destination. Montreal showed me that a city could be a place to enjoy in itself, not merely anonymous space that you travel through between home and work and school.

But it was later—appropriately enough, on my honeymoon—that I fell in love with cities. My wife, Julie, and I toured Paris, Venice and Milan along with lesser-known delights like Luxembourg City and Freiburg, Germany. We came home wondering why American cities—most particularly, our hometown of Minneapolis—didn't instill us with the same sense of wonder. At first, we

*Source:* Jay Walljasper, "New Lessons from the Old World: The European Model for Falling in Love with Your Hometown," *E Magazine* 16 (March/April 2005), pp. 27–33. First published in *E/The Environmental Magazine.*

accepted the conventional wisdom that it was because European cities are so much older, with street plans locked in place before the arrival of the automobile. Yet on subsequent trips abroad, we came to realize that there was something more at work. What explains the fact that most European cities gracefully end at some point, giving way to green countryside at their edges, unlike the endless miles of sprawl in America? How is it that public life and street culture feel so much richer? Why do you seldom see slums?

Intrigued by these questions, I have returned to Europe over a number of years seeking answers. In scores of interviews with urban planners, transportation authorities, politicians, activists, and everyday citizens, I learned that a clear set of public policies accounts for the different spirit of European metropolitan centers. It's not just the antiquity of the towns, but also the way people there think about urban life.

In fact, many of the Europeans I talked to worried about the impact of increasing auto traffic and creeping sprawl on the health of their cities. But rather than accepting these changes as the inevitable march of progress, as many Americans do, they were taking action to maintain the vitality of their hometowns. Urban decay was being reversed, pollution reduced, historic neighborhoods protected, transit systems improved, pedestrian zones expanded, green spaces preserved, bike lanes added, pedestrian amenities installed, and development guidelines enacted to head off ugly outbreaks of sprawl.

## EUROPEAN EPIPHANIES

Throughout my travels, I was frequently thunderstruck at some sight (a beautiful plaza, comfortable public buses, a street crowded with bicycles) that was amazing to an American, but to Europeans simply a part of day-to-day life. These moments would depress me at first—why can't we do this at home?—and then rouse me. Of course we can! Americans are an enterprising people, restless in pursuit of improving their lives. If Europe's successes in making cities more livable and lovable were more widely known, people would insist on doing something similar here. Maybe even better.

This notion first hit me when I entered the central train station in the Dutch city of The Hague. In America, I marveled, this building would qualify as one of the world's wonders. Not for its ultramodern architecture; we have suburban office parks from Tampa to Tacoma that can match it for glitz. It was the building's basic function that startled me: the large-scale movement of human beings by means other than the automobile. Streetcars wheeled right into the station, unloading and loading throngs of commuters while an underground parking facility accommodated 3,000 bicycles. I consulted the electronic schedule board and counted more than 20 trains an hour departing for destinations all over the Netherlands and Europe—this in a city about the size of Chattanooga, Tennessee.

A transportation network like the Netherlands' would be beyond the wildest dreams of commuters, environmentalists and city lovers across North

America. In Amsterdam, for instance, only 20 percent of people's trips around the city are in a car; 36 percent are made on foot, another 31 percent on bikes, and 11 percent on transit. In the Dutch city of Groningen, 47 percent of all urban trips are on bikes, 26 percent on foot, and 23 percent by car.

But that's not good enough for the Dutch. Alarmed by studies showing sizable increases in traffic in the years to come, government officials have worked to boost alternative transportation. Voters in Amsterdam approved an ambitious plan to eliminate most automobiles in a three-square-mile section of the center city, an idea later adopted in a number of other Dutch towns. Increased public funding has been invested in heavy and light rail, and major employers are now required to locate new facilities near transit stops. New housing and commercial developments are not approved without close scrutiny of their impact on traffic congestion.

With studies showing that people are much more willing to walk or take transit when the pedestrian environment is attractive, attention is being given to sprucing up train stations and making nearby neighborhoods more pleasant places to walk. Forward-looking transportation planners advocate expanded home delivery of goods and increased availability of public storage lockers, recognizing that some people stick with their cars because it's difficult to carry and stow belongings when they're biking, walking or riding transit.

## CITIES WITH CENTERS

On a trip to Germany, I sat in the ornate town hall of Heidelberg—a small city known widely as the setting of the beer-garden romance *The Student Prince*—while Bert-Olaf Rieck pointed out the window to a public square so picturesque it might have been used as a set for the famous operetta. He explained that it was where he parked his car while he was a linguistics student at the university. Now that he is a city official, it's his job to help clear cars out of the central city and make Heidelberg known for bike riding just as much as beer drinking and dueling.

Rieck recently had been appointed Heidelberg's bicycle commissioner, a new position arising out of the city's determination to reduce auto traffic in its historic streets. That's why Rieck was plucked out of the ranks of a bicycle activist group and installed at city hall. He was busy working on ways to make bicycles the vehicle of choice for at least one-third of all trips (up from 20 percent) around the city—an ambitious goal already achieved by Copenhagen and the German city of Munster. In the Dutch cities of Groningen, Harderwijk, Houten, Veenendaal and Zwolle, bicyclists account for 40 percent or more of urban trips.

To put bikes on par with cars, Rieck planned a major expansion of the city's bike paths. He had already succeeded in adding 1,500 new parking spots for bikes outside the main train station and snatched a lane of traffic from cars on a main thoroughfare. He proudly led Julie and me down this street on bicycles the city had recently purchased for its employees to use on trips around town. For a frequent bike commuter like me, it was nothing short of euphoric to pedal down a busy avenue in the safety of my own lane.

Heidelberg has a way to go to match the accomplishments of another German town, Freiburg, a city of 200,000 in the Black Forest. Freiburg showed the way for many European cities with its early efforts to incorporate environmental and quality-of-life concerns into its transportation planning. In the early 1970s, it made the radical moves of not scrapping its streetcars, as most cities across the continent had been doing, and establishing one of Germany's first pedestrian zones.

The pedestrian district is now the bustling heart of the city, filled with folks strolling between department stores, an open-air market and numerous sidewalk cafés. The city has also built a new network of bicycle lanes and overhauled its streetcars into a modern light rail system. While people hopped into their autos for 60 percent of all vehicle trips around the city in the 1970s, cars accounted for less than half of those trips 20 years later—with bikes increasing from 18 to 27 percent of all trips and light rail moving ahead from 22 to 26 percent.

Freiburg's success provides a firm answer to American naysayers who contend that people will never leave their cars at home and who deny that what happens in densely populated Old World cities is applicable to our own spread-out metropolitan areas. Freiburg is one of Germany's fastest-growing cities with new development stretching across a wide valley. You see packs of bicyclists waiting at red lights in its expanding suburbs and light rail trains gliding past single-family homes on ample lots.

Freiburg also has promoted many other environmental initiatives. It banned pesticides for urban uses and built a biochemical plant to recycle organic wastes from the city's garbage. The city established a hot line to answer citizens' questions about environmental matters, and it now subjects all new development projects to an in-depth environmental review.

What makes this small city so eager to buck business as usual in favor of environmental innovation? The presence of 30,000 university students helps, but most observers point to the citizens' deep regional pride. People cherish the city's historical charm (the center city was painstakingly rebuilt after suffering substantial damage in World War II) and the natural beauty of the Black Forest, which itself is under assault by pollution.

## BIKING TO TIVOLI

The Danish capital of Copenhagen is, as Danny Kaye sang in an old movie about Hans Christian Andersen, "wonderful, wonderful." It rivals Paris and Amsterdam for charm, with lively streets, tidy parks, vibrant neighborhoods, cosmopolitan culture, relaxed cafés and cheerful citizens. But Copenhagen's wonderfulness stems not from some happily-ever-after magic but from inspired thinking and hard work in response to real-world urban conditions.

One of the first things a visitor notices about Copenhagen is the bicycles. They're everywhere. You see prim, briefcase-toting business executives on bikes. Fashionable women in formidable high heels on bikes. Old people, schoolkids and parents with toddlers on bikes. Half of all people who work in the central city arrive by bicycle in the summertime, and, despite Copenhagen's chilly, rainy and sometimes icy weather, almost a third do in the winter.

All these bicycles, in addition to a good train system and an extensive network of pedestrian streets, explain why Copenhagen feels like such a pleasant, comfortable place. This is not just the luck of an ancient city unsuited for modern roadways. (Indeed, Copenhagen is no older than most East Coast American cities, having been completely rebuilt after 1807 when the British navy burned it to the ground.) It is the happy result of sensible urban planning with a strong emphasis on making the town attractive to pedestrians.

Ever since a street in the heart of town was first closed off to traffic in 1962, planners have added additional blocks to the lively pedestrian zone each year, eliminated parking spots and turned traffic lanes into bike lanes. Slowly, central Copenhagen has been transformed from a noisy, dirty, exhaust-choked downtown into a pleasant spot where you just naturally want to hang out. Jan Gehl, head of the urban design department at the Royal Danish Academy of Fine Arts, pointed to extensive studies showing that social and recreational use of the city center has tripled over the past 30 years. And he noted that the streets are just as lively when the shops are closed in the evenings and on Sundays: "A good city is like a good party," Gehl explained. "People don't want to leave early."

Copenhagen's initial plans to create a pedestrian zone were met with just as much skepticism as we would hear about similar plans in America today. "We are Danes, not Italians," Gehl recalled the newspapers complaining. "We will not use public space. We will never leave our cars. The city will die if you take out any cars." But the pedestrian zone was popular from the first day, he noted, and downtown business leaders eventually took credit for a plan they once adamantly opposed. One key to the success of Copenhagen's efforts, Gehl said, is that they have been implemented gradually over 40 years. Drastic changes all at once provoke overreactions, he said.

On the national level, Denmark has worked to halt sprawl with legislation that requires nearly all new stores to be built within existing commercial centers of cities, towns or villages.

## URBAN DECAY . . . IN EUROPE?

Strolling away from the charming pedestrian streets and wonderfully preserved buildings of central Copenhagen on my first visit, I stumbled upon a sight familiar to urban Americans: a district of rundown apartment buildings, poor families, hookers, and drug and alcohol casualties. Middle-class flight to the suburbs in the 1960s and 1970s combined with cutbacks in blue-collar jobs brought dramatic changes to an area known as Vesterbro, and to other inner-city Copenhagen neighborhoods.

In America, urban decline is generally attributed to people's overwhelming preference for suburban amenities, but Denmark's policy makers bring a broad regional perspective to issues of struggling city neighborhoods. According to Jan Engell, an official in Copenhagen's planning department, the inner city is seen as an incubator where young people and immigrants can live cheaply as they launch their careers. And if many of them choose to move to bigger homes in out-lying areas as they prosper and raise families, this is interpreted not as the failure of city life, but as a sign of its success.

This view of the metropolitan region as a single, unified community in which people choose to live in various areas at different times in their lives has led to an enlightened policy in which local tax revenues are shared between wealthier and poorer municipalities. Responsibility for the higher proportion of low-income, immigrant, elderly, mentally ill and chemically dependent peo-ple who live in the inner city and require more government services is borne not just by Copenhagen taxpayers but by everyone in the region.

Imagine what a difference it would make if Westchester County or Chicago's North Shore suburbs chipped in some of their local tax proceeds to boost public schools or drug treatment programs in the Bronx or the South Side! This is a key reason, along with higher levels of social benefits in general, why even Copenhagen's shabbiest quarters don't feel nearly as dangerous or as desperate as American ghettos. Vesterbro, despite its sex shops and drug ad-dicts, remained at the time of my first visit a popular place for students, artists and others attracted to the gritty energy of city life.

On later visits to Copenhagen I have seen the effects of an ambitious revi-talization effort that aims to improve Vesterbro without driving away the peo-ple who live there. The Danish parliament allotted an ample pot of money for the city, working with landlords and in some cases tenants to fix up blocks of century-old apartment buildings.

All these plans are being carried out in close cooperation with community groups, and tenants have the right to opt out of certain improvements they think will jack up their rents. "This is a democracy experiment as much as a so-cial one," said planning official Jan Engell, noting, for example, that the empha-sis on installing sophisticated energy and water conservation systems in the buildings came from residents themselves more than from city hall.

The Vesterbro redevelopment is drawing on lessons learned from the nearby Nørrebro neighborhood, where the city's efforts to make Copenhagen more attractive to middle-class families touched off riots during the 1980s. "Residents felt they were being forced out of the neighborhood," Storskov ex-plained. People were outraged when old buildings were bulldozed and 19th-century streets were reconfigured to meet modern specifications. The new apartment buildings are now far less popular than the old ones left standing, Storskov admitted. "That is why we began to renew houses rather than tear them down, even though it costs more."

What's happening in Vesterbro ought to remind Americans that urban re-
vitalization does not have to mean gentrification—and, indeed, that low-
income people often know best what works in their own neighborhoods.

## PLACES FOR PEOPLE

All across Northern Europe, cities are exploring ways to boost their vitality and
livability. Most cities now have bustling pedestrian zones, and bikeways criss-
cross even the most crowded metropolises. The Norwegian cities of Oslo,
Bergen and Trondheim (borrowing an idea from Singapore) levy a toll on all
cars entering the city. Oslo used some of this money to reroute a harborside
highway through a new tunnel, which gave the city a waterfront pedestrian
plaza that's become a favorite hangout for local residents. London recently
adopted a similar traffic-pricing measure with surprising success.

"Until recently, American cities with their wide lanes and fast traffic were
the model for us," said Joachim Schultis, an urban planning professor in Heidelberg. "But all that has now changed."

Being able to get around by strolling, biking or taking a train without always dodging trucks and cars enhances urban life in ways that are hard to
imagine until you've experienced them. The more I visited Europe, the more
charged up I got about wanting to see innovations like these back home.
There's no reason why our cities can't follow suit, transferring themselves from
conduits for cars into places for people. But the first step, I instinctively understood, was finding new ways for Americans to look at the places where they
live. We need to fall in love with our hometowns.

Americans have always harbored a bit of mistrust toward cities—these
crowded, complex and creatively chaotic places. Going all the way back to
Thomas Jefferson's exaltation of yeoman farmers as the backbone of democratic
culture, country life has been seen as the American ideal. Generations of conser-
vationists and environmentalists have reinforced these views. Tracing their roots
back to Henry David Thoreau and John Muir, ecology activists have sought re-
demption from ecological devastation in the untrammeled lands. Blessed with far
more wilderness than any European nation, Americans generally have viewed
any landscape shaped by human hands as somehow tainted. That's why protecting wilderness and saving wetlands are more often the focus of environmental
organizations than curbing sprawl or revitalizing inner-city neighborhoods.

Yet our unease about cities—we see them as unnatural, unhealthy, almost
un-American—has spawned one of the most spectacular environmental
disasters in history: sprawl. Over the past 60 years, millions of Americans have
forsaken compact neighborhoods for sprawling acreage outside town. Closer
connection to nature among the green lawns may have been the dream, but the
truth is that suburban living often means countless hours in the car, cruising
down endless miles of pavement, passing ceaseless stretches of new sub-
divisions and strip malls, all of which depend on limitless supplies of land, fossil
fuel, lumber and other environmentally precious resources.

In terms of the environment, cities clearly offer the most Earth-friendly lifestyle. A resident of an inner-city neighborhood who takes public transit to work, walks to local businesses, and shares a modest home with family or friends imposes far less damage on the environment than most Americans do. Of course, an urban address does not automatically confer an enhanced ecological consciousness; indeed, city dwellers are capable of merrily plundering the planet the same as anyone else. But city life does at least offer the opportunity to walk, bike or take the bus to your destinations, and to conserve resources by living in a compact neighborhood. Those things are impossible in most suburbs, where autos are the only way to get from point A to point B. Houses are cut off from stores by impassable swaths of pavement. Schools, day-care centers, libraries and workplaces all sit isolated amid a sea of roaring traffic.

The environment is not the only victim of this all-for-the-auto way of designing our communities. Children can't wander down to the park or skip over to the candy store. Sometimes they can't even cross the street to see neighbor kids. To go anywhere, they have to wait for someone to chauffeur them. Old people and the disabled, many of whom can't drive or have trouble walking across wide busy streets, are similarly placed under a sort of house arrest.

James Howard Kunstler, the author of *The Geography of Nowhere: The Rise and Decline of America's Man-Made Landscape,* insists that there is an even deeper way we pay for this folly of poor urban planning. "It matters that our cities are primarily auto storage depots," he says. "It matters that our junior high schools look like insecticide factories. It matters that our libraries look like beverage distribution warehouses."

When so much of what you see on a typical day is so drab, it's hard to care about what happens to these places. I have fallen in love with Paris, Stockholm, Oxford, Florence and Gouda, Netherlands, as well as New York, New Orleans and even Madison, Wisconsin, because they stir something in my soul. It's more than scenic charm; it's a feeling they inspire as I walk around them with my family or soak up their atmosphere just sitting at a café table or on a public bench.

It's been 15 years since I began roaming European cities in search of ideas that we could take advantage of here in America, and I am happy to report that I'm not alone. Many people, it seems, have returned from Barcelona, Sydney, Buenos Aires, Toronto or Portland, Oregon fired up by what they've seen and wanting to do something like it at home. Historic preservation and sidewalk cafés, tapas bars and Irish pubs, bicycle lanes and farmers' markets all owe some of their popularity to inspiration from abroad.

## RECAPTURING THE CITIES

A growing legion of citizens is slowly changing the face of America with the message that there are other ways to build our communities besides the all-too-familiar patterns of sprawl. Architect and town planner Andres Duany argues, "Everything you build should be either a neighborhood or a village."

He says great cities are nothing more than a series of villages artfully stitched together. These traditional villages and neighborhoods, he says, provide the basics within walking distance—a grocery, cleaners, café, pharmacy, bakery, park, day-care center, schools and perhaps a bookshop, ice cream parlor, movie house and other social amenities. They should also offer a mix of housing types that can accommodate people of all ages and incomes. Ideally, a transit stop sits in the middle of things, and all parts of the neighborhood are within a five-minute walk of the center.

This simple wisdom, which guided the building of towns and cities for all of human history, was forgotten in America during the post-World War II years when it was assumed that all travel would be by auto. Over the past 50 years, our federal, state and local governments have been preoccupied with building new and faster roads. We've spent billions to widen streets and highways in almost every urban neighborhood and rural township. Millions of trees have been chopped down, tens of thousands of houses torn down and communities everywhere ripped apart, all to meet the needs of the ever-escalating volume and speed of traffic.

But now, in place after place across North America, citizens are speaking out, holding meetings, and fighting city hall (and in some cases working with city hall) on the issue of slowing down traffic. They are fed up that the time-honored tradition of taking a walk has become a frustrating, unpleasant and dangerous pastime. They are tired of worrying about the safety of their children, their pets and their elderly and disabled friends. They are determined to restore a sense of peace and community to their neighborhoods by taking the streets back from the automobile.

Speeding traffic sets in motion a vicious cycle in which people who might prefer to walk or bike end up driving out of fear for their safety. Numerous studies have shown that the speed of traffic, much more than the volume, is what poses a threat to pedestrians. One study conducted by the British government found that pedestrians were killed 85 percent of the time when they were hit by cars traveling 40 miles an hour compared to only five percent of the time when vehicles were traveling at 20 miles per hour.

Lowering speed limits is one logical response. Most German cities have posted 30-kilometer-per-hour (19 mph) limits on all residential streets. But many observers note that people pay less attention to speed limits than to the look of a street in determining how fast they drive. Wide, open streets encourage motorists to zoom ahead. Many people herald the new idea of traffic calming as a more effective way of slowing drivers because it's enforced 24 hours a day, not just when a police car is on the scene. Traffic calming was born in the late 1960s in Delft, Netherlands, when a group of neighbors, frustrated with cars roaring in front of their homes, placed furniture and other large objects at strategic spots in the street, which forced motorists to slow down. City officials, called out to clear these illegal obstacles, knew a good thing when they saw one and began installing their own more sophisticated traffic-calming devices. The idea spread across Europe and Australia, and now has come to North America.

Traffic calming encompasses a whole set of street designs that increase safety and aesthetic satisfaction for pedestrians. The aim is twofold: to slow the speed of traffic and to give drivers a visual reminder that they must share the street with people. Speed bumps, narrowed streets, four-way stop signs, brightly painted crosswalks, on-street parking, median strips, bans on right turns at red lights, crosswalks raised a few inches above the roadway, and curbs that extend a ways into intersections all help make the streets safer and more pleasant for pedestrians.

Opponents claim that traffic calming simply shoves speeding traffic onto someone else's street. But numerous studies have shown that traffic calming measures not only reduce speeds but can actually decrease traffic in general as people make fewer auto trips, either by handling a number of errands on one outing or by switching sometimes to biking, walking or taking public transit. Transportation officials in Nuremberg, Germany found in 1989 when they closed a major downtown street that traffic on nearby streets *decreased*—exactly the opposite of what opponents of the plan had warned.

Many American communities are rethinking traffic issues. Eugene, Oregon, which used to require that all streets be at least 28 feet wide, now allows some to be as narrow as 20 feet. Wellesley, Massachusetts, faced with a plan to widen its congested main street, instead chose to narrow it and expand the sidewalks to encourage walking. Even in auto happy Southern California, the cities of San Bernardino, Riverside and Beverly Hills have narrowed major commercial streets.

In neighborhood after neighborhood across my home city of Minneapolis, citizens have risen up with new ideas about how to make it a better place to live. A vocal supporter of street narrowing was elected mayor, unseating an incumbent in large part because of his vigorous urban-livability platform. Many streets around town have been narrowed or now have speed bumps. A series of new bike paths wind around the city and suburbs. A light rail line has opened to great success. New developments, reflecting the best of classic Minneapolis architecture, are popping up all over the metropolitan region. Independent and idiosyncratic coffee shops have blossomed all over town, giving a village feel to many neighborhoods. New investment has flowed into once-rundown parts of the city, bringing a new sense of hope.

But most important of all, the citizens of Minneapolis have a new appreciation for their home. They understand that the city will thrive if it nurtures its special urban qualities and will fall on its face if it merely tries to imitate suburbia by widening streets, developing strip malls, and adding parking lots. Minneapolis has become proud to be a city once again. It is far different from the disheartened town Julie and I came home to from our honeymoon. Minneapolis now feels like a city whose residents care about it. We've fallen back in love with our hometown.

# 27

# I Love Paris on a Bus, a Bike, a Train and in Anything but a Car

**Serge Schmemann**

*This New York Times essay shows how a major urban place, in this case Paris, can manage traffic and automobile pollution. These answers—small cars, high gasoline cost, improved public transportation, barriers to automobiles, and encouragement of bicycles—are lessons to be learned and applied in the United States.*

Now that Michael Moore has broken a taboo by holding up France as a model for national health care, maybe it's safe to point out other things France seems to do right. Like how Paris is trying to manage traffic and auto pollution.

What Paris has done right is to make it awful to get around by car and awfully easy to get around by public transportation or by bike. Any tourist in a rent-a-car who's circumnavigated the Arc de Triomphe most likely will never drive in Paris again. But there are plenty of Parisians who do it all the time—far too many, in fact. So Mayor Bertrand Delanoë, a Socialist, vowed in coming to office in 2001 to reduce car traffic by 40 percent by 2020.

He's serious about it. I live near the Boulevard St. Michel, and two years ago the city laid down a granite divider strip between the bus-only lane and the cars, squeezing private cars from three lanes to two. Taxis and bicycles may use the bus lane.

At the same time, every bus stop was newly equipped with a screen that told you how long the wait was for the bus. During rush hour, when the cars stand still along Boul' Mich, there's nothing better than zooming past them in a bus.

Bus routes reach the most obscure corners of Paris. There's also the Metro—and especially the great Line No. 1, which runs on tires under the Champs-Élysées and beyond. Then there's a nifty new tramway that runs along the southern rim of the city and several suburban train lines that can be used for rapid transport within the city.

In short, public transportation will take you where you want to go, and you can use it all you want on an electronic card that can be paid by the week or by the month (about $70 these days). Taxis, of course, can also be summoned anywhere by phone.

The lesson for big-city mayors: If you're going to squeeze the cars, first primp the public ride.

Mayor Delanoë's latest front in the anti-car war is the bicycle. Last week, more than 10,000 stolid, gray-painted bicycles (no Tour de France speedsters) became available for rent at 750 self-service locations across Paris. The cost is modest, less than $1.50 for a one-day pass, about $7.50 for a week and about $43.50 for a year—and the bikes can be dropped off at any docking station. The number of bikes is supposed to double by the end of the year. Already in their first week, the bikes are all over central Paris, many carrying commuters—and, yes, some New Yorkers. (An outdoor advertising company paid for everything in return for exclusive use of city-owned billboards.)

Lesson for all big cities: This is an idea whose time has come.

Now, a word about cars. In American cities, it's "big."

Parisians overwhelmingly buy small cars. And it's not because people are petite, but because fuel is drop-dead expensive. Gasoline costs more than twice as much in Paris as in New York.

But the price of diesel fuel is deliberately set far lower. That's because diesel-powered cars produce about 30 percent less greenhouse gas pollution than equivalent gasoline-powered engines. So car-buyers in Paris get small, diesel cars not because the French are virtuous (a separate topic), but because it makes economic good sense.

Many of these small cars have ample room for full-size people and have no trouble maintaining (or seriously exceeding) the 130 kilometers-per-hour (about 80 m.p.h.) limit on the national highways and are as clean and almost as quiet as gasoline engines.

The lesson for the next U.S. president: raise the taxes on fuel. A lot.

# 12

# Environment

## THE UNITED STATES CONTEXT

The United States has 4.5 percent of the world's population, yet it uses about 25 percent of the world's energy—and in doing so produces 30.3 percent of the greenhouse gases that cause global warming (more than the combined contributions of South America, Africa, the Middle East, Australia, Japan, and all of Asia) (Gore, 2006:250). In contrast, the European Union accounts for 20 percent of world GDP (gross domestic product), while consuming only 16 percent of the world's energy. "What these figures boil down to is that for every dollar's worth of goods and services the United States produces, it consumes 40 percent more energy than other industrialized nations" (Walter, 2001:1). Moreover, emissions from U.S. power plants alone exceed the total emissions of 146 other nations combined, which represent 75 percent of the world's population (Gergen, 2001).

The United States also produces more garbage than any other nation, on average 4.4 pounds per person per day, most of which is placed in landfills. The European nations, because they are much better at recycling waste, generate only about half the amount of solid waste per capita as the United States.

A critical health danger is related to the production and disposal of toxic wastes (lead, asbestos, detergents, solvents, acids, and ammonia), fertilizers, herbicides, and pesticides that pollute the air, land, and water.

## References

Gergen, David. 2001. "It's Not Can We, But Will We?" *U.S. News & World Report* (September 24):60.

Gore, Al. 2006. *An Inconvenient Truth.* New York: Rodale.

Walter, Norbert. 2001. "Gobbling Energy and Wasting It, Too." *New York Times* (June 13). Online: www.nytimes.com/2001/106/13/opinion/13WALT.htm

# 28

■■■

# Flush with Energy

## Thomas L. Friedman

*Pulitzer Prize winning writer Thomas L. Friedman shows how Denmark has reduced energy demands. For example, Denmark has reduced its use of Middle East energy from 99 percent in 1973 to zero today. It has accomplished this energy independence by imposing high gasoline and carbon dioxide taxes, applying building and appliance efficiency standards, recycling waste heat, and getting 20 percent of its electricity from wind.*

The Arctic Hotel in Ilulissat, Greenland, is a charming little place on the West Coast, but no one would ever confuse it for a Four Seasons—maybe a One Seasons. But when my wife and I walked back to our room after dinner the other night and turned down our dim hallway, the hall light went on. It was triggered by an energy-saving motion detector. Our toilet even had two different flushing powers depending on—how do I say this delicately—what exactly you're flushing. A two-gear toilet! I've never found any of this at an American hotel. Oh, if only we could be as energy efficient as Greenland!

A day later, I flew back to Denmark. After appointments here in Copenhagen, I was riding in a car back to my hotel at the 6 p.m. rush hour. And boy, you knew it was rush hour because 50 percent of the traffic in every intersection was bicycles. That is roughly the percentage of Danes who use two-wheelers to go to and from work or school every day here. If I lived in a city that had dedicated bike lanes everywhere, including one to the airport, I'd go to work that way, too. It means less traffic, less pollution and less obesity.

What was most impressive about this day, though, was that it was raining. No matter. The Danes simply donned rain jackets and pants for biking. If only we could be as energy smart as Denmark!

Unlike America, Denmark, which was so badly hammered by the 1973 Arab oil embargo that it banned all Sunday driving for a while, responded to that crisis in such a sustained, focused and systematic way that today it is energy independent. (And it didn't happen by Danish politicians making their people stupid by telling them the solution was simply more offshore drilling.)

What was the trick? To be sure, Denmark is much smaller than us and was lucky to discover some oil in the North Sea. But despite that, Danes imposed on themselves a set of gasoline taxes, $CO_2$ taxes and building-and-appliance efficiency standards that allowed them to grow their economy—while barely growing their energy consumption—and gave birth to a Danish clean-power industry that is one of the most competitive in the world today. Denmark today gets nearly 20 percent of its electricity from wind. America? About 1 percent.

And did Danes suffer from their government shaping the market with energy taxes to stimulate innovations in clean power? In one word, said Connie Hedegaard, Denmark's minister of climate and energy: "No." It just forced them to innovate more—like the way Danes recycle waste heat from their coal-fired power plants and use it for home heating and hot water, or the way they incinerate their trash in central stations to provide home heating. (There are virtually no landfills here.)

There is little whining here about Denmark having $10-a-gallon gasoline because of high energy taxes. The shaping of the market with high energy standards and taxes on fossil fuels by the Danish government has actually had "a positive impact on job creation," added Hedegaard. "For example, the wind industry—it was nothing in the 1970s. Today, one-third of all terrestrial wind turbines in the world come from Denmark." In the last 10 years, Denmark's exports of energy efficiency products have tripled. Energy technology exports rose 8 percent in 2007 to more than $10.5 billion in 2006, compared with a 2 percent rise in 2007 for Danish exports as a whole.

"It is one of our fastest-growing export areas," said Hedegaard. It is one reason that unemployment in Denmark today is 1.6 percent. In 1973, said Hedegaard, "we got 99 percent of our energy from the Middle East. Today it is zero."

Frankly, when you compare how America has responded to the 1973 oil shock and how Denmark has responded, we look pathetic.

"I have observed that in all other countries, including in America, people are complaining about how prices of [gasoline] are going up," Denmark's prime minister, Anders Fogh Rasmussen, told me. "The cure is not to reduce the price, but, on the contrary, to raise it even higher to break our addiction to oil. We are going to introduce a new tax reform in the direction of even higher taxation on energy and the revenue generated on that will be used to cut taxes on personal income—so we will improve incentives to work and improve incentives to save energy and develop renewable energy."

Because it was smart taxes and incentives that spurred Danish energy companies to innovate, Ditlev Engel, the president of Vestas—Denmark's and the world's biggest wind turbine company—told me that he simply can't understand how the U.S. Congress could have just failed to extend the production tax credits for wind development in America.

Why should you care?

"We've had 35 new competitors coming out of China in the last 18 months," said Engel, "and not one out of the U.S."

# 29

# Scandinavia Gets Serious on Global Warming

**Bruce E. Johansen**

*This article shows the many innovative ways in which Sweden
and Denmark conserve energy, and in doing so reduce the
problem of global warming.*

Sweden and Norway have some of the highest liquor taxes in the world, provoking large-scale smuggling from Denmark. Until recently, gold-and-blue-capped Swedish Customs officers poured the contraband booze down the drain. These days, however, a million illicit bottles a year are trucked to a sparkling new high-tech plant about eighty miles from Stockholm that manufactures biogas fuel. Every busted booze smuggler has been drafted into Sweden's war against oil dependence and greenhouse gases.

The Linköping plant also accepts packing-plant waste. This swill produces biofuel for buses, taxis, garbage trucks, and private cars, as well as a methane-propelled "biogas train." The train's boosters (not squeamish vegetarians, from the sound of it) have figured that the entrails from one dead cow buy 2.5 miles on the train.

The color of consensus in Sweden today is green. A growing web of pedestrian malls allows tens of thousands of people to traverse downtown Stockholm on foot every day—down a gentle hill, northwest to southeast, along Drottninggatan, past the Riksdag (Parliament) and the King's Palace, merging with Vasterlanggatan, into the Old Town—for more than two miles. More and more streets across the city are gradually being placed off-limits to motor traffic.

*Source:* Bruce E. Johansen, "Scandinavia Gets Serious on Global Warming," *The Progressive* 71 (July 2007), pp. 22–24. Reprinted by permission from *The Progressive*, 409 E Main St, Madison, WI 53703. www.progressive.org.

To reduce oil consumption and greenhouse-gas emissions, Swedes are being encouraged to avoid commuting altogether. Teleconferencing is in. When they do commute, more Swedes now use public transport, hybrid vehicles, and biodiesel cars, as well as bicycles.

Stockholm will introduce a fleet of Swedish-made electric hybrid buses in its public transport system on a trial basis in 2008. These buses will use ethanol-powered internal-combustion engines and electric motors, an interim step toward development of entirely "clean" vehicles. The vehicles' diesel engines will use ethanol.

Ulf Perbo, who heads BIL Sweden, the national association for the automobile industry, says even automakers there want to end oil dependency. "It is not in our interest to be dependent on oil, with regard to the production and sales of cars," he says. "Oil is not what interests us; cars are. And oil is going to be a limitation in the future." All Swedish gas stations are required by an act of parliament to offer at least one alternative fuel. Every fifth car in Stockholm now drives at least partially on alternative fuels, mostly ethanol.

The proportion of oil-heated homes in Sweden has fallen to 8 percent, as many neighborhoods use hot water from central plants that burn biofuels, often wood-based pellets. Since the beginning of 2006, householders have been paid to replace oil-burning furnaces with environmentally friendly heating systems. Such financial incentives already were available to libraries, pools, and hospitals that wanted to switch to more efficient renewable energy.

Per Bolund, one of nineteen Green Party members in Sweden's 349-member Riksdag, says there may be less here than meets the eye. When Swedish officials brag that they have reduced the use of oil in home heating to almost zero, he says, they are ignoring the fact that half that total is from nuclear plants, and most of the other half from often-inefficient hydropower. "Any time you see the government claiming that oil use for heating has been minimized to nearly zero you have to say—yes, but!" Don't stereotype Sweden as a green-power heaven, Bolund says. "We have a long way to go."

But the Swedes are moving in the right direction, however. Another conservation measure, "congestion charging," which levies a toll on cars entering downtown Stockholm, became a controversial issue in the Swedish general election during the late summer of 2006. The congestion charge of up to $7 a day narrowly passed in a referendum on September 17, 2006.

The congestion charge reduced auto traffic 20 to 25 percent, while use of trains, buses, and Stockholm's extensive subway system increased. Emissions of carbon dioxide declined 10 to 14 percent in the inner city and 2 to 3 percent in Stockholm County. The project also increased the use of environmentally friendly cars, which are exempt from congestion taxes. The Stockholm congestion tax will become permanent this summer.

The Green Party favored a Stockholm congestion charge for decades, as conservatives blocked it. Ironically, the congestion charge will be imposed under the country's present conservative-oriented coalition government.

Sweden's Commission on Oil Independence, a government panel, also was a longtime Green Party initiative that is now embraced across the Swedish political spectrum. "The Social Democrats stole it from us," Bolund says. He then grins, saying that the Greens must be prepared to be mimicked across the political mainstream to succeed.

The Swedish government recently adopted another Green Party idea: a vehicle tax based on carbon dioxide emissions rather than weight. Bolund pointed out that some cars (such as hybrids) are heavy, but relatively low in fossil-fuel emissions. This is the latest wrinkle in a sixteen-year-old Swedish movement toward carbon-based taxation. The country was the first in the world to adopt a carbon tax, in 1991. Today, nearly half of the Swedish income tax burden has been phased out and replaced by levies based in some manner on fossil-fuel consumption.

Everywhere in Stockholm you see little energy-saving tricks. Many renovated Stockholm hotel rooms and apartments have a door slot for key cards that must be activated to turn on the lights. When you leave your room, the lights automatically turn off. The escalators and moving sidewalks in the Riksdag stop when no one uses them. And signs in the Riksdag cafeteria advertise that food scraps can have a useful second life as biogas.

Sweden is not alone. The Danish Crown slaughterhouse uses the fat of 50,000 pigs a week to generate biogas. The entire Danish Crown plant has been redesigned with an eye to saving energy, part of a thirty-year Danish effort to eliminate waste, conserve energy, and reduce consumption of fossil fuels, as *The Wall Street Journal* reports.

Surplus heat from Danish power plants is delivered to nearby homes, via insulated pipes. Large parts of Denmark have undergone a nearly total makeover of basic energy infrastructure. The new system now heats almost two-thirds of Danish homes. Power plants have been radically reduced in size and built closer to people's homes and offices to reduce power loss during transmission. In the mid-1980s, Denmark had fifteen large power plants; it now has several hundred small ones.

Danish building codes enacted in 1979 (and tightened several times since) also require thick home insulation and tightly sealed windows. Between 1975 and 2001, Denmark's national heating bill fell 20 percent, even as the amount of heated space increased by 30 percent. Denmark's gross domestic product has doubled on stable energy usage during the last thirty years. The average Dane now uses 6,600 kilowatt hours of electricity a year, less than half of the U.S. average, according to *The Wall Street Journal*.

Denmark has become a world leader in wind-turbine technology. Turbines generate electricity that competes in price with oil, coal, and nuclear power, and they provide several thousand jobs. Some wind turbines now have blades almost 300 feet wide—the length of a football field.

During January, a very stormy month, Denmark harvested 36 percent of its electricity from wind, almost double the usual. In the United States, the comparable figure is one-quarter of 1 percent.

Urban life in Denmark is being recast with the automobile as antithesis. Drivers are free to buy an SUV, but the bill includes a registration tax up to

180 percent of the purchase price. Denmark's taxation system has become an environmental exclamation point. Imagine, for example, paying more than $80,000 in taxes (as well as $6 a gallon for gasoline) to buy and drive a Hummer H2—that, and pesky bicyclists may ridicule your elegantly pimped ride as an environmental atrocity.

Bicycles have become privileged personal urban transport. To sample bicycle gridlock, come to Copenhagen, which has deployed 2,000 bikes around the city for free use. The city's environmental chief, Klaus Bondam, commutes by bicycle. Helmets are not required, despite the occasional bout of two-wheeled road rage as bicyclists clip each other on crowded streets. People ride bikes while drinking coffee or smoking. Rain or shine, they use a wide array of baskets to carry groceries and briefcases.

Many Danish companies offer indoor bike parking, as well as locker rooms. Employees ride company-owned bikes to off-site meetings. People tote children on extra bike seats. Members of parliament ride to work, as do CEOs of some major companies. Lars Rebien Sorensen, head of the pharmaceutical firm Novo Nordisk, even conducts media interviews from his bike saddle.

Imagine a CEO in the United States doing that, or a Senator. We are falling way behind Sweden and Denmark and many other European countries in taking serious steps to combat global warming. It may be a while before the U.S. Senate cafeteria carries a sign urging colleagues to recycle scraps for biogas. But we don't have a while to wait.

# 30

# The $6.66-a-Gallon Solution

**Simon Romero**

*Although Norway is the third-largest oil exporter, it has the most expensive gasoline. The high cost of gasoline has positive effects for the environment: (1) lower per capita consumption of gasoline; (2) lower car ownership rates; (3) more fuel-efficient vehicles; and (4) fewer emissions of greenhouse gases. Also the high taxes included in the cost of gasoline (about $519 per capita annually) produces revenue to support Norway's extensive social benefits.*

OSLO, April 23—Car owners in the United States may grumble as the price of gasoline hovers around $2.25 a gallon. Here in Norway, home to perhaps the world's most expensive gasoline, drivers greeted higher pump prices of $6.66 a gallon with little more than a shrug.

Yes, there was a protest from the Norwegian Automobile Association, which said, "Enough is enough."

And a right-wing party in Parliament, the Progress Party, once again called for a cut in gasoline taxes, which account for about 67 percent of the price.

But "those critics are but voices in the wilderness," said Torgald Sorli, a radio announcer with the Norwegian Broadcasting Corporation who often discusses transportation issues. "We Norwegians are resigned to expensive gasoline. There is no political will to change the system."

Norway, the world's third-largest oil exporter, behind Saudi Arabia and Russia, has been made wealthy by oil. Last year alone, oil export revenue surged 19 percent, to $38 billion.

But no other major oil exporter has tried to reel in its own fuel consumption with as much zeal as Norway. These policies have resulted in Norwegians consuming much less oil per capita than Americans—1.9 gallons a day versus almost 3 gallons a day in the United States—and low car ownership rates. On

*Source:* Simon Romero, "The $6.66-a-Gallon Solution," *New York Times* (April 30, 2005), pp. C1, C10.

city streets and rural roads, fuel-efficient Volkswagens and Peugeots far out-number big sport utility vehicles.

[Norway's gasoline policies stand in contrast to those in the United States, where President Bush made cheaper gasoline a priority during his discussion of energy policy at his news conference on Thursday.]

Gasoline, of course, is not the only expensive commodity in Norway, a traditionally frugal and highly taxed nation. At a pub in Oslo, for instance, a pint of beer might cost the equivalent of $12 and an individual frozen pizza $16. But expensive gasoline is rare among large oil-producing countries that often subsidize fuel for their citizens. Gasoline prices in Norway—with a currency, the krone, strong in comparison with the dollar—have climbed 30 percent since 1998, outpacing a 15 percent increase in the consumer price index in that period, the national statistics bureau said.

Having the world's highest gasoline prices is just one strategy to combat greenhouse gases in this redoubt of welfare capitalism and strict environmental laws. Overall energy consumption, especially of electricity, is quite high, how-ever, with Norway blessed with not just oil but ample hydropower resources.

Norway not only taxes its gasoline. Norwegians also pay automobile taxes as high as $395 a year for each vehicle, and in Oslo there is even a "studded-tire" fee of about $160 for vehicles with all-terrain tires that tear up asphalt more quickly in the winter.

Then there are the taxes on new passenger vehicles that can increase the price of imported automobiles. Norway has no auto manufacturing industry aside from an experiment to produce electric cars, and economists have sug-gested that that has made it easier to limit automobile use in Norway because there is no domestic industry to lobby against such decisions as in neighboring Sweden, home of Saab and Volvo.

Norway designed the duties to make large-engine sport utility vehicles much costlier than compact cars. For instance, a high-end Toyota Land Cruiser that costs $80,000 in the United States might run as much as $100,000 in Norway.

Economists argue that gasoline prices and other auto taxes in Norway are not so expensive when measured against the annual incomes of Norwegians, among the world's highest at about $51,700 a person, or the shorter workweek of about 37.5 hours that is the norm here. (Norwegians also get five weeks of vacation a year.) The government frequently makes such arguments when re-sponding to criticism over high fuel prices.

"We do not want such a system," Per-Kristian Foss, the finance minister, said in a curt response to the calls for lower gasoline taxes this month in Parliament.

Other European countries have also placed high taxes on gasoline, and some like Britain and the Netherlands have gasoline prices that rival or at times surpass Norway's. In Oslo, as in other European capitals, there is ample public transportation, including an express airport train that whisks travelers to the international airport from downtown in 20 minutes. Yet Norway, with a popu-lation of just 4.8 million, differs from much of Europe in its breadth, with an ex-tensive network of roads, tunnels and bridges spread over an area slightly larger than New Mexico.

"Rural areas without good public transportation alternatives are hit a little harder," said Knut Sandberg Eriksen, a senior research economist at the Institute of Transport Economics here who estimates the government collects about $2.4 billion in fuel taxes alone each year, or about $519 for every Norwegian. Some of the revenue supports Norway's social benefits.

"Our government has been grateful to use the automobile as a supreme tax object," Mr. Eriksen said. "The car is its milking cow."

Perhaps as a result of such policies, Norway has lower levels of car ownership than other European countries, with 427 cars per 1,000 people in 2003 compared with more than 500 cars per 1,000 people in both France and Germany, according to the Economist Intelligence Unit. The United States has more than 700 cars per 1,000 people.

The average age of a passenger car in Norway is 18 years when it is scrapped, though this might be changing in a strong economy with the lowest interest rates in 50 years. Registrations of new passenger cars last year climbed 20 percent from 2003. But the frugality of some Norwegians, even in rural areas, suggests older cars will remain at many households.

"Personally I have no need for a new vehicle; I'm proud to hold on to my own for as long as I can," said Johannes Rode, 69, a retired art and music teacher and owner of a 29-year-old red Volkswagen Beetle in Ramberg, a coastal town in northern Norway. "To do otherwise would be wasteful and play into the oil industry's hands."

Caution about oil's risks is common in Norway. The government created the Petroleum Fund more than a decade ago as a repository for most of the royalties it receives from oil production. The $165 billion fund, overseen by the central bank, is intended for the day when oil resources in the North Sea start to dry up.

Meanwhile, unlike other large oil producers like Saudi Arabia, Iran or Venezuela, Norway has done little to encourage domestic petroleum consumption. In part because high gasoline prices deter such a luxury, Norway consumes little more than 200,000 barrels a day of oil while exporting nearly its entire production of 8.3 million barrels a day. This confounds some Norwegians.

"Norway is a rich, oil-producing country with no foreign debt," said Egli Otter, a spokesman for the Norwegian Automobile Association, a sister organization to AAA. "We think that Norway, with its enormous and complicated geography and distances, deserves pump prices at an average European level. Motorists find it very difficult to be taxed into these extremes."

Such opinions contrast with the quick defense of high gasoline prices often voiced around Norway, which is celebrating its 100th year of independence from neighboring Sweden and so far has opted out of joining the European Union.

Sverre Lodgaard, director of the Norwegian Institute of International Affairs, said Norway had a responsibility to manage its oil resources soberly because of its support of world-wide limitations on greenhouse-gas emissions.

"We are engaged on this front," Mr. Lodgaard said. "It is difficult for us to view the example of the United States, which is overconsuming to an incredible extent."

**FILLING THE TANK**

Norway and other European nations discourage gas consumption by taxing heavily at the pump. By contrast, the United States is looking to lower the cost of gasoline.

| | Typical Price for a Gallon of Gasoline | Gallons Used Each Day per Person |
|---|---|---|
| Norway | $6.66 | 1.9 |
| Netherlands | 6.55 | 2.3 |
| Britain | 6.17 | 1.2 |
| Germany | 5.98 | 1.4 |
| Italy | 5.94 | 1.4 |
| France | 5.68 | 1.4 |
| Singapore | 3.50 | 7.3* |
| Brazil | 3.35 | 0.5 |
| India | 3.29 | 0.1 |
| Mexico | 3.20 | 0.8 |
| South Africa | 3.13 | 0.4 |
| United States | 2.26 | 2.9 |
| Russia | 2.05 | 0.8 |
| China | 1.78 | 0.2 |
| Nigeria | 1.48 | 0.1 |
| Iran | 0.47 | 0.8 |

*So high because the economy relies heavily on oil refining, petrochemicals and shipping industries, which use a lot of oil.

*Source:* Reuters; Energy Information Administration

The United States, which uses about a quarter of the world's daily oil consumption, had the cheapest gasoline prices of the 27 industrial countries measured by the International Energy Agency in its most recent analysis of fuel prices. Taxes accounted on average for just 20 percent of the price of gasoline in the United States, the agency said.

Even amid Norway's bluster on gasoline prices, however, environmentalists suggest the nation could do more to achieve greater energy efficiency. One sore point is the consumption of electricity, traditionally generated by hydropower but soon to depend more on a fossil fuel, natural gas.

Producing oil for export in Norway requires large amounts of electricity, and homes in the country, with much of its territory above the Arctic Circle, use electricity for heating, creating much higher electricity consumption levels than elsewhere in Europe. It is not uncommon to drive on well-lighted roads even in remote areas.

"There are areas in which we have done O.K.," said Dag Nagoda, a coordinator in the Oslo office of the WWF, formerly known as the World Wildlife Fund. "And there are areas in which we can do better."

PART

# Individual Deviance

PART

5

# Individual Deviance

# 13

# Crime and Crime Control

## THE UNITED STATES CONTEXT

International comparisons of crime data, while inexact, do provide rough approximations of how crime is patterned geographically. What is known is that among the industrialized nations there is not much difference in burglaries, bicycle thefts, and other property crimes. What is striking, however, is that among these nations, the United States has much higher rates of violent crimes (robberies, assaults, murders, and rapes). "For at least a century and probably longer we have been the most murderous 'developed' society on earth" (Harwood, 1997:27). Criminologists are in general agreement that the extraordinarily high rate of violent crime in the United States is the result of the confluence of at least five major forces. First, countries where there is a wide gap between the rich and poor have the highest levels of violent crime. The United States, as we have noted, has the greatest inequality gap among the industrialized nations.

Second, the greater the proportion of the population living in poverty, the higher the rate of violent crime. Criminologist Elliott Currie says, "[We] know that the links between disadvantage and violence are strongest for the poorest and the most neglected of the poor. . . . [The] people locked into the most permanent forms of economic marginality in the most impoverished and disrupted communities [have] the highest concentrations of serious violent crime" (Currie, 1998:127).

Third, violent crime is worse in those societies with weak "safety nets" for the poor. As Currie puts it: "[The United States,] though generally quite wealthy, is also far more unequal and far less committed to including the vulnerable into a common level of social life than any other developed nation" (Currie, 1998:120).

Fourth, the government's "war on drugs" is partly responsible. By making certain drugs illegal, it drives up their prices, making the manufacture, transport, and sale of illicit drugs lucrative. Organized crime syndicates and gangs, in turn, use violent means to control their territories.

And, fifth, the greater the availability of guns in a society, the higher the level of violent crime. Without question, the United States has more guns per capita than in any other industrialized nation—an estimated 240 million guns and adding about 4 million more annually in a population of 306 million. In fiscal 2000–2001, there were 73 gun homicides in England and Wales. The United States, with about five times the population, had 8,719 firearm murders (Associated Press, 2003).

The U.S. solution to crime ignores these sources of criminal behavior and instead focuses on imprisoning criminals. While the United States has just four and a half percent of the world's population, the number of U.S. prison/jail inmates amounts to 23 percent of the world's prisoners, with a higher proportion of its citizens imprisoned than in any other country. The U.S. incarceration rate in 2006 (per 100,000) was 738, compared to 78 in Sweden, 196 in Mexico, and 607 in Russia (Hartney, 2006). In 2004, the member nations of the European Union averaged only 87 prisoners per 100,000 population (Rifkin, 2004:82).

## References

Associated Press. 2003. "Blair Proposes Minimum of 5 Years for Gun Violence." (January 7).
Currie, Elliott. 1998. *Crime and Punishment in America*. New York: Metropolitan Books.
Hartney, Christopher. 2006. "The U.S. Rates of Incarceration: A Global Perspective." *Council on Crime and Delinquency Fact Sheet* (November).
Harwood, Richard. 1997. "America's Unchecked Epidemic." *Washington Post National Weekly Edition* (December 8):27.
Rifkin, Jeremy. 2004. *The European Dream*. New York: Jeremy P. Tarcher/Penguin.

# 31

■ ■ ■

# Lawless, but Gunless

### Ken MacQueen

*Canadians are just as likely to commit crimes as Americans—
except murder, where the rate in the United States is three
times that in Canada. This is mainly due to the availability of
guns in the United States. There are 30 guns per every 100
people in Canada, compared to 90 per every 100 people in the
United States.*

When it comes to crime, Canadians smugly draw the line between civility and
chaos along the 49th parallel. Sure, Canada has its share of crime, but it's nothing
like those crazy American cities, right? Well, it isn't that simple. Perhaps it comes
from an unhealthy diet of American crime shows, but it's borderline delusional
to think that Canadians are more law-abiding than their southern neighbours.

Canadians are just as larcenous, and sometimes more so. A comparison of
crime stats from both countries (see Table 31.1) reveals that your car is actually
more likely to be stolen in Canada. You are more likely to be a victim of arson.
You are more likely to be burglarized. Most any crime, in fact, that doesn't involve guns is just as likely to befall Canadians as Americans. This is especially
true in the Canadian West, which has chronically higher crime rates than the
rest of the country.

British Columbia has been Canada's crime leader for most of the past
decade, with rates that would rank it among the worst cities in America, says
the B.C. Progress Board, a provincial agency that tracks economic and social indicators. The board, in a little-noticed report last year, charted crime rates in 61
Canadian and American jurisdictions, combining both non-violent property
crimes—a particular problem in B.C.—and violent personal crimes, from homicide to robbery. Its conclusion: "B.C.'s property crime rate is the highest in
North America at 6,534 crimes per 100,000 citizens. The province's violent

*Source:* Ken MacQueen, "Lawless, but Gunless," *Maclean's* (July 7, 2008), pp. 58–59. Reprinted by
permission.

### TABLE 31.1    Who Has Higher Crime Rates? In Many Cases, It's Canada

Canadians are just as larcenous as Americans. In fact, when you look at crimes that don't involve guns, the Canadian rates tend to be higher. But when it comes to violent crimes, such as homicide, Americans have us beat. Why? Mainly because they have a lot more guns.

|  | Canada | United States |
|---|---|---|
| **Guns per 100 People** | 30 | 90 |
| **Crimes That Tend Not to Involve Guns** | | |
| Auto thefts per 100,000 population | 487 | 398 |
| Break and enters per 100,000 population* | 768 | 729 |
| Arsons per 100,000 population | 41 | 27 |
| **Crimes That Tend to Involve Guns** | | |
| Gun murders per 100,000 population | 0.6 | 3.4 |
| Murders (all causes) per 100,000 population | 1.9 | 5.7 |
| Robberies per 100,000 population | 94 | 149 |

*Break and enters are referred to as burglaries in the United States.

*Sources:* Gun ownership numbers (2007): *Small Arms Survey 2007,* Graduate Institute of International Studies in Geneva; crime rate numbers (all 2006); Statistics Canada, FBI's *Crime in the United States 2006* and *Crime in Metropolitan America: City Crime Rankings,* QC Press.

crime rate is fourth among the jurisdictions in question." B.C.'s combined personal and property crime rate is the second worst of all 61 jurisdictions, the board concluded, "surpassed only by the District of Columbia."

That said, danger levels in the worst of America's "anarchic" inner cities, where many crimes go unreported, are higher than anything in Canada, says Neil Boyd, a criminologist at Simon Fraser University. "In the United States there are places in many cities where you cannot walk safely at night, and that's not true in Canada," he says. "In terms of the danger that crime presents to citizens, in the United States, especially in deprived urban areas—urban ghettos, essentially—the environment is still much more out of control than it is in Canada."

The worst of American violent crime is concentrated in these inner cities, and much of it is black-on-black violence. Blacks, who represent 12 per cent of the American population, are more likely to be convicted of murder, and six times more likely to be murdered, than the general population. But Canada has its own pockets of deprivation. Levels of victimization and incarceration among Aboriginal Canadians, who represent about three per cent of the population, are grossly disproportionate. The Aboriginal homicide rate is almost seven times higher than the non-Aboriginal population; the rate of incarceration is nine times higher.

Still, murder is one crime where Canadians lag behind our neighbours—mercifully. Oh, some of us try, and succeed far too often, but we aren't as efficient as Americans—mainly because there aren't as many guns. There are 30 guns per every 100 people in Canada, and a host of restrictions on licensing, carrying and transporting firearms. The U.S.—the world's most heavily armed society—has 90 guns per every 100 people. As a result, in Canada firearms only account for one-third of homicides, while more than two-thirds of American murders involve guns. Partly because of that, Americans have had a murder rate about three times higher than Canada for the last decade (an improvement from four times higher in 1980). The Canadian Centre for Justice Statistics, using data from 2000, neatly sums up the difference: "the U.S. has much higher rates of violent crime, while Canada generally has much higher rates of property crime."

One thing both countries share is a fear of crime ruled more by perception than reality—especially if violent inner-city crime rates are stripped from the equation. Both countries have had a profound drop in their crime rates over the past three decades. American rates have levelled off this decade at the lowest levels since the Bureau of Justice Statistics began collecting data in 1972. Canadian rates have fallen in tandem. Headlines notwithstanding, the rate of gun homicides in Canada in 2006 was about half of what it was 30 years ago. That reality isn't reflected in political debates in either country, in opinion polls, or in the news media, where "the pornography of grief," as Boyd puts it, is often the story of the day.

It's just one more thing we have in common with our neighbours. An airport limo driver in Los Angeles neatly summed it up while bestowing a tip-worthy compliment on a Canadian customer. "We're really not much different," he said. "You folks are just disarmed Americans."

# 32

# Reducing Crime by Harnessing International Best Practices

### Irvin Waller and Brandon C. Welsh

*Unfortunately, the best knowledge available regarding how to prevent crime is seldom used in the United States. Exacerbating this problem is the fact that many Western governments, the United States included, are reducing expenditures and eliminating existing crime prevention programs for political reasons or to save costs. The authors of this article argue that employing the best practices of other countries, such as the family-based intervention programs of the United Kingdom, will prove most cost-effective in the long run by reducing spending on prisons and the need for additional police.*

A great deal is now known about what works to prevent crime. Landmark reviews of scientific evidence by Sherman and his colleagues for the National Institute of Justice[1] and by Loeber and Farrington for the Office of Juvenile Justice and Delinquency Prevention[2] demonstrate that a great deal does indeed work and much more is promising.

Since 1994, the International Centre for the Prevention of Crime (ICPC),[3] based in Montreal, Canada, has been harnessing this U.S.-based knowledge and the evidence on what works from other countries to help solve local crime problems. Making crime prevention knowledge available and tailoring preventive actions to local conditions in cities and countries is a powerful tool in the effort to fight crime. Failure to use the best know-how to reduce crime slows human and economic development, particularly in fast-growing cities, which are the economic motors of most countries.

*Source:* Irvin Waller and Brandon C. Welsh, "Reducing Crime by Harnessing International Best Practices," *National Institute of Justice Journal* (October 1998), pp. 26–31.

ICPC assists cities and countries in reducing delinquency, violence, and insecurity by investing in people and communities in more affordable and sustainable ways. As the central pillar of its efforts to harness crime prevention best practice globally, ICPC supports a Best Practice Bureau to systematically identify, compile, and disseminate information on successful crime prevention practice. It has designed a best practice program to encourage concrete implementation and has launched its "Towards the Use of Best Practice World Wide" Internet site and report.[4] As well, the Centre operates a comparative crime prevention research program to assess the successes, benefits, and directions of crime prevention cross-nationally.

This article summarizes the work program of ICPC to assist cities and countries in reducing delinquency, violence, and insecurity. It reports on the Centre's approach to the prevention of crime, describes a number of proven and promising crime prevention practices around the world, and presents some of the evidence on the comparative economic advantages of investing in crime prevention.

## CRIME PREVENTION AS A PROCESS

Successful crime prevention at the community level begins with a rigorous planning model—a process. It is characterized by a systematic analysis of the crime problem and the conditions that generate it, a review of the services and activities in place to tackle those conditions and ways to improve them, rigorous implementation of the program, and evaluation of the impact of the program on crime and its implementation so that improvements can be made. We view prevention activities that adhere to this model as "problem-solving partnerships"—measures developed as a result of a careful effort to identify causal factors while mobilizing the agencies able to influence those factors.

There is a need for this planning model to include efforts to forecast developments in crime, policing, and the social demography in which these occur. It is also important that these exercises are themselves collaborative so that the agencies that can influence the undesirable trends are involved from the beginning of the process.

Many models exist to help guide these efforts, and some are tailored to specific circumstances, such as high-crime neighborhoods. The European Forum for Urban Security, created by the Council of Europe in 1987 to act as the permanent crime prevention structure for Europe, has articulated the following guidelines for effective crime prevention policy and practice:

- The use of a central coalition to define problems and provide needed resources to address them, prepare action programs and the required staffing needs, and tailor local policy to changing conditions.
- The need for a technical coordinator to oversee and maintain the coalition's problem-solving partnership approach.
- Ongoing surveys of victimization, citizens' views of crime problems, and actions taken to keep the preventive practices up-to-date and targeted at local priorities and needs.[5]

There is also a need for strategies by central-government agencies to foster crime prevention at the local level. Research by ICPC[6] has identified the following core elements as important for the success of a central strategy that will foster effective local crime prevention:

- A central secretariat, with these characteristics:
  —Staff, reporting to a senior official, with a budget for development.
  —Capacity to mobilize key partners.
  —Ability to propose strategies based on an analysis of crime problems and preventive practices.
- Delivery of preventive practices made possible through:
  —Collaboration with other government departments.
  —Development of local problem-solving partnerships.
  —Involvement of citizens.

## BEST PRACTICE IN CRIME PREVENTION

Many different types of crime prevention projects in various countries have reduced levels of delinquency and violent crime by tackling the causes—those that are conducive to victimization as well as those that generate criminal behavior—and by forming real partnerships at the local level.

For ICPC, crime prevention involves a range of strategies successfully pioneered in Europe, North America, and elsewhere. They involve initiatives by central and local governments as well as activities of the private sector, city management, urban planning, policing, the judiciary, schools, housing, social services, youth services, women's affairs, public health, universities, and the media. Figure 32.1 illustrates the impact of several examples of successful programs drawn from the three crime prevention strategies described below.

Projects selected for discussion are not limited to those where scientific evaluations have demonstrated a reduction in crime "beyond a reasonable doubt." Instead, we also have included projects where the "balance of probabilities" is that they reduced crime.[7]

## FOSTERING BETTER DESIGN

Fostering better design is about the improvement of buildings, products, and communities to make it harder, more risky, or less rewarding for offenders to commit crime. This strategy is better known as situational crime prevention.[8] Two projects described below illustrate the extent to which residential burglary can be reduced through situational crime prevention techniques. Each of these projects evolved from an analysis of the causes of crime in which public and private agencies with the solutions were involved. No significant displacement of the crimes to the surrounding areas was found. However, some diffusion of benefits—unanticipated reductions in nontargeted crimes—occurred in adjacent areas.

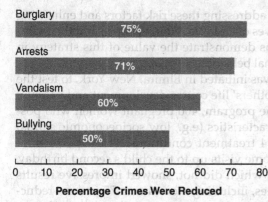

Burglary — 75% — Fostering better design: cocoon neighborhood watch, target hardening (Kirkholt housing project, Rochdale, England)

Arrests — 71% — Mobilizing agencies: incentives for youths to complete school (Quantum Opportunities Program, United States)

Vandalism — 60% — Facilitating partnerships: promoting responsibility with intelligent sanctions for juvenile offenders (HALT Program, the Netherlands)

Bullying — 50% — Mobilizing agencies: parents and teachers targeting causes of school bullying (Norway)

0   10   20   30   40   50   60   70   80

**Percentage Crimes Were Reduced**

**FIGURE 32.1**  Problem-Solving Partnerships That Work

*Source:* For Kirkholt, see note 9; for Quantum, see note 14; for HALT, see note 15; for Norway, see note 13.

In the late 1980s, a project team of city officials, police, social workers, and university researchers undertook to tackle repeat victimization in the Kirkholt housing project in Rochdale, England. Burglary victims were offered assistance in removing coin-operated electric and gas meters; in target hardening by upgrading home security with improved locks and bolts; and in establishing a "cocoon" neighborhood watch program in which six or more residents surrounding a victimized dwelling were asked to participate by watching and reporting anything suspicious. Before-after measures showed a 58-percent reduction in burglaries in the first year and a 75-percent reduction by the end of the third.[9]

In 1991, the Dutch safe housing label was initiated by police in the Rotterdam-Leiden-The Hague triangle. The label was introduced nationally in 1996. When housing project developers or housing associations apply for a police secured label, their project and its environment must be approved by the police as meeting standards relating to residents' participation and responsibility, neighborhood management, home watch, and building design. In Rotterdam, a 70-percent reduction in burglaries was observed following the program's first year in a comparison of participating and nonparticipating households.[10]

## MOBILIZING AGENCIES

Poverty experienced during formative years, inconsistent and uncaring childrearing techniques, and parental conflict are some of the problems that place young people at increased risk for involvement in delinquency. Efforts to address these key risk factors and prevent child victimization in the home and at school at an early age can produce important short- and long-term downstream benefits in the form of reduced delinquency, later offending, and other related social problems. The crime prevention strategy of mobilizing agencies is about bringing together stakeholders, such as schools, housing, and social services, that have a role to play in addressing these risk factors and enhancing protective factors to improve the lives of children, young people, and their families. The following three programs demonstrate the value of this strategy in preventing delinquency and criminal behavior.

In the late 1970s, a program was initiated in Elmira, New York, to test the efficacy of nurse home visits on mothers' life course development and parental care of children. At the onset of the program, 400 pregnant women who possessed one or more high-risk characteristics (e.g., low socioeconomic status) were randomly assigned to 1 of 4 treatment conditions. The experimental group, which received postnatal home visits up to the child's second birthday, compared with the control group, which did not, showed impressive results across a range of prosocial outcomes, including more than a 75-percent reduction in child abuse and neglect (4 percent versus 19 percent).[11] A 13-year followup postintervention, when the children were 15 years old, confirmed a significant sustained reduction in child abuse and neglect.[12]

In 1983, a comprehensive antibullying program was initiated in 42 elementary schools across Norway. Key components of the program included a booklet for school personnel describing bully/victim problems and how to intervene effectively, information and advice for parents on how to deal with their child if a bully or a victim, and access to an informational video on bullying and its impact for the public. After 2 years, the project had reduced the prevalence of bullying by 50 percent.[13]

The Quantum Opportunities Program, which operated in five U.S. cities (San Antonio, Philadelphia, Milwaukee, Saginaw [Michigan], and Oklahoma City) from 1989 to 1993, offered disadvantaged teenagers afterschool activities for which they received small hourly stipends and a matching amount of funds in a college-fund account. The youths were encouraged to complete school through activities such as computer-assisted instruction, peer tutoring, homework assistance, community service and public event project activities, and development activities such as curriculum on life/family skills and college and job planning. In each city, 50 youths were randomly assigned to either a program group that received the intervention or a control group that did not. After 4 years, the program group achieved a 71-percent reduction in self-reported arrests compared with the control group. Program group members also were less likely to have dropped out of school (23 percent versus 50 percent) and were more likely to have graduated from high school (63 percent versus 42 percent).[14]

## FACILITATING PARTNERSHIPS

The crime prevention strategy of facilitating partnerships is about bringing together police, justice services, and those concerned with social development to solve crime problems and promote effective and intelligent sanctions for offenders. In many cases, promoting responsibility is a central feature of programs adopting this strategy. The active ingredient is a focus on increasing the responsibility one holds for one's actions to the victim and the wider society.

Two of the three projects reviewed below illustrate the potential crime reductions that can be achieved by this strategy.

In the Netherlands, the HALT Program was created to respond to the problem of youth vandalism. It involves collaboration between police, prosecutors, municipal authorities, victims, and the community to ensure that young offenders repair vandalism damage they have caused and to assist young people in resolving employment, housing, and education problems. After 1 year, the program group, compared with a matched control group, was more likely to have ceased involvement in vandalism (63 percent versus 25 percent)—a 60 percent overall reduction.[15] As a result of the program's success, it has been expanded to more than 40 sites across the country.

In the early 1990s in Scotland, a reeducation program for men convicted of violence against their female partners was started as a condition of a probation order. The program involved weekly group sessions over a period of 6 to 7 months. A quasi-experimental design was used to assess the effectiveness of the program compared with other criminal sanctions (e.g., prison, probation, fines). One year after intervention, female partners of men in the reeducation program (n=27) reported a much lower prevalence (occurrence of at least one incident), 33 percent versus 75 percent, and lower frequency (five or more incidents), 7 percent versus 37 percent, of violence perpetrated by their male partners compared with female partners of men who did not receive the intervention (n=59). This translates into a 56-percent decrease in the prevalence of violence and an 81-percent decrease in frequency.[16]

Throughout France, neighborhood justice "houses" and "offices" have been set up by the Ministry of Justice and local associations to address minor crimes and other legal problems through alternative justice approaches. Staff are trained to provide victim-offender mediation and are legally empowered to deal with cases. It is reported, although not proved, that everywhere they have been set up, they have relieved the courts and settled cases faster.

## COST-EFFECTIVENESS OF CRIME PREVENTION

In Europe, North America, and other regions of the world, governments have been forced to find ways to reduce expenditures, restructure departments, and identify investments that will best meet the needs of their citizens. Major reforms have been implemented in areas such as health and education that are vital to citizens. For crime control, the strategic issues are only just beginning to be faced through efforts such as the Comprehensive Spending Review in the United Kingdom, which has reviewed effectiveness arguments in crime reduction and examined the comparative monetary advantages of spending on prisons vis-à-vis family-based intervention programs, for example.[17]

A recent study by The RAND Corporation[18] compared the estimated number of crimes that would be prevented by a $1 million investment in various strategies of intervening at different developmental stages in the lives of at-risk children with the number averted by California's three-strikes law. The study found that more monetary benefits from reduced crime were achieved from spending on parent training and graduation incentive strategies (see Quantum Opportunities Program above) than on the combined strategy of home visits and day care or probation or the three-strikes law.

In 1994, the newly elected government of the Netherlands dedicated an annual budget of 160 million guilders ($100 million) for local crime prevention efforts to tackle the early risk factors for delinquency and later criminal offending. This decision was based largely on scientific research carried out by the Dutch Ministry of Justice.[19] A simulation model using historical crime and crime control trends was developed to forecast the effects of four hypothetical scenarios on government spending on public safety (see Figure 32.2):

- Adding 1,000 extra police officers to a force of 27,620 officers.
- Extrapolating current trends (doing the same).
- Strengthening network criminality prevention—for example, police working with social agencies to address youth crime—to achieve a 10-percent decrease in crime.
- Increasing investment in situational crime prevention by 30 percent.

The situational prevention scenario was predicted to have the strongest effect on reducing criminal justice spending over time and was the most cost-effective. Network criminality prevention was predicted to be the next most effective strategy. The police scenario had the most undesirable impact. Its poor showing had to do with the direct contribution it made to criminal justice spending and its ineffectiveness in dealing with an hypothesized increase in violent crimes—the most expensive category of offenses. Furthermore, after 7 years— by the year 2000—adding more police was estimated to cost the government 100 million guilders (approximately $60 million) more had they done nothing.

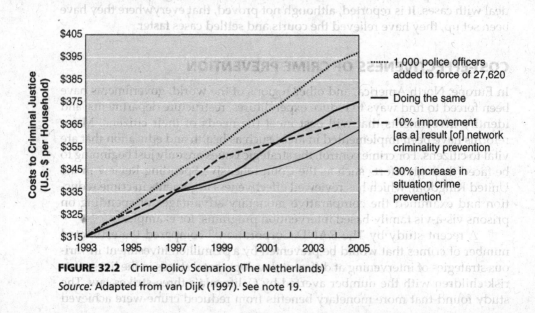

**FIGURE 32.2**  Crime Policy Scenarios (The Netherlands)

*Source:* Adapted from van Dijk (1997). See note 19.

## MOVING FROM RHETORIC TO EFFECTIVE ACTION

In the last decade, prevention has achieved a prominent position in crime reduction thinking and practice around the world. Efforts to foster better design, mobilize agencies, and facilitate partnerships have become synonymous with best practice in crime reduction. In many crime-ridden cities and communities where these strategies have been employed, substantial and lasting reductions in delinquency, violence, and insecurity have been achieved; a greater quality of life has been realized; and community and economic growth has flourished.

However, crime prevention remains more rhetoric than action. Governmental investment in crime prevention is extremely low in most industrialized countries—between 2 and 3 percent of criminal justice spending—and is nonexistent in most developing countries and countries in transition.[20] The traditional, reactive approaches to dealing with crime—police, courts, and corrections—continue to dominate national crime policies. Little attention has been paid to the scientific conclusions and the international consensus on what works most effectively to reduce crime.

The International Centre for the Prevention of Crime was set up to help overcome this inaction through its central mission of harnessing international best practice from around the world to solve crime problems. It engages in the exchange of international expertise to promote, for example, the efforts of its U.S.-based partners—the National Crime Prevention Council and the U.S. Conference of Mayors—in working with cities and communities through such well-known and successful projects as the Texas City Action Plan to Prevent Crime and the Comprehensive Communities Program. It offers technical assistance—strategic action-oriented analyses—at the national, local, and political levels to reduce crime more effectively and is a member of the White Paper team for the Minister of Safety and Security in South Africa.

ICPC also harnesses best practice in crime prevention by providing tools to raise awareness of crime prevention's impact. Such tools stress the importance of leadership, the affordability and cost-benefit of crime prevention, and the contribution of prevention strategies and programs to the sustainable development of cities and countries. With these efforts, ICPC is hopeful that effective action in reducing crime will replace the rhetoric that stands in the way of building safer communities and societies.

## Notes

1. Sherman, L. W., D. Gottfredson, D. MacKenzie, J. Eck, P. Reuter, and S. Bushway, *Preventing Crime: What Works, What Doesn't, What's Promising*, Office of Justice Programs Research Report, Washington, DC: U.S. Department of Justice, National Institute of Justice, 1997, NCJ 165366.
2. Loeber, R., and D. P. Farrington, eds., *Serious and Violent Juvenile Offenders: Risk Factors and Successful Interventions*, Thousand Oaks, CA: Sage Publications, Inc., 1998.

3. ICPC is a not-for-profit, nongovernmental organization. It is governed by a board of directors, combining the competencies of cities, prevention experts, the private sector, and specialized institutes from around the world, including the U.S. National Crime Prevention Council and the U.S. Conference of Mayors. It receives support from the governments of Belgium, Canada, France, the Netherlands, the United Kingdom, and the Province of Quebec, which make up an advisory and policy committee.

4. International Centre for the Prevention of Crime, *Towards the Use of Best Practice World Wide*, Montreal, Canada: International Centre for the Prevention of Crime, 1997. The key sections of this report are also available on the Internet at www.crime-prevention-intl.org.

5. European Forum for Urban Security, *Urban Security Practices*, Paris, France: European Forum for Urban Security, 1996.

6. Waller, I., B. C. Welsh, and D. Sansfaçon, *Crime Prevention Digest 1997. Successes, Benefits and Directions from Seven Countries*, Montreal, Canada: International Centre for the Prevention of Crime, 1997. This report is also available on the Internet at www.crime-prevention-intl.org. On the basis of an ICPC analysis of crime prevention strategies by central governments in seven industrialized countries, including the United States, ICPC regarded the listed elements as core because, among other reasons, government agencies using those elements have shown proven and promising results in preventing crime.

7. To meet the "balance of probabilities" criterion, a project or program must (1) use a problem-solving partnership approach (as defined in this article's section entitled "Crime prevention as a process") and (2) yield results based on at least one of the following: (a) a temporal sequence between the program and the crime or risk outcome clearly observed, or (b) a comparison group present without demonstrated comparability with the treatment group.

8. See Clarke, R. V., ed., *Situational Crime Prevention: Successful Case Studies*, 2d ed., Guilderland, NY: Harrow and Heston, 1997.

9. Forrester, D., S. Frenz, M. O'Connell, and K. Pease, *The Kirkholt Burglary Prevention Project: Phase II*, Crime Prevention Unit Paper, No. 23, London, England: Home Office, 1990.

10. Scherpenisse, R., "The Police Label for Secured Housing: Initial Results in the Netherlands," paper presented at the European Union Conference, "Crime Prevention: Towards A European Level," May 11–14, 1997, Noordwijk, Netherlands, 1997.

11. Olds, D. L., C. R. Henderson, R. Chamberlin, and R. Tatelbaum, "Preventing Child Abuse and Neglect: A Randomized Trial of Nurse Home Visitation," *Pediatrics* 78 (1986): 65–78.

12. Olds, D. L., J. Eckenrode, C. R. Henderson, H. Kitzman, J. Powers, R. Cole, K. Sidora, P. Morris, L. M. Pettitt, and D. Luckey, "Long-Term Effects of Home Visitation on Maternal Life Course and Child Abuse and Neglect: Fifteen-Year Follow-Up of a Randomized Trial," *Journal of the American Medical Association* 278 (1997): 637–643.

13. Olweus, D., "Bully/Victim Problems Among School Children: Basic Facts and Effects of a School Based Intervention Program," in *The Development and Treatment of Childhood Aggression*, ed. D. J. Pepler and K. H. Rubin, Hillsdale, NJ: Lawrence Erlbaum Associates, 1991: 411–448.

14. Hahn, A., *Evaluation of the Quantum Opportunities Program (QOP): Did the Program Work?*, Waltham, MA: Brandeis University, 1994.
15. Kruissink, M., *The HALT Program: Diversion of Juvenile Vandals*, Dutch Penal Law and Policy, The Hague, Netherlands: Research and Documentation Centre, Ministry of Justice, 1990. The control group numbered 90, the program group 179.
16. Dobash, R., R. Dobash, K. Cavanagh, and R. Lewis, *Research Evaluation of Programmes for Violent Men*, Edinburgh, Scotland: Scottish Office Central Research Unit, 1996.
17. Goldblatt, P., and C. Lewis, eds., *Reducing Offending: An Assessment of Research Evidence on Ways of Dealing With Offending Behaviour*, London, England: Home Office Research and Statistics Directorate, 1998.
18. Greenwood, P. W., K. E. Model, C. P. Rydell, and J. Chiesa, *Diverting Children from a Life of Crime: Measuring Costs and Benefits*, Santa Monica, CA: The RAND Corporation, 1996.
19. van Dijk, J. J. M., "Towards a Research-based Crime Reduction Policy: Crime Prevention as a Cost-effective Policy Option," *European Journal on Criminal Policy and Research* 5 (1997): 13–27
20. Waller, Welsh, and Sansfaçon, *Crime Prevention Digest 1997*.

# 14

Lessons from Holland,

# Drugs

## THE UNITED STATES CONTEXT

The United States has defined some drugs as legal and others as illegal. The contradiction in this policy arises in that the legality of a drug is not correlated with its health consequences. The most dangerous drugs—nicotine and alcohol—are legal even though they are responsible for hundreds of thousands of deaths annually. Alcohol alone kills 25 times as many as all illegal drugs combined. Yet it (and tobacco) remain legal and the government wages a costly war against the drugs defined as illegal.

The prohibition against heroin, cocaine, marijuana, methamphetamine, and others and the official policies to combat their use are intended to deter crime, but they have the opposite effect. By making drugs illegal and dangerous to produce, transport, and sell, the price is many times greater than if the drugs were legal. Thus, many users turn to crime to sustain their costly habit. Crime is also encouraged as organized crime imports, processes, and distributes the illicit drugs through its networks. This in turn promotes more crime as violence between rival gangs develops over disputed territorial boundaries. Moreover, the huge amounts of money involved sometimes corrupt police and other government agents. At another level, making drug use illegal creates crime by creating criminals. By labeling and treating these people as criminals, the justice system creates further crime by stigmatizing them, which makes reintegration into society after prison very difficult (about one-third of the prison population are drug offenders). The result, typically, is for the drug users to join together in a deviant drug subculture.

Another irony is that the drug war is intended to reduce the use of illicit drugs by the populace, yet it does not. It turns out that the nations with the most lenient approach (the Netherlands, for example) have *lower* drug use than found in the United States.

# 33

...

# Does Europe Do It Better?
# Lessons from Holland,
# Britain, and Switzerland

Robert J. MacCoun and Peter Reuter

*This article debunks some common myths associated with
so-called liberal drug policies in Europe. The authors discuss
innovative programs in Europe that use decriminalization,
legalization, and drug maintenance to address problems associated with drug use.*

Listen to a debate among drug policy advocates and you're likely to hear im-
passioned claims about the brilliant success (or dismal failure) of more "liberal"
approaches in certain European countries. Frequently, however, such claims are
based on false assumptions. For example, we are told that marijuana has been
legalized in the Netherlands. Or that addicts receive heroin by prescription in
Great Britain.

Pruned of erroneous or excessive claims, the experience in Europe points
to both the feasibility of successful reform of US drug laws and the drawbacks
of radical change. What follows are descriptions of some innovative approaches being tried over there, with judgments of their applicability over here.
They fall into three broad categories: eliminating user sanctions (decriminalization), allowing commercial sales (legalization) and medical provision of heroin
to addicts (maintenance).

*Source:* Robert J. MacCoun and Peter Reuter, "Does Europe Do It Better? Lessons from Holland,
Britain, and Switzerland," *The Nation* (September 20, 1999), pp. 28–30. Reprinted with permission
from the September 20, 1999 issue of *The Nation*. For subscription information, call 1-800-333-8536.
Portions of each week's Nation magazine can be accessed at www.thenation.com.

# DECRIMINALIZING MARIJUANA: THE CASE OF THE DUTCH COFFEE SHOPS

Dutch cannabis policy and its effects are routinely mischaracterized by both sides in the US drug debate. Much of the confusion hinges on a failure to distinguish between two very different eras in Dutch policy. In compliance with international treaty obligations, Dutch law states unequivocally that cannabis is illegal. Yet in 1976 the Dutch adopted a formal written policy of nonenforcement for violations involving possession or sale of up to thirty grams (five grams since 1995) of cannabis—a sizable quantity, since one gram is sufficient for two joints. Police and prosecutors were forbidden to act against users, and officials adopted a set of rules that effectively allowed the technically illicit sale of small amounts in licensed coffee shops and nightclubs. The Dutch implemented this system to avoid excessive punishment of casual users and to weaken the link between the soft and hard drug markets; the coffee shops would allow marijuana users to avoid street dealers, who may also traffic in other drugs. Despite some recent tightenings in response to domestic and international pressure (particularly from the hard-line French), the Dutch have shown little intention of abandoning their course.

In the initial decriminalization phase, which lasted from the mid-seventies to the mid-eighties, marijuana was not very accessible, sold in a few out-of-the-way places. Surveys show no increase in the number of Dutch marijuana smokers from 1976 to about 1984. Likewise, in the United States during the seventies, twelve US states removed criminal penalties for possession of small amounts of marijuana, and studies indicate that this change had at most a very limited effect on the number of users. More recent evidence from South Australia suggests the same.

From the mid-eighties Dutch policy evolved from the simple decriminalization of cannabis to the active commercialization of it. Between 1980 and 1988, the number of coffee shops selling cannabis in Amsterdam increased tenfold; the shops spread to more prominent and accessible locations in the central city and began to promote the drug more openly. Today, somewhere between 1,200 and 1,500 coffee shops (about one per 12,000 inhabitants) sell cannabis products in the Netherlands; much of their business involves tourists. Coffee shops account for perhaps a third of all cannabis purchases among minors and supply most of the adult market.

As commercial access and promotion increased in the eighties, the Netherlands saw rapid growth in the number of cannabis users, an increase not mirrored in other nations. Whereas in 1984 15 percent of 18- to 20-year-olds reported having used marijuana at some point in their life, the figure had more than doubled to 33 percent in 1992, essentially identical to the US figure. That increase might have been coincidental, but it is certainly consistent with other evidence (from alcohol, tobacco and legal gambling markets) that commercial promotion of such activities increases consumption. Since 1992 the Dutch figure has continued to rise, but that growth is paralleled in the United States and most other rich Western nations despite very different drug policies—apparently the result of shifts in global youth culture.

The rise in marijuana use has not led to a worsening of the Dutch heroin problem. Although the Netherlands had an epidemic of heroin use in the early seventies, there has been little growth in the addict population since 1976; indeed, the heroin problem is now largely one of managing the health problems of aging (but still criminally active) addicts. Cocaine use is not particularly high by European standards, and a smaller fraction of marijuana users go on to use cocaine or heroin in the Netherlands than in the United States. Even cannabis commercialization does not seem to increase other drug problems.

## TREATING HEROIN ADDICTS IN BRITAIN

The British experience in allowing doctors to prescribe heroin for maintenance has been criticized for more than two decades in the United States. In a 1926 British report, the blue-ribbon Rolleston Committee concluded that "morphine and heroin addiction must be regarded as a manifestation of disease and not as a mere form of vicious indulgence," and hence that "the indefinitely prolonged administration of morphine and heroin" might be necessary for such patients. This perspective—already quite distinct from US views in the twenties—led Britain to adopt, or at least formalize, a system in which physicians could prescribe heroin to addicted patients for maintenance purposes. With a small population of several hundred patients, most of whom became addicted while under medical treatment, the system muddled along for four decades with few problems. Then, in the early sixties, a handful of physicians began to prescribe irresponsibly and a few heroin users began taking the drug purely for recreational purposes, recruiting others like themselves. What followed was a sharp relative increase in heroin addiction in the mid-sixties, though the problem remained small in absolute numbers (about 1,500 known addicts in 1967).

In response to the increase, the Dangerous Drugs Act of 1967 greatly curtailed access to heroin maintenance, limiting long-term prescriptions to a small number of specially licensed drug-treatment specialists. At the same time, oral methadone became available as an alternative maintenance drug. By 1975, just 12 percent of maintained opiate addicts were receiving heroin; today, fewer than 1 percent of maintenance clients receive heroin. Specialists are still allowed to maintain their addicted patients on heroin if they wish; most choose not to do so—in part because the government reimbursement for heroin maintenance is low, but also because of a widespread reluctance to take on a role that is difficult to reconcile with traditional norms of medical practice. Thus, one can hardly claim that heroin maintenance was a failure in Britain. When it was the primary mode of treatment, the heroin problem was small. The problem grew larger even as there was a sharp decline in heroin maintenance, for many reasons unrelated to the policy.

## "HEROIN-ASSISTED TREATMENT": THE SWISS EXPERIENCE

What the British dropped, the Swiss took up. Although less widely known, the Swiss experience is in fact more informative. By the mid-eighties it was clear that Switzerland had a major heroin problem, compounded by a very high rate of HIV infection. A generally tough policy, with arrest rates approaching those in the United States, was seen as a failure. The first response was from Zurich, which opened a "zone of tolerance" for addicts at the so-called "Needle Park" (the Platzspitz) in 1987. This area, in which police permitted the open buying and selling of small quantities of drugs, attracted many users and sellers, and was regarded by the citizens of Zurich as unsightly and embarrassing. The Platzspitz was closed in 1992.

Then in January 1994 Swiss authorities opened the first heroin maintenance clinics, part of a three-year national trial of heroin maintenance as a supplement to the large methadone maintenance program that had been operating for more than a decade. The motivation for these trials was complex. They were an obvious next step in combating AIDS, but they also represented an effort to reduce the unsightliness of the drug scene and to forestall a strong legalization movement. The program worked as follows: Each addict could choose the amount he or she wanted and inject it in the clinic under the care of a nurse up to three times a day, seven days a week. The drug could not be taken out of the clinic. Sixteen small clinics were scattered around the country, including one in a prison. Patients had to be over 18, have injected heroin for two years and have failed at least two treatment episodes. In fact, most of them had more than ten years of heroin addiction and many treatment failures. They were among the most troubled heroin addicts with the most chaotic lives.

By the end of the trials, more than 800 patients had received heroin on a regular basis without any leakage into the illicit market. No overdoses were reported among participants while they stayed in the program. A large majority of participants had maintained the regime of daily attendance at the clinic; 69 percent were in treatment eighteen months after admission. This was a high rate relative to those found in methadone programs. About half of the "dropouts" switched to other forms of treatment, some choosing methadone and others abstinence-based therapies. The crime rate among all patients dropped over the course of treatment, use of nonprescribed heroin dipped sharply and unemployment fell from 44 to 20 percent. Cocaine use remained high. The prospect of free, easily obtainable heroin would seem to be wondrously attractive to addicts who spend much of their days hustling for a fix, but initially the trial program had trouble recruiting patients. Some addicts saw it as a recourse for losers who were unable to make their own way on the street. For some participants the discovery that a ready supply of heroin did not make life wonderful led to a new interest in sobriety.

Critics, such as an independent review panel of the World Health Organization (also based in Switzerland), reasonably asked whether the claimed success was a result of the heroin or the many additional services provided to trial participants. And the evaluation relied primarily on the patients' own reports, with few objective measures. Nevertheless, despite the methodological weaknesses, the results of the Swiss trials provide evidence of the feasibility and effectiveness of this approach. In late 1997 the Swiss government approved a large-scale expansion of the program, potentially accommodating 15 percent of the nation's estimated 30,000 heroin addicts.

Americans are loath to learn from other nations. This is but another symptom of "American exceptionalism." Yet European drug-policy experiences have a lot to offer. The Dutch experience with decriminalization provides support for those who want to lift US criminal penalties for marijuana possession. It is hard to identify differences between the United States and the Netherlands that would make marijuana decriminalization more dangerous here than there. Because the Dutch went further with decriminalization than the few states in this country that tried it—lifting even civil penalties—the burden is on US drug hawks to show what this nation could possibly gain from continuing a policy that results in 700,000 marijuana arrests annually. Marijuana is not harmless, but surely it is less damaging than arrest and a possible jail sentence; claims that reduced penalties would "send the wrong message" ring hollow if in fact levels of pot use are unlikely to escalate and use of cocaine and heroin are unaffected.

The Swiss heroin trials are perhaps even more important. American heroin addicts, even though most are over 35, continue to be the source of much crime and disease. A lot would be gained if heroin maintenance would lead, say, the 10 percent who cause the most harm to more stable and socially integrated lives. Swiss addicts may be different from those in the United States, and the trials there are not enough of a basis for implementing heroin maintenance here. But the Swiss experience does provide grounds for thinking about similar tests in the United States.

Much is dysfunctional about other social policies in this country, compared with Europe—the schools are unequal, the rate of violent crime is high and many people are deprived of adequate access to health services. But we are quick to draw broad conclusions from apparent failures of social programs in Europe (for example, that the cost of an elaborate social safety net is prohibitive), while we are all too ready to attribute their successes to some characteristic of their population or traditions that we could not achieve or would not want—a homogeneous population, more conformity, more intrusive government and the like. It's time we rose above such provincialism.

The benefits of Europe's drug policy innovations are by no means decisively demonstrated, not for Europe and surely not for the United States. But the results thus far show the plausibility of a wide range of variations—both inside and at the edges of a prohibition framework—that merit more serious consideration in this country.

# 34

# Europe: Curing, Not Punishing, Addicts

**Rick Steves**

*In contrast to U.S. drug policy, European countries focus on
harm reduction—and it works. Most notably, the percentage of
Europeans who use illicit drugs is about half that of Americans.
The European countries treat drug abuse not as crime but as an
illness.*

Europe has a drug problem, and knows it. But the Europeans' approach to it is
quite different from the American "war on drugs." I spend 120 days a year in
Europe as a travel writer, so I decided to see for myself how it's working. I
talked with locals, researched European drug policies and even visited a smoky
marijuana "coffee shop" in Amsterdam. I got a close look at the alternative to a
war on drugs.

Europeans are well aware of the U.S. track record against illegal drug use.
Since President Nixon first declared the war on drugs in 1971, our country has
locked up millions of its citizens and spent hundreds of billions of dollars
(many claim that if incarceration costs are figured in, a *trillion* dollars) waging
this "war." Despite these efforts, U.S. government figures show the overall rate
of illicit drug use has remained about the same.

By contrast, according to the 2007 U.N. World Drug Report, the percentage of Europeans who use illicit drugs is about half that of Americans. (Europe
also has fewer than half as many deaths from overdoses.) How have they managed that—in Europe, no less, which shocks some American sensibilities with
its underage drinking, marijuana tolerance and heroin-friendly "needle
parks"?

*Source:* Rick Steves, "Europe: Curing, Not Punishing, Addicts," *Los Angeles Times* (October 12, 2007).
Online: http://articles/latimes.com/2007/oct/12/news/OE-STEVES12. Rick Steves is a best-
selling travel guidebook author and host of public television's "Rick Steves' Europe." You can learn
more about Rick at ricksteves.com.

Recently, in Zurich, Switzerland, I walked into a public toilet that had only blue lights. Why? So junkies can't find their veins. A short walk away, I saw a heroin maintenance clinic that gives junkies counseling, clean needles and a safe alternative to shooting up in the streets. Need a syringe? Cigarette machines have been retooled to sell clean, government-subsidized syringes.

While each European nation has its own drug laws and policies, they seem to share a pragmatic approach. They treat drug abuse not as a crime but as an illness. And they measure the effectiveness of their drug policy not in arrests but in harm reduction.

Generally, Europeans employ a three-pronged strategy of police, educators and doctors. Police zero in on dealers—not users—to limit the supply of drugs. Users often get off with a warning and are directed to get treatment. Anti-drug education programs warn people (especially young people) of the dangers of drugs, but they get beyond the "zero tolerance" and "three strikes" rhetoric that may sound good to voters but rings hollow with addicts and at-risk teens. And finally, the medical community steps in to battle health problems associated with drug use (especially HIV and hepatitis C) and help addicts get back their lives.

Contrast this approach with the American war on drugs. As during Prohibition in the 1930s, the U.S. spends its resources on police and prisons to lock up dealers and users alike. American drug education (such as the now-discredited DARE program) seemed like propaganda, and therefore its messengers lost credibility.

Perhaps the biggest difference between European and American drug policy is how each deals with marijuana. When I visited the Amsterdam coffee shop that openly sells pot, I sat and observed: People were chatting; a female customer perused a fanciful array of "loaner" bongs. An older couple (who apparently didn't enjoy the edgy ambience) parked their bikes and dropped in for a baggie to go. An underage customer was shooed away. A policeman stepped inside, but only to post a warning about the latest danger from chemical drugs on the streets. In the Netherlands, it's cheaper to get high than drunk, and drug-related crimes are rare.

After 10 years of allowed recreational marijuana use, Dutch anti-drug abuse professionals agree that there has been no significant increase in pot smoking among young people and that overall cannabis use has increased only slightly. Meanwhile, in the U.S., it's easier for a 15-year-old to buy marijuana than tobacco or alcohol—because no one gets carded when buying something on the street. . . .

The Netherlands' policies are the most liberal, but across Europe no one is locked away for discreetly smoking a joint. The priority is on reducing abuse of such hard drugs as heroin and cocaine. The only reference to marijuana I found among the pages of the European Union's drug policy was a reference to counseling for "problem cannabis use."

Meanwhile, according to FBI statistics, in recent years about 40% of the roughly 80,000 annual drug arrests were for marijuana—the majority (well over 80%) for possession.

In short, Europe is making sure that the cure isn't more costly than the problem. While the U.S. spends tax dollars on police, courts and prisons, Europe spends its taxes on doctors, counselors and clinics. EU policymakers estimate that they save 15 euros in police and health costs for each euro invested in drug education and counseling.

European leaders understand that a society has a choice: tolerate alternative lifestyles or build more prisons. They've made their choice. We're still building more prisons.

In short, Europe is making sure that the cure isn't more costly than the problem. While the U.S. spends tax dollars on police, courts and prisons, Europe spends its taxes on doctors, counselors and clinics. EU policymakers estimate that they save 15 euros in police and health costs for each euro invested in drug education and counseling.

European leaders understand that a society has a choice: tolerate alternative lifestyles or build more prisons. They've made their choice. We're still building more prisons.